Live *in* Love

Live *in* Love

Growing Together
Through Life's Changes

LAUREN AKINS

with Mark Dagostino

Ballantine Books
New York

Published in the United States by Ballantine Books,
an imprint of Random House,
a division of Penguin Random House LLC, New York.

BALLANTINE and the HOUSE colophon are registered trademarks of
Penguin Random House LLC.

Grateful acknowledgment is made to Capitol CMG, Inc. for permission to reprint
an excerpt from "Oceans (Where Feet May Fail)" by Joel Houston, Matt Crocker,
and Salomon Ligthelm, copyright © 2013 by Hillsong Music Publishing (APRA)
(adm. in the US and Canada at CapitolCMGPublishing.com).
All rights reserved. Used by permission.

LIBRARY OF CONGRESS CATALOGING-IN-PUBLICATION DATA

Names: Akins, Lauren, author. | Dagostino, Mark, author.
Title: Live in love: growing together through life's changes /
Lauren Akins with Mark Dagostino.
Description: New York: Ballantine Group, 2020.
Identifiers: LCCN 2019051124 (print) | LCCN 2019051125 (ebook) |
ISBN 9780593129043 (hardcover) | ISBN 9780593129029 (ebook)
Subjects: LCSH: Rhett, Thomas, 1990– | Akins, Lauren. | Country
musicians—United States—Biography. | Country musicians'
spouses—United States—Biography.
Classification: LCC ML420.R4307 A75 2020 (print) | LCC
ML420.R4307 (ebook) | DDC 782.421642092/2 [B]—dc23
LC record available at https://lccn.loc.gov/2019051124
LC ebook record available at https://lccn.loc.gov/2019051125

Printed in the United States of America on acid-free paper

randomhousebooks.com

2 4 6 8 9 7 5 3 1

First Edition

Book design by Virginia Norey

For ALL of my unmistakable and irreplaceable family and friends—because without y'all, there wouldn't be much of a book for me to write.

And so we know and rely on the love God has for us. God is love. Whoever lives in love lives in God, and God in them.

—1 John 4:16

Just so no one gets confused or thinks I'm being impersonal: Please note that Thomas Rhett's full name is Thomas Rhett Akins. We grew up in the South, where everyone we know says his middle name as if it's a part of his first name. I'm talking me, his mom, my parents, our friends from school, *everybody*. We all call him "Thomas Rhett." So that's the way I'll be referring to my bestie and husband throughout the pages of this book. —*Lauren*

Contents

With Love, from Me to You . . .

A few years ago, just before the release of my husband's second album, before anyone outside of our country music family had heard the first note of his #1 single, "Die a Happy Man," my life took a drastic turn.

Like a lot of wives, I had happily let my own goals take a back seat to my husband's. Ever since we'd been together as a couple—a couple for the second time, which is a whole other story—I'd been at Thomas Rhett's side. Squeezing into a single bunk on the tour bus, watching him play concerts from the side stage, holding his hand before he stepped in front of the cameras for press interviews and TV appearances . . . I was right there for all of it.

Before Thomas Rhett and I got married, I'd gone to college and trained to be a nurse. But I wasn't practicing as a nurse. As his career took off, mine never had the opportunity to get started. We'd dreamed about starting a family, and we hadn't done that yet, either. I'd always imagined that someday we'd live in a neighborhood where everyone's doors were unlocked and our kids could play in the streets, just the way I'd grown up in my little Tennessee hometown. But since Thomas Rhett was on his way to becoming a big name in country music, my hopes for a normal suburban family life seemed increasingly out of reach. Don't get me wrong: I'm not complaining! It filled my heart to see the love of my life come closer and closer to achieving his dreams. My husband is amazing, and

I fully support him, and because I supported him and helped him reach his goals I've been blessed to live out the rewards. This journey we were on was exciting and wonderful, but it was also forcing me to leave more than a little bit of myself behind. Letting go of the dreams I once had for a certain type of life in favor of the new kind of life that Thomas Rhett seemed to be headed for—that was hard. I was feeling lost.

Just as Thomas Rhett was getting ready to release his second album, though, God led me to an opportunity to do something I'd wanted to do ever since I was a little girl. He gave me a chance to go on a mission trip to Haiti, to put my medical training to use in the best way I could ever imagine: helping children.

So the very week *Tangled Up* was released, I gave up my chance to stay in five-star hotels and live the fancy life of a country music star's wife, and went on a mission trip to one of the most impoverished nations on Earth. A mission trip that would change everything for us.

"Die a Happy Man" changed everything for us, too. The personal love song and video (with me in it) that was released as the album's second single led me and my husband into a shocking whirlwind of press and social media attention. Magazines and big TV shows that I'd read and watched all my life were suddenly featuring not just him, but *us* in their pages and on their stages. And the public's expectations of us and their imaginations about us seemed to reach new peaks. Everywhere we looked people talked about "Thomas Rhett & Lauren Akins" as if we were one entity, the "perfect couple"; as if the video and the song were the embodiment of a fairy-tale romance come true. And in a way, they were. The fact that I'd married my lifelong friend, the fact that we'd dated as teenagers and then gotten together again in college, the fact that our families are really close and love each other, the fact that he writes songs for me—all of it is romantic, and sometimes even dreamy. But when people started posting our Instagram pictures all over social media with the hashtags #RelationshipGoals and #MarriageGoals, I just kept thinking, "Does anyone have any idea how hard it's been? Does anyone understand how long it's taken us to get things right? Does anyone understand what really goes on behind the scenes of a so-called perfect marriage?"

Then something even bigger happened: Thomas Rhett and I became the parents of two incredible little girls. First came Willa Gray, the beautiful baby Thomas Rhett and I fell in love with and adopted while I was on a mission trip to Uganda; and then our amazing Ada James, whom I gave birth to in Nashville just three months after we brought Willa Gray home. (We also found out we had a third baby girl on the way when I was right in the middle of writing this book!)

What we never expected was how much people would love seeing pictures of our little family. We gained more social media followers and more press attention for the arrival of our two babies than almost anything else that had ever happened in Thomas Rhett's career. I can't explain it. It's not anything we courted. We didn't go and put our family on some reality TV show or anything, yet the interest has kept on rising to this day.

I don't sing, I don't dance, I don't act. I'm a wife and mother, and I never wanted to be in the spotlight, but I have *fans* now. It's so strange to me. And every day those fans ask me for details about this life I'm leading. They also ask for all kinds of advice, thinking maybe I can give them some insight into how they can lead a life like this, too. They want to know how to find (and keep) a good husband, how to keep romance alive in a marriage, about adopting babies, and raising kids right, and all kinds of things.

I asked myself a million times, "Why?" And one day, it occurred to me that I was asking the wrong person. In our family, we try to start our days with God. God first, and then us. And once I asked Him the question, I came to embrace the possibility that maybe all this attention was part of God's plan. That maybe I have been given an opportunity to do some good with all of this—by sharing our story with y'all, struggles and all.

The thought of it terrifies me! I mean, who am I to think that I've lived enough to be able to give advice to *anyone*? But this isn't the first time God's led me to the edge of a cliff and told me to jump with faith into the unknown. So even though I've never done this before, and even though it makes me nervous, here goes.

My hope is that through sharing my story and the story of my family, *Live in Love* will serve as whatever you need in this moment: a self-help book, a romantic escape, a marriage book, a family guide, a beacon of faith, a behind-the-curtain peek at a country music couple, an inside look at the trials of the international adoption process, or just a light- and love-filled distraction from the darkness that seems to fill up the news these days. With any luck, it'll be all of those things all at once.

This is the *real* story of who we are, what we believe, what our passions are, and why we do what we do. I hope it's a reminder that having faith is a good thing, that a healthy marriage is a good thing, that standing up for one another is a good thing, and that valuing one another as human beings is a *very* good thing. And my greatest hope is that it inspires you to seek out your *own* good things, while you love, love, love on the people in your life.

Finding our path hasn't been easy, but the journey has taught us a lot. A happy marriage, a happy career, a happy *life*—it's all possible. Living the *dream* is possible. But it doesn't get handed to you. It takes time. It takes faith. It takes effort. It takes making good choices, and making tough choices, too.

And all of that takes support. It takes a Crew. It takes family, and friendship, and . . . well, by the end of this book, I think you'll see the whole picture.

How do I know any of this? How can I say any of this with confidence? Because I'm living it.

With Love,

Lauren
Akins

In a coffee shop with Thomas Rhett in Vancouver

Live *in* Love

Prologue

His Dream Come True

"And the ACM Single Record of the Year is . . ."

This was it. The big moment. We didn't have any expectation that he might win, mostly because the other nominees in his category were so huge. We're talking songs like "Take Your Time" by Sam Hunt and "Girl Crush" by Little Big Town. How could this personal little love song that Thomas Rhett wrote for me possibly win against that kind of competition?

Still, we couldn't help but fantasize about it just a little bit. I mean, *was* this it? Was this the moment that would change everything? Was this the night that would prove that all of my husband's wildest dreams were actually coming true?

Just being in that audience felt like a dream. Because he had been nominated in such a big category, we were seated near the front, right on the aisle, just behind the guys from Florida Georgia Line. The first-name-only crowd—Keith and Nicole, Tim and Faith—were in the front row, of course, but that wasn't all that far from us. I could look to my left or right and just a couple of rows ahead or behind and see Lady Antebellum, and Luke Bryan, and Carrie Underwood, and Jason Aldean.

"Can you believe this?" I said right out loud when they showed us to our seats.

Thomas Rhett just shook his head and smiled.

Country star Jake Owen, a friend of ours, was the presenter for the category, and when he ripped the envelope open my stomach started doing backflips. I thought, "I might actually throw up right here in front of all these people on national TV." If Thomas Rhett won, then this was the culmination of everything he had ever wanted. Everything he'd ever worked for. I was so proud and nervous at the same time I could barely contain myself. A cameraman pointed his lens right at us as I gripped his hand. My sweet husband. My best friend.

This wasn't our first award show. It wasn't our first time sitting in an audience full of superstar musicians and celebrities, either. Some of these big stars were our friends now. They'd been to our house, and we'd been to theirs. We were doing *life* together. Still for some reason, Thomas Rhett and I were real nervous.

We'd done everything we'd planned to do to get ready for the big day, including going to bed early the night before. Contrary to what people might imagine, the life of a country singer isn't all late nights and parties and drinking beers in the back of some pickup truck. Thomas Rhett needed to take care of his voice, to be ready and well rested, and so I went to bed early right alongside him. He got up in the morning and got a workout in, and we even made time for a little coffee date in the quiet of our hotel room at the Mandalay Bay before the craziness started.

Then came the knock at the door. At 11 a.m. sharp, the glam squad arrived. My husband took care of some business with his management team while I gave myself over to my sweet friend Ali, a hair and makeup guru who promised to make me look good. Anyone who knows me knows I'm not one who cares very much about what my hair and makeup look like on any given day, but it's hard not to feel just a little bit like a princess as a team of professional beauty makers buzz around you and hand you your second mimosa to keep you laughing during all of that primping.

Before I knew it, it was time to go. I gave myself a quick look in the mirror and could hardly believe my eyes. "Dang! We sure do clean up nice," I said, all dressed up in a gorgeous white gown. But there wasn't any time to say "thank you" any more than I already had, which was

On the red carpet
at the ACMs
in 2016

about eight hundred times. I pulled on my sparkly high heels and our manager whisked us into the elevator and down to a private underground garage, one where celebrities and high rollers get to climb into limousines far from public view. It was still hard for me to believe we were a part of that particular club, but that's where our car picked us up to take us to the red carpet at the MGM Grand.

When Thomas Rhett's first album came out, he was nominated for a whole series of Best New Artist awards. It was such an honor, and we got so excited and had the time of our lives going to those first few award shows—but he lost every time. So by now, we were pretty used to losing. And on this night in 2016, at the Academy of Country Music Awards, with nothing but A-list competition, we were sure his chances of losing were bigger than ever.

What's crazy is the song Thomas Rhett was nominated for was "Die a Happy Man," a love song that he had written for *me*. He had even convinced me to shoot the video with him, despite the fact that I'm not an actress, I can be super awkward, and I wanted nothing to do with the spotlight. And that's on top of the fact that I'm not super comfortable with PDA, which is what I figured this video would be. But Thomas Rhett not only talked me into it, he made it easy. We shot it in Hawaii, while we were on vacation. This was before we had kids, when life was still about as carefree as it can get for a couple of newlyweds. We basically hung out in the ocean together and walked on the beach while a good friend of ours shot the video around us. To my pleasant surprise it was natural as could be. Nothing showy or over-the-top—well, minus the bareback horse riding, because I'm pretty sure that was the first horse Thomas Rhett had ever ridden.

If nothing else, I thought, it would be nice to have a professional video of the two of us together. Maybe we'd look back at it and smile someday when we were old and gray. I never expected that video to become a viral sensation, but that's exactly what happened. It was crazy! The video was viewed tens of millions of times, and hundreds of thousands of people searched my name and started following me on Instagram. After that video, Thomas Rhett started joking that he should set up a meet-and-greet line at his concerts just so his fans could meet *me*.

"It's nuts," he told me. "People are like, 'Yeah, yeah. Nice to meet you. Can we meet your wife?'"

After years spent riding on the tour bus with him, squeezing in together in a single bunk, and always staying comfortably behind the scenes, it did feel kinda good to be recognized as a part of my husband's success. But it also didn't seem real—until that night when Jake Owen stood on-stage next to Miss America in that giant arena at the MGM Grand with millions of people watching on TVs all over the world and said, "And the ACM Single Record of the Year is . . . 'Die a Happy Man,' Thomas Rhett!"

My jaw basically hit the floor. Thomas Rhett dropped his head on my shoulder for a second, and then we looked at each other like, "I cannot believe this is happening!" He went in to kiss me and my mouth was still wide open, so he kind of bumped his lips into my teeth, and we laughed. And I finally looked at him like, "Okay, they're waiting for you! You have *got to* go up there!"

And that's when I watched my husband climb the stairs onto that big stage and take that statue in his hands. It was like a dream. It *was* his dream. We'd watched people do this on TV our entire lives, and now he was that guy! It blew my mind. He was actually living it—and I got to be right there to see it happen.

Thomas Rhett stood in front of the whole world for a moment like he didn't know what to do. He was clearly in as much shock as I was. And when he stepped up to the microphone to give his acceptance speech, my lipstick on his face and all, the first thing he said was, "Holy crap, God!"

The whole audience laughed.

"Wait a second, that didn't come out right," he said. I watched as he took a breath and gathered his thoughts.

Thomas Rhett made sure to give proper thanks to God after that, and he ended up giving a beautiful speech full of gratitude to everyone who had helped him reach that pinnacle—including me. I was in awe.

Quietly, in my mind, I gave thanks to God, too, for everything that had led us to that day.

Thomas Rhett was the toast of the town that night, and as we went party hopping it seemed like every door in Las Vegas, and maybe the whole world, was suddenly open. It didn't matter what we had planned for the next day. There isn't any going to bed early when you're riding that big of a high. At three in the morning my husband was still saying, "Where to next? Want to play some blackjack?!"

I was thrilled for him, down to the bottom of my heart. I loved this man with everything in me, and his dreams were all coming true.

But wouldn't you know it? Right there in the middle of all that excitement and celebration, a familiar question came bubbling up into my mind. A question I'd been struggling with for at least a couple of years.

I looked around at the glittering lights and I wondered . . .

"What about *my* dreams?"

1

Camp Gregory

At some point, most of us develop at least *some* idea of what we think our lives are going to be like when we grow up. But how often do we stop and take a moment to look back and think about where those dreams came from?

So much of what we want as adults gets formed in our hearts when we're little kids, and yet, do any of us really remember how we first came

Practicing for the future?

up with the particular set of expectations we have for our own lives? I mean, when did those dreams and desires first set in? Was it just our families and upbringings that taught us what to like, or what not to like? Was it school that pointed us in one direction or another? Was it friends? Or church? Or something we barely even remember?

Were we even paying attention when God put those dreams in our hearts?

When I think back on my childhood, the first thing I see is an evening in the early summer. It's dusk, when the lights are just starting to come on in the front yards, and the first few lightning bugs are starting to glow.

A dozen or more kids from our neighborhood are at my house playing kickball in the front yard. We're midgame when we hear a voice call out from the front porch of a house just down the street.

"Y'all come home for supper!"

That would be Laurie, my friend Hunter's mom, who also happened to be best friends with *my* mom. And without missing a beat, Hunter would yell back: "Five more minutes! We're almost done!" Every kid would follow his lead and beg for the same thing. "Five more minutes. Just five more minutes!" Eventually Laurie and sometimes one or two of the other parents would just give up and let their kids stay at our house as long as they wanted.

Laurie would come walking down the street with whatever dishes she was going to serve at her own house that night, and I swear I can still smell the charcoal burning as she and my mom would get to work throwing hamburgers on the grill on our back porch.

"How many we got tonight?" my mom would yell. "Ten?"

The more the merrier in the Gregory household.

We'd keep on playing until it got so dark that we couldn't see the ball anymore. Then everyone who was staying for supper would pile into the house, tired and hungry, with brown feet—'cause we never wore shoes.

We'd wash our hands (and maybe our feet) and form a line through the kitchen, loading up our plates and sitting ourselves down at the dining room table, where my dad would ask us all to hold hands before anyone was allowed to touch the food.

"Dear God," he'd pray, "thank you so much for this great country we live in, where we get to worship you freely without risk of people coming after us and trying to kill us—"

My dad told it like it was. To everyone. Even God.

"Thank you so much for all the people out there on the front lines who protect us and allow us to have these freedoms," he'd continue. "And thank you so much for Hailey and Hunter and Hannah and Kamron and

Kara for being here with us tonight. Keep them safe as they go back to their own homes later, *where they live,* and bless all of our family and friends, and continue to give us health and safety and happiness in the future. Thank you so much for this food and bless it to the nourishment of our bodies."

We'd be dying to dig into the food when he'd ask every one of us to go around the table and tell God something we were thankful for that day.

Hunter might say, "Hamburgers!" My sister Macy would chime in, "Sunshine!" I'd add, "Winning in kickball!" And on and on.

It didn't matter if it was something small, something funny, or something profound. Everybody was grateful for *something.*

When it finally came back around to him, my dad would wrap it up, saying, "Please God, forgive us our sins, and help us to do better every day. In Jesus' name. Amen."

And we'd all reply, as loud and fast as we could, "Amen!" as we dug in.

On lots of those nights, Laurie's kids, Hailey and Hunter and Hannah, and Kamron and Kara (friends who lived across the street and just up the road in the opposite direction), and whoever else was there never even went back to their own houses. They'd end up sleeping over, sometimes along with a few other friends from the neighborhood, or kids from other far-off neighborhoods who we knew from school. We would get all of our extra quilts, blankets, and pillows and lay them on the floor, and all the boys would sleep in one room and all the girls in another, and as far as my parents were concerned, all were welcome.

We lived "up the hill," north of Nashville, in a town so small it's lucky to have its own post office. The nearest grocery store is fifteen minutes down the road, but we could get to downtown Nashville in twenty minutes if my parents managed to avoid rush-hour traffic.

We may not have lived in the city where everybody was close to everybody, but that didn't matter, because everyone we knew wanted to come to our neighborhood, and especially to our house.

We all had big back yards surrounded by woods, where us kids would spend hours and hours exploring. Our front yards were big enough for kickball and capture the flag, and playing all kinds of games we'd make up on the spot. I can remember a bunch of us tying our bikes together with ropes to make a big bike-train one day, with our little siblings in the red wagon as the caboose. And everybody's dogs were always running around off-leash, too, right out in the streets, just like us. The streets were small enough, the cars moved slow enough, and the neighbors were close enough that the chances of anything bad happening seemed small.

There were hardly any fences. Kids didn't call each other to see who was home. We'd just go knock. I can't even imagine how many times my mom opened the door to see some boy's or girl's face and hear, "Is Lauren home?"

If I was, she'd let 'em in. And if I wasn't, if I was at soccer practice or something, they would ask, "Well, is Macy home?" and they'd end up coming in to play with my little sister.

Everybody knew everybody, and everybody watched out for everybody. And I know that sounds like something straight out of the 1950s, not the 1990s, as if I grew up in some kind of idyllic small-town neighborhood straight out of the American Dream, but honestly, that's kind of what it felt like.

Our home was a red brick, ranch-style, one-story house with four small bedrooms. It was one of the smaller homes in the neighborhood, actually, which made it all the more fun that it was so full of people all the time. We had a big back porch, and a little front porch, and just enough space in the back yard to fit a trampoline before we hit the woods, which sloped down to a creek. Every time I walked in the front door the house smelled like good food and clean sheets. Not a soapy clean or sterilized clean, more like a place where you just want to stay. Like, "Mmmm. What is that smell? I don't know if I want to eat it or wash with it!"

Our house was almost as full of kids in the wintertime as it was in summertime. Our neighborhood was up a little higher in elevation than Nashville, which meant it was always a few degrees colder and that we'd get more snow. And because we had all kinds of hills in our neighborhood, it was a perfect place to go sledding. So whenever the weatherman predicted there was a snowstorm coming, we would bring a slew of kids

home with us from school. They'd all
tell their parents, "We are going
to the Gregorys' tonight because
we're supposed to have a snow
day tomorrow!" and at the end
of the school day, Dad would
load up our big ol' Chevy Suburban with all the friends we could fit.
Even when all the seats were full I'd

Macy, me, and Dad

open the window and yell, "We can fit three more in our car!" Then we'd
call more people the moment we got home and ask, "Can you come
spend the night?"

There'd be so many kids packed into our house all the time that everyone started calling it "Camp Gregory." In the hallway at school I'd over-
hear kids asking their friends, "Y'all going to Camp Gregory tonight?"

"Yeah," they'd answer. "Of course. It's gonna snow!"

My mom and dad embraced every kid that came over. I could bring
someone home who looked different or talked different, even if they
went to a different church or didn't go to church at all, and I was never
nervous to introduce them to my parents. I never once thought, "Oh, this
person is really different, I don't know how my parents are gonna react."

One of the Gregory House Rules was that everybody is on the same
playing field. My parents simply loved people, and they modeled that the
whole time we were growing up.

They extended grace to everyone they met. We would run into people
in the grocery store, and my mom would have conversations with them,
and even if I could tell that they talked too long about something my
mom didn't really want to talk about, afterward she wouldn't complain.
She would say something to me like, "Gosh, she's so sweet. I just love
her," and she'd really mean it. So many times I would watch my dad interact with all kinds of people, too, and he'd always walk away saying, "What
a great guy!"

My parents' conversations never seemed to revolve around pointing
out differences or faults or flaws in anybody, or about what other people

could do for them or how successful they were, or any of that kind of stuff. What mattered to my parents was how you treat people. And they modeled that by treating people well.

That grace extended to me, to my little sister Macy, who's two and a half years younger than me, and to our little brother, Grayson, who wouldn't be born until I was almost eight years old.

The simple fact that they showed us how to value true beauty for what it is, by accepting people and appreciating them for who they are, is one of the many reasons I knew they would always love me. I never had to wonder if they might stop loving me if I didn't do well on a test or if I didn't make the soccer team, because I never felt like my worth came from any other place than from what really matters: who I am in my heart, and how I treat others.

My parents started a family pretty young. They met when my dad went to visit a friend, who turned out to be a friend of my mom's, at my mom's college. They fell for each other hard, and it wasn't long before my mom moved from Texas to Nashville, in her sophomore year, just to be closer to my dad. They married soon after that, and she was pregnant with me by the time she graduated from Lipscomb University with her degree in social work, which technically means I was on a college graduation stage before I was even born.

My dad loves his family, and he made that clear to us all the time. Getting to watch my dad love on my mom and love on us so much was his greatest gift to me and my siblings. I mean, everyone occasionally has bad days where things aren't going well at work or whatever it may be, but no matter what else was going on in his life, my dad was always so clear about how proud and grateful he was to have us as his family. That's what mattered to him. And it showed.

He loved nature, and he took us on a ton of camping trips growing up. We piled our friends into the Suburban, and he'd bring freeze-dried food and beef jerky, and a water-filter pump so we could make clean water from a river, and he taught us survival skills in the forest. It was intense.

But it was also beautiful, just laying out there under the stars, breathing the fresh air, experiencing nature all up close and personal. Our friends would get to experience that with us, and that made it so much fun for everyone. Looking back, I'm sure it made it easier and more fun for Mom and Dad, too, because we always had friends around to keep us entertained.

What mattered most to my parents was spending time with us kids and our friends, so that all of us could make memories together.

It was in our neighborhood where Mom first met Laurie, who lived in the house on the corner within shouting distance just diagonally across the street. It seemed like fate. They were both pregnant at the time, my mom with me, and Laurie with her and her husband John's first child, Hailey. They started taking walks together every day, which means Hailey and I started hanging out before we were born.

Two years later, Laurie gave birth to Hailey's little brother, Hunter, and then my mom gave birth to my little sister Macy. They were born just a few months apart, which meant Laurie and Lisa were two moms with two sets of kids in diapers. They still laugh to this day about how hard it was raising little ones so close in age, and how they never would have made it without each other.

Hunter was an especially difficult baby. I know this because Laurie talked about it to us as we were growing up. He just cried and cried, to the point where sometimes Laurie couldn't take it. So she'd walk over to our house and beg my mom, "Lisa, please, can you take him for a little while? I just need a *break*," and my mom would happily say, "Sure!" Once Hunter was at our house, in a different environment, doted on by me and crawling around with my sister, he was happy as could be. And so were we.

Laurie was so grateful, she would return the favor anytime Mom needed. If Mom had to run to the store, she'd drop us girls off for a little while at Laurie's. They'd check in with each other every day, and pick up milk or eggs for each other while they were at the grocery just to save the other one the trouble. All that leaning on each other seemed to make the toughest job in the world a lot more enjoyable.

As Hunter got a little older, he stopped his crying, but he turned into a bit of a wild child. He was always getting into some kind of trouble or doing some crazy thing. When he learned to ride bikes, he was the first one to build a ramp and jump it—and I happily followed in his tracks. When we all went out exploring in the woods, he'd be the one to pick up the plywood we found on the ground and uncover a mysterious big hole underneath. Or when we found the place we called The Pit—a ginormous cutout in the side of the hill, like a big abandoned rock quarry or

Me, Macy, Hunter, and Hailey jumping on our new trampoline— clearly not taking Dad's rules seriously

something, which wasn't an uncommon thing to find in the landscape in this hilly part of our state—Hunter was the first to challenge us to see who could start at the bottom and climb up the highest without rolling down in the mud. That was when we were a little older, of course, but even when we were super little, I always took him up on whatever he challenged me to do. It didn't matter if it was something like, "Who can sit on the sticker bush the longest?" (that's a "pricker bush"

for those not in our neck of the woods), we'd manage to turn everything into a game.

I didn't want to be shown up just because I was a girl, so I did whatever I could to keep up with the boys and beat them at their own games. Plus, Hunter was just the sweetest child. He was handsome, even as a kid. Everybody adored him. And even though he was younger than me, it was hard to say no to him. He made everything, *everything,* even the craziest thing or the forbidden thing, sound like it was a good idea. Like this one time, all the way back in kindergarten, when my grandparents bought us a trampoline. Not just any trampoline, but a big, Texas-sized, rectangular trampoline that my dad got upset about, because he insisted somebody was gonna get hurt on it. He made all kinds of rules to try to keep us safe on that thing, and first and foremost was we could never have more than two kids jumping on it at once. Well, one day right after we got it, when all the neighborhood kids were lined up waiting to take a turn, Hunter, who was already jumping on it with another one of our friends, said, "Lauren, Lauren, come on. Come up!"

"No. I can't. We're not allowed!" I said.

"Oh, come on," Hunter replied. "I *dare* you!"

I didn't realize it yet, but saying "yes" to dares was in my blood. So I did it. I broke Dad's rule. I climbed on up, and Hunter figured out that by jumping right next to me and by timing it just right, we could bounce way higher than we could by ourselves. We started goofing off and laughing like crazy, going higher and higher, timing it just right so we could launch each other up, as if we were jumping on one side of a see-saw or something and catapulting the other person into the air. At one point we hit it just right and I bounced way, *way* up. I felt like I was flying. But we were too close together. Hunter bounced up just as I was coming down—and I planted my two front teeth into his skull.

It was horrible. "Ow!" he screamed, and everyone gasped out loud as his head started bleeding. I could hear him crying as I collapsed to the mat of the trampoline, holding my face.

I laid there and didn't move, and a couple of the other kids were like, "Oh, Lauren, get up. You're fine." But I *wasn't* fine. I was just quiet because I needed a minute to wake up from the shock of the pain or something. When I pulled my hands away from my mouth, the blood came spurting out of me like my face was a fountain. It gushed *everywhere.*

Everybody started screaming. One of my front teeth, which wasn't even a little bit loose, got knocked right out of my mouth. Hunter took one look at me and his tears dried up: "Oh, dang," he said with his eyes really wide. "That's way worse than what I got."

Hailey ran inside screaming, "Lisa, Lisa! Lauren's bleeding *everywhere!*"

Mom came running out and I could see the panic on her face the moment she laid eyes on me. She couldn't even tell where the blood was coming from 'cause there was so much of it. She sent some kids inside to grab some towels and then tried to wipe me off to find where the blood was coming from. She carried me into the kitchen and called her parents, my grandparents, who had moved into a house just up the street from us, and next thing I knew they both came rushing down. They wet a wash-cloth and held it tight against my gums, and it seemed like the bleeding was slowing down, but as soon as they took it off to check, more blood spurted all over the kitchen.

Suddenly the washcloth was back in my mouth and they were telling me to bite on it and putting me in the back seat of the car as we went rushing off to an emergency dentist. My second front tooth fell out while we were driving, and I was so out of it by the time we got there, I don't even remember what the dentist did to fix me.

My dad apparently got home from work just a few minutes after we left. I can't imagine what he must've thought as he walked into the house and saw blood spatter all over the kitchen, and Mimi, my grandmother, there trying to clean it up.

"What happened?" he asked. And she told him—and he flew off the handle. "I told y'all this was gonna happen!" he yelled.

He was livid.

He was still livid when we got home.

After making sure I was alright, and doing his best to calm my mom down, he put his hands on my shoulders and looked me in the eye and asked me, "Lauren, what were you thinking?"

I started bawling. I was just so upset, thinking he was never gonna for-give me.

"I don't know, Daddy!" I cried. "I didn't mean to do it. I didn't think it was gonna happen!"

"I know you didn't think it was going to happen, Lauren. But you're a kid! I'm the grown-up. I *knew* it was going to happen! That's why I put those rules in place. Rules that you didn't listen to," he said.

"I know. I'm sorry. I'm *sorry*," I cried.

He hugged me and said, "Alright, alright. Calm down. I know you didn't mean for this to happen. We all mess up sometimes, Lauren. All of us. I'm just glad you and Hunter didn't hurt yourselves any worse than you did."

After a moment of quiet in his arms, my tears dried up a little bit and I got up the courage to ask him the one thing that was foremost in my mind.

"Daddy?"

"Yes, Lauren."

"Are you gonna take the trampoline away?"

I started crying at the very thought of it, and my dad let out a sigh.

"Now what good would it do to take the trampoline away *now*?" he said. "Does it make any sense that I would throw it away *after* you learned your lesson? You did learn your lesson, right?"

"Yes," I said.

"And you'll do better next time?"

"Yes."

"You'll follow the rules and make sure that all your *friends* follow the rules?"

"Yes," I said.

"Well, good," he said. "When you make mistakes, learn from 'em. Do better next time. Do a little better tomorrow. I just wish you'd listened to me in the first place, because I've already made a lot of mistakes in my

All I want for 'Halloween' is my two front teeth

life, and if you'll listen to me, maybe you won't have to make those mistakes yourself. You know what I mean?"

"Uh-huh," I said, nodding.

I really didn't know what he meant by that. Dad said things like "Nobody's perfect" and "Everybody makes mistakes" all the time. But at that age, I couldn't see it. It felt to me like my mom and dad *were* perfect. They were just so good to everybody. They were so loving, and they always seemed to know right from wrong—honestly, that was a lot to live up to. Seeing how disappointed my dad was when I broke his rule, that hurt bad.

I think that feeling of disappointing him

hurt worse than my mouth did. I wasn't even that upset about my two front teeth being gone, mostly because my mom kept reminding me how

cute I looked with my two teeth missing. I also got to eat mashed potatoes through a straw, which was fun, at least for the first few days. But poor Hunter. He ended up with a permanent scar on the top of his head. It's like I branded him with my mouth!

Four generations on the couch: Bemaw, Mimi, and Mom with Macy and me

None of that scared us. The two of us got back up on our trampoline a few days later. *Just* the two of us. On opposite ends of it. As far apart as we could get without falling over the edge. And I don't remember having any problems with the trampoline after that. My dad was right: We'd learned our lesson. Throwing the trampoline away wouldn't have done any good at that point. That trampoline was fun! We just needed to learn to respect it, and to respect Dad's rules, which were there for our own good. And we did.

Skinned knees, stubbed toes, bumps, bruises, and missing teeth were just part of the way I learned my lessons. The hard way. Through firsthand experience.

My daring, tomboy spirit had been passed down to me by not one, but *both* of my parents.

My mom, Lisa, was the "fun mom"—the athletic one who'd take us anywhere we wanted to go and do just about anything we wanted to do. Some parents even called her the "crazy mom" for all of the messes she'd let us make in her home and the things she'd let us get away with in our neighborhood. Her particular style of parenting made all my friends fall in love with her, though, and it would only get bigger and bolder in the years ahead.

But my dad? Steve? For all of his rules and worrying, he was the bigger risk-taker. For one thing, he flew planes for a living. He'd made a solid run at flying *Top Gun*–style fighter jets for the Navy, with his heart set on becoming an astronaut. For real. An astronaut—until he was restricted from flying at extremely high altitudes due to a rare medical condition called sickle cell trait. He didn't let that stop him, though. After being honorably discharged, then re-enlisting, then getting honorably discharged again, he started flying private jets for a living when I was just a baby.

Sitting at the edge of our woods with Dad

That's not all. He also wrangled snakes just for fun. Truly. Before he and Mom met, he was a regular participant in the annual Rattlesnake Roundups in Texas, and he taught me how to wrangle snakes at such an early age that I barely remember a time before I knew how to do it.

Why would any man teach his little girl to wrangle snakes, you might ask? The answer is simple: 'cause he wanted me to be capable. He wanted me to know things. He didn't want me to be scared of a harmless garden snake, or to feel helpless when I came across one of the venomous copperheads that are pretty common in rural Tennessee. "You just get a stick or something, and come at it from behind," he'd tell me while he showed me how to do it on some random snake we'd come up on in the woods in our back yard. "And right up on their neck, just pin them down with whatever you've got. Not hard enough to hurt 'em, but just enough to walk up to it and grab them behind their head." And then he'd let me try it myself.

The first time I grabbed the head of a good-sized snake and it started wrapping its tail all around my forearm, I'm not gonna lie, it scared me half to death!

"Hold its head. I mean, they can wrap their tail around you as much as they want to, but as long as you've got control of their head, they're not gonna hurt you. Trust me."

Kara (Kamron's sister) and me with one of the first snakes I caught in our back yard

I did what he told me, and I didn't get hurt.

I watched my dad take a whole nest full of copperheads down from a tree at a friend's house near the end of our street one day. And the older I got, the more my friends and their moms started calling on *me* to come get snakes out of their yards, too. I'm in my college friend Amber's phone as "Snake Girl," just because I got a snake out of her mom's yard one day—all because my dad taught me to not be afraid of things I didn't need to be afraid of.

He was like that with everything. Like, "You don't have to be afraid." If he was teaching us to climb a tree or to rock climb or whatever it was, he would always say, "I'm not gonna let you fall. I got you. Trust me."

I did.

If my dad said, "Trust me," whatever he was talking about, I knew I was gonna be fine.

He may not have been a teacher by trade, but he was definitely a teacher by calling.

And for all of his daring and adventurousness, Dad was kind of a nerd at heart. He never let go of his dream of becoming an astronaut, which means he knew all kinds of stuff about NASA and astronomy. One of his great joys in life was waking me up in the middle of the night and taking me out into the middle of the street, where it was dark enough to lay back and look up into a treeless sky during the peak of the annual Perseid meteor shower. He would point to all of the constellations as we waited for our eyes to adjust, and then the two of us would gasp in surprise at every one of those flares of stardust as they burned through the atmosphere and streaked across the sky. Some of 'em were so big, I almost thought I could hear them make a *whoooosh* as they flew over.

My dad taught me that the night sky in the summertime gives us the greatest show on Earth.

It was on one of those August nights when I remember looking up the street to Hailey and Hunter's house and catching the glow of a cigarette in the dark. It took a few seconds for my eyes to make out the two figures on the porch, and I realized that while my dad and I were laying in the middle of the street, John had woken Hunter up to watch the very same meteor shower.

Even at nine or ten years old, I knew that was something special. I remember thinking how cool it was that we were laying in the middle of the street at the center of our neighborhood, watching a meteor shower in the middle of the night, and we had friends right next door who were up doing the exact same thing.

As I got older, even when there wasn't a meteor shower, if friends came over and we didn't have plans and someone said, "What do you want to do?" a lot of times I'd say, "You wanna get a blanket and go lay outside and look at the stars?" New friends might have thought it was kind of a weird idea at first, but I guarantee you they didn't think it was weird by the time we'd gone and done it. I think most of the friends I knew growing up would still pick that activity over a million other things we could do with our time. It didn't matter if it was two of us, or ten of us. There was nothing better than those random conversations we'd end up having under the stars.

I don't think there was anything I loved to do more when I was a kid.

Brown feet, lightning bugs, good friends, family, open doors, open hearts, night skies . . .

A simple life.

Even as a little girl I remember thinking, "It doesn't get much better than this."

2

Listening

Of course, life isn't *always* simple. It doesn't matter how much you try to keep it simple, either. Life gets complicated. And it seems to get more and more complicated the older you get.

Finding a way to hold on to the life you have, or to get to the life you want—a life that matters to you and holds meaning for you, no matter what that life may be—that's where the challenges lie. And I think one of the biggest lessons I learned growing up is that, thankfully, none of us have to face those challenges alone.

I was lucky to have my parents and Macy around me all the time. And my dad's parents, and my mom's parents, especially after they moved in up the street. We had cousins around all the time, too: My dad's sister's daughters, my cousins Karlie and Allie Brooke, lived nearby, and they were like a second set of sisters to me. And growing up with Hailey and Hunter just across the street, and my friends Kamron and his older sister Kara, and so many other kids my age, gave me an incredible community of love and support throughout my childhood. All of these people formed what I came to call "the Crew"—a tight-knit group of friends and family that seemed to sprout in our neighborhood and kept growing in ever-expanding circles through school and church communities as we all got older.

My sister and I, and eventually our little brother, Grayson, all went to

Goodpasture Christian School, a private K-through-12 school where my dad had gone when he was a kid. It's a small campus, with the kindergarten set off in a little red schoolhouse out past the playing fields, and the larger, brick elementary, middle school, and high school buildings with blue-painted accents all just a few steps from each other. We only had eighty or so students per class, so it was a really close community. A lot of the moms and dads got to know each other just waiting in line to pick us up at the end of the day, or when we all sat next to each other in the stands watching the high school kids play football on Friday nights. There were generational connections, too, since quite a few of the kids who went there were the sons and daughters of Goodpasture alumni. Some of the coaches who coached my dad were still around when I was there, and over the years I'd end up with a couple of the same teachers he had, too. There was something nice about having all of those connections—as if there were always people looking out for us, who knew us and our parents, everywhere we turned.

Hailey and Hunter and Kamron and Kara didn't go to the same school we did. They went to Davidson Academy, another private school about four miles from Goodpasture. But we ended up getting to know all of their friends from Davidson, and soon their Davidson friends became our friends and our Goodpasture friends became *their* friends.

And then we made even more connections through our church. Our family went to Madison Church of Christ during this time, a traditional, I would say straitlaced church in a big brick building, also not far from the Goodpasture campus. We were there like clockwork every Sunday morning, listening to sermons about the Word of God and the importance of the very real presence of Jesus in our lives. We also went on Wednesday nights when our parents took us to youth group, which was a little bit more relaxed. Sometimes we'd have speakers come in to tell us about the mission trips they'd been on, spreading the Word and helping children and families in faraway corners of the world. I always loved listening to those talks, and I imagined myself traveling on mission trips when I was old enough to go myself. Those Wednesday nights led to us making even more friends with kids from other schools and other neighborhoods, too.

One friend I haven't mentioned, because he wasn't part of our Crew yet, was a dark-haired boy named Thomas Rhett Akins. Thomas Rhett and I first crossed paths when he moved to the area and started going to Goodpasture in first grade. We didn't have the same teacher that year, so I didn't *really* get to know him. In fact, I'm pretty sure the first time I really noticed him was when a lot of other people noticed him, too: in the third grade, when he played the lead in the school Christmas play, *A Christmas Carol.*

Thomas Rhett played Scrooge, and he was great. He really nailed the "bah humbug" part.

Everyone at Goodpasture, including me, recognized that that boy had talent to spare. Beyond that, I didn't think much of anything about him. Thomas Rhett's mom, Paige, and my mom got to know each other before Thomas Rhett and I ever became friends. Paige and my mom would see each other at pickup at the end of the day, and since she and Thomas Rhett went to Madison Church, too, we'd cross paths and say hello before or after church. But for a long time, that's all our connection to each other really was.

The only reason I even bring up those early years is to make the point that you never really know who you're *not* paying attention to, right now. You can just never know who might end up being really important to you later in life.

And the bigger point I'm trying to make is that I had a lot of people around me: my family, my neighborhood Crew, my school community, my church community, people I didn't even realize would be there for me later on, and all of that was an extension of the biggest support system of all. The one I was just beginning to understand: the relationship between me and God.

One of my earliest lessons in understanding the power of God's influence in our lives came in that very same third-grade school year.

For most of my childhood, I thought my family was just going to be the four of us: Mom, Dad, Macy, and me. (Plus our extended family, and our

neighborhood family, and our school family, and our church family . . .)
But when I was six, maybe going on seven, our neighbor Laurie got pregnant with her third child, and something changed around our house.

Our family of four, with a new tree we planted

My mom started say-
ing things like, "I just
know I'm supposed to
have a third baby," and
my dad was like, "Nope.
No, we're not. We are
good."

It started out kind of
lighthearted and funny.
My mom would bring
up Laurie, and how
they'd had their first two kids around the same time, and she'd say to my
dad, "Don't you want a boy, or at least to *try* for a boy?" But my dad always said, "No."

It got to the point where it started to get real tense between them. My
dad truly did not want another child, and he really dug his heels in. I didn't
know this whole story at the time, but I later learned that he actually went
to Laurie and asked her, "Please do not talk to Lisa about being pregnant.
Do not let her touch your belly. We are *not* having a third baby. We're
done with two," and he meant it.

My mom prayed to God, over and over, begging God to change his
mind, and one day at lunch, while Macy and I were in school, my mom
came right out and begged my dad.

"No," he insisted. "We've already been through this. We are not having
a third baby!"

Mom started crying so hard she nearly choked on her soup. "Please,
Steve. Please!"

He just wouldn't budge.

My mom cried all the way back to Goodpasture, and she was still wip-
ing her eyes in the pickup line when, clear as day, she heard a voice in her
head that she knew in her heart was the voice of God. She had never

heard Him speak to her directly before that moment, and I don't think she's heard His voice so audibly ever since. But right then and there, God told her, "Lisa, you are going to have a third baby."

She took a quick breath, and she *knew*.

"Oh my gosh," she thought. "Okay, okay, it's happening. It's *happening*."

She was at peace about it from that moment on, and she said Dad walked in the house that night from work and he came in and hugged her while Macy and I were off playing somewhere and he had completely changed his mind. He held her in his arms and said, "Well, do you want to start trying tonight?" And she was floored.

"Yes!" she said.

Of course, I didn't learn all of these details until I was a little older, but that "yes" led to Mom and Dad sitting Macy and me down a couple of months later to tell us that God had blessed our family: We had a little brother or sister on the way.

Laurie's third child, Hannah, was born right around that time, and she immediately felt like a little sister to Macy and me. And when our baby

New baby Grayson with his new big sisters

brother Grayson was born the following July, we all just fell in love with him. Those first few months with a new baby brother were one of the happiest periods I can remember from my whole childhood. I turned eight years old that November, and heading into the holiday season, experiencing all of the love around the Thanksgiving table, and the lights and the magic of Christmas through the eyes of a little bright-eyed baby just made everything sparkle even brighter than it had before. And believe me, Christmastime always sparkled in our family. Like, I mean, *Christmas* is a verb to us. We Christmas *hard*.

We all helped out decorating, with as many lights as the electrical outlets would hold. And it was always a huge outing to go pick out our Christmas tree, which we'd get flocked, so it looked like it was covered in freshly fallen snow. We decorated the tree all together with all kinds of ornaments we collected and cherished and reminisced about over hot chocolate every year.

My mom carried little Grayson in her arms as we trekked out on our annual pre-Christmas tradition of

In front of all the dreamy Opryland lights

going to Opryland to see the Christmas lights, and Macy and I were so excited for him to see it all, it's like it doubled the excitement of the whole experience for the two of us. For those who don't know, Gaylord Opryland is this massive resort and conference center in Nashville, right near the Grand Ole Opry stage, that's all spread out over a few acres. And inside, there's a giant, glassed-in atrium with a man-made river, and fountains, and trees, and gardens, with all kinds of bars and restaurants spread around in that beautiful setting. It's a magical place to visit just about any time of year, but at Christmastime, they go over the top. They decorate the whole facility, inside and out, with what has to be well over a million Christmas lights. They turn the whole facility into a winter wonderland. My parents had brought me there every year since I was born. And of course the Gregorys never travel alone. We always bring the Crew. So we had grandparents, cousins, friends, and their families come with us, and we'd take in all the sights and sounds of that wonderland together.

There were carriages drawn by Clydesdales, those big, giant workhorses, all dressed in jingle bells. And there was a place where we could write a letter to Santa and put it in a mailbox that delivered straight to the North Pole. And out front there's a Nativity scene, and all kinds of shimmering angels, and what looks like a giant Christmas tree made entirely of lights—ginormous strands of lights strung from the ground up to the top of a giant pole that rises from the ground like a skyscraper. And even though no one is supposed to step inside that "tree," our family made a tradition of stepping over the little knee-high fence and looking straight up into all of those lights and spinning round and round until some of us got dizzy and fell to the ground laughing.

Macy and I were just so excited to share all of this with our new little brother that when Christmas morning came, we woke up super early and woke up our parents and just about jumped out of our matching pajamas waiting for our grandparents to show up before we ran to the tree to see what Santa had brought us.

My mom and her parents were super close. She was adopted, and they never made a big deal about that. They never considered theirs any "different" from any other parent-child relationship. To them, adoption was just another way of having a baby, a different sort of "birth story" they might tell, the same way my mom and dad might tell the birth story of Macy, or me, or Grayson. You wouldn't know it or even think about it if they had not told you.

I'm sure their closeness and the way my mom and grandparents treated her adoption as such a normal part of life rubbed off on me, though. It was almost like they all silently recognized that God had put them together to make a family where there might not have been one otherwise.

My mom had a real close relationship with her dad. They were like best friends in some ways. She was so happy when they moved up the street from us, and both Mimi and Granddaddy (as I called my mom's parents) were always so joyful around all of us kids. I'll just never forget the way Granddaddy looked at Grayson on his very first Christmas. He whispered in the sweetest voice, "Hello, Grayson. Merry Christmas," as he held my baby brother close in his arms.

I give my parents a lot of credit for teaching us kids to recognize just how fortunate we were to be alive, and to live in a free country where we were free to worship as we pleased, and especially just to be in each other's company. I think sometimes it's easy to take those things for granted, but we didn't. We cherished them. And I think that's why our Christmas traditions were so sacred. The familiarity of gathering around that tree every year, going to Opryland, exchanging gifts, enjoying Christmas breakfast together before making cookies and watching classic Christmas movies from beanbag chairs with new pairs of cozy socks on our feet, spending the whole day hanging out with family, together—it mattered. Every bit of it mattered. It was all important to us. And it was fun! That was the way we were raised, and there was just no way any of us were going to miss any of that. *Ever.*

In our little kitchen with Granddaddy and Mom

It's not like I was taught to be such a homebody that I didn't dream about doing other things with my life in the future. I used to dream I'd grow up to be a California surfer girl, even though I'd never been out west and never stepped foot on a surfboard. I used to dream of traveling to Africa someday, too. I don't know why. I was just drawn to that far-off continent, even though I'd never traveled all that far from Nashville. There were lots of dreams like that, which I never really thought would come true because they were just too far from the life I knew or would cost too much money to accomplish, but they definitely lived in my heart. And even when I dreamed of those things, I could not imagine ever spending Christmas anywhere but right there where I was, surrounded by the people I loved.

Now, I know all of this makes it seem like my parents are these really special, amazing people who worked real hard to create this idyllic life for their children. And they absolutely are! But what I don't want anyone thinking is that my parents were somehow "perfect." Because they absolutely were not. And I'm not saying this to put them down in any way. It's just that, as Dad told us all the time, "Nobody's perfect! We all mess up." And my parents messed up plenty before us kids were around, and after. But, like my dad also said, those mistakes are the things that teach us some pretty important life lessons—and sometimes the things that go wrong are just God stepping in to try to lead us in a better direction.

I mentioned earlier that my dad always called it like he saw it. He was blunt. He was honest. And as I got old enough to understand a little bit more, he explained to me why he was like that: "Because there were a lot of things I had to figure out on my own when I was younger," he said. "So I figure, by telling you all the things I had to learn the hard way, and by being honest with you about everything I went through, you won't have to suffer as much as I did just to figure out how life works."

You could call it *open-book parenting*. Basically, my dad told us everything. *Everything*. Even things that made my mom blush.

For instance, really early on, like from the moment I was old enough to ask how Mom and Dad met, my dad told us that he had previously been engaged to another woman. I don't think a lot of other parents would talk about that kind of thing, but he did—because he wanted us to learn from the story.

Basically, Dad thought that woman was the love of his life. He was head-over-heels for her, but then she broke up with him, and he was devastated. He thought his whole world had come to an end. He just couldn't get over it. He found himself depressed and living in West Texas, drilling for oil and wrangling rattlesnakes and, basically, feeling lost in life.

Then one day, thanks to some prompting from a friend of his, he started praying for God to bring him new love. He started praying to God every night when he got home from work. When he found himself getting too sleepy to pray, he would get on his knees and pray. That's when he realized that kneeling kind of hurt, which kept him awake and kept his mind a little sharper, and he thought, "Huh. I guess that's why so many people kneel when they pray!" And over time, he turned his prayer into more of a meditation, trying to quiet his mind and focus on one good thing (like it says in the Bible), all while asking God to bring new love into his life.

Then one night, he had a dream, and in that dream he saw a woman standing about eight or ten feet away from him, surrounded by light. He was taken by the shape of her backlit hair, and the way she held herself, and how her hands were held down by her waist, and the color of her clothes, and he woke straight up out of that dream and said out loud in his otherwise empty apartment, "That's her! That's her!"

He used to tell us this story all the time, and swear that he knew for certain that what God had shown him in that dream was the woman he was going to marry.

Well, it wasn't two weeks later when his friend Brent, who happened to be student body president at Abilene Christian University, invited him to come hear him speak at the church on campus. And as they were leaving that night, walking down a flight of stairs, my dad looked ahead at a group of college girls who were standing there in the lobby of the building, and one of them looked just like the girl in his dream. My dad thought, "Is that her?"

My dad wasn't the type to approach strange women out of the blue, but in that moment, he walked straight up to her and said, "Hey, I know it's unorthodox, you don't know me, but my name's Steve. I wanted to introduce myself." The girl's friends were all looking at him like he was crazy, but he kept talking. "I'm here to ask you out," he said. "I know it's kinda forward, but I'd like to go out with you."

Well, that girl and her friends all thought it was hilarious. They started laughing so loud everybody turned and looked. But Dad didn't let up. He knew this was the girl from his dream.

"I have a boyfriend, and we're practically engaged!" she told him.

And my dad said, "Yeah, well, you're gonna be tested. Because if you're really gonna marry this guy, it's gotta be for real, and you're gonna need to be tested—and I'm gonna be your test."

They laughed even louder at that point.

My dad didn't flinch. He handed her a card and said, "This is my number."

"I'm not going out with you!" the girl insisted.

To which my dad replied, "You will at some point. I'm not gonna bug you anymore, but you will. Trust me."

He turned and walked away, and met back up with his friend Brent, who hadn't heard any of this conversation (except for the laughter from across the room), and the girl suddenly called after them: "Brent! Wait. Do you *know* him?" she asked.

Brent said, "Steve? Yeah. He's a good friend of mine. Why?"

My dad quickly asked Brent how he knew her, and Brent said, "That's Lisa Dunaway. She's like my sister. We grew up down the street from each other."

My dad just smiled. At that moment he knew for sure that this was all meant to be.

Next thing he knew, Lisa called out, "Wait a minute." She left her girl-friends standing there, walked right over to my dad, and said, "I changed my mind. I wanna go out with you," and her friends' jaws just about hit the floor.

The next day, my dad took Lisa Dunaway up in a plane on their very first date. He rolled the plane and pulled some Gs in it just to kind of test her out, and my mom never threw up or anything.

That was the start of it all.

From that day forward, my dad said he understood that being dumped by his ex-fiancée hadn't been a bad thing. It was a *good* thing, "because obviously I wasn't meant to marry her. I was meant to marry your mom, and to have you kids, and now, I'm the happiest man alive."

The point of him telling us this story was to teach us that all of that heartbreak he went through was actually something to celebrate. It was a good thing, in the end. It was what God wanted and it was what was meant to be.

"And so maybe, when things go wrong in our lives," he said, "we ought to be grateful, and to think about how those bad things might actually be pointing us toward something much better."

Of course, not every story he told had that much meaning to it. Some-times he just opened up because he felt like opening up. Like when he told us stories about dating my mom, which made it seem like some sort of miracle that the two of them ever matured enough to get married and start a family in the first place.

Before I tell this story, let me just preface this by saying that my parents celebrated their thirty-second anniversary while I was working on this book, so they've clearly got the whole marriage thing figured out just fine. I think we could all learn a thing or two from a couple who've managed to stay together for that many years. But before my mom and dad had any of us kids, they used to make a game out of daring each other to do really gross things.

It all started innocently one day when the two of them were visiting my mom's grandparents' farm in Texas. The two of them were sharing a sandwich out in a field, and one of them dropped it, and it fell right onto a dried-up cow patty. That's when my dad said, "I bet you won't pick it up and still eat it." And my mom said, "Yes, I will!"

And she *did*. She brushed it off a little bit and she ate it! She did it just to prove him wrong, and she walked away feeling victorious.

Their dares got so gross after that, I'll do my parents a favor and not describe them here. But, like I said, saying "yes" to dares is in my blood. For better or worse.

Even after us kids came along and the gross-out games stopped, they still egged each other on with all kinds of dares and bets. During the winter of my third-grade year, it snowed one day, and our whole back yard, which was mostly rocks and twigs because the grass doesn't really grow back there, wound up covered in a thick layer of snow. My dad turned to my mom in front of us kids and our friends and said, "Lisa, I bet you won't put your bikini on and roll all the way down the hill in the snow." And Mom was like, "Yes, I will. For a price." So he said, "Okay. Would you do it for a hundred dollars?" And she said, "Absolutely!"

It was sixteen degrees out, and Mom put her bikini on, and rolled down the entirety of our back yard in the snow, over all those rocks and twigs, and at the bottom of the slope she slammed into one of those Fisher-Price car toys that toddlers ride. She said she didn't even feel it—because by that time, her whole body was just completely *numb*.

She ran back inside and all of us kids got a bunch of blankets and tried to wrap her up. "Mom!" "Miss Lisa!" "Lay down!" we yelled as she came in shivering and headed for the recliner, but when we tried to hug her in those blankets she screamed, "Don't touch me. Nobody *touch* me!" Apparently running an ice-cold body straight into the heat of the house hurt a whole lot worse than running into a Fisher-Price car.

She won her hundred dollars, though, and that made her smile through the pain, which inspired me and my friend Kara to come up with a few of our own challenges. The two of us ran into my bedroom and put bikinis on and dared each other to do back handsprings on the trampoline. This was at night. After dark. And my parents were right there videotaping the whole thing from the warmth of our living room, laughing with us while we froze our butts off.

Mom and me at the beach in Destin, Florida

I think most people would look at my parents like they're fairly sophisticated, well-educated people, which makes all of this crazy behavior even funnier to me as I look back on it. But life with my parents is the only life I ever knew, so to me, laughter and silliness are just part of a happy home.

In fact, I hardly remember a time before that third-grade year when laughter wasn't the dominant sound in our home.

That was all about to change.

Macy and I were playing over at our grandparents' house one day that winter of 1998. We used to play Monopoly a lot in the room up above their garage, and I was just finishing up a good long game with Mimi when I realized that Granddaddy had been gone a long time. My sister had gone up to Hunter's house to play, and Granddaddy had gone downstairs to watch her walk up the street and to finish up some work on his pickup truck. At least that's what we thought.

An hour or so had passed when I asked Mimi, "Where is Granddaddy?"

"I think he's still working on the truck," she said.

I walked over and looked out the window, and sure enough, I could see him laying down underneath his truck.

I stood there for a few seconds, and kept looking—and he didn't move an inch.

"Mimi," I said. "Granddaddy's not moving."

She came and stood next to me and looked out the window, and she started panicking.

"What is he doing?" I asked.

She didn't answer. She could clearly tell that something was wrong. She ran downstairs and out the door and got down on the ground and shook him a little bit. Then she ran right back in, went straight to the phone, and dialed 911 as I ran downstairs, opened the door to the garage, and yelled, "Granddaddy?"

He didn't move. So I screamed for him: *"Granddaddy!"*

My grandmother pulled me back inside the house and told me to stay put. She ran outside, got down on her knees, and tried to pull him out from under the truck, but he wasn't moving. He wasn't moving at all. She started crying the most painful cry I'd ever heard.

And so did I.

My Granddaddy never got up that day.

He was gone.

For the first time I could recall, our house filled with silence and tears. It still filled up with people, though. Friends came calling. Family. People we knew from church. People we knew from school. They said things like, "I'm so sorry," and "He was a great man."

Mostly they were just quiet, and sad.

My mom was devastated. She didn't cry a whole lot. She was never much of a crier, and neither was I. But I could feel the weight of her sadness.

There were times when she would hold us so tight it felt like she might break us. And there were times when she just didn't want anyone to touch her, as if her body had gone numb and the pain of a warm hug from her

Granddaddy came to Goodpasture to watch me in a school program

husband or children was too much to take. So I leaned on my dad, and he held me and Macy and little Grayson. Grayson, who was seven months old and too young to understand, and who would grow up without remembering the sound of our granddaddy's voice, how his whiskers felt on our cheek when he'd give us a kiss, or what it felt like when he gave us one of his big bear hugs.

My dad was our rock through it all. He said it would all be okay. He said Mom would be okay, she just needed some time. And I knew well enough at that point that I could trust his word.

It was only at my grandfather's funeral that I learned something I'd never known: My parents and grandmother were thankful he'd lived as long as he did.

Granddaddy had come close to death once before. Many years earlier, when my mom was just sixteen years old, he had suffered a heart attack. Before the ambulance arrived that day, Mimi got down on her knees and prayed, "Please, God. Don't take him now. Let him live long enough to see his grandchildren. Please!"

God answered that prayer.

Grayson would be my mother's last child. My granddaddy's last grandchild. And he lived long enough to see him. To hold him in his arms.

Hearing that gave me an eerie feeling. Almost like, "Be careful what you wish for." It struck me that my grandmother's very specific prayer was answered very specifically. My grandfather had lived long enough to see all of his grandchildren, but that was it. Maybe she should have prayed to let him see all of his grandchildren grow up, or graduate from high school, or why not pray to let him live till he was a hundred and three?

I was still young and naïve and trying to come to grips with the loss of one of the best men I ever knew. My first loss of a family member. My first experience with death at all. It was the first real concrete reason I had to believe that heaven is someplace real, which meant that Granddaddy was now at peace.

A snow day at home before church, with Macy, on the back porch

The deeper lesson, the lesson I'd been learning pretty steadily my whole life without even realizing it, though, was one that settled into my heart in a way it never had before that moment. I'd listened to the story of my mom praying for a third baby, and I knew how God answered that prayer. I'd listened to my dad's story of praying to find new love, and I knew how God had answered that prayer, too. And now I knew clearly that God had answered my grandmother's prayer as well. Which meant that the lessons I'd learned from my parents, the words I'd heard from preachers and at youth group—they were *true*. They were *real*.

God answers prayers.

He *listens*.

He's listening right now, I thought.

God's listening.

3

First Crushes

After Granddaddy passed, Mom started volunteering at school more often, and she'd offer to take even more kids home to play with us than she used to.

When a bunch of us kids were playing in the yard, instead of staying inside the house, she'd come out and play with us. She'd hike with us in the woods, all the way out to The Pit. She'd take us to the movies, even on a school night. Or she'd get us all in the kitchen making dozens and dozens of cookies or muffins together to share with everybody we knew.

She became twice the "fun mom" she'd ever been.

She even took us out rolling. I think they call it "TP-ing" in other parts of the country, but we called it rolling—when you go and cover all the trees in the front yard of somebody's house with toilet paper. And for us, it wasn't a mean thing. It was more of a prank, and almost a badge of honor. It was almost like a popularity thing. Like, "Oh. You got rolled!" We would be at school the next day saying, "Oh my gosh. Who do you think did it?"

"Well, I heard so-and-so spent the night at so-and-so's house. I bet it was them." It was *fun*. And I *loved* it. Sometimes we would do it in our neighborhood, but other times, if it was a house we had to drive to, Mom would drive us late at night.

First she would take us to the grocery store, where we would get expired meat for cheap at the deli. And then we'd have one person on dog duty, feeding that meat to any loose dogs at the house so they would be quiet. And we'd make sure to have some baseball players with us so they could throw the toilet paper all the way up in the top of the trees. And Mom wasn't just driving, she was throwing those rolls up and over the branches right alongside us, trying not to laugh too loud and wake anyone up.

And when we got rolled back? It was almost like Christmas morning. If Mom was first up in the morning and looked outside and we had toilet paper all in the trees, she would wake us up excited, like, "Oh my gosh. We got rolled!"

"Get the trash bags," she'd say, and we'd trek outside to clean it all up. We had to climb way up in the trees to get it all out, and that was just part of the fun. The worst was when it rained, though, 'cause the paper would just cling to everything and ended up being there for a long time.

Honestly, it's like my mom turned into a great big kid in the years after Granddaddy died, and it made all of my friends want to be around her more than ever. She just seemed to be smiling and laughing all the time, and that definitely sunk in with me. I took it to mean that after losing her dad, she just wanted to live every day to the fullest. As if his death had reminded her that she didn't want to waste one minute of her life doing anything less than enjoying the life she had, with her kids, and her husband, and her friends—her whole Crew.

She never said anything about any of that to me. I came up with that theory all by myself. And I didn't really think about it a whole lot. I mean, I was *eight*. But after seeing her so sad, I was so glad to see her smiling all the time, and I'm pretty sure I tucked that example of how she handled herself somewhere in the back of my mind for future reference—just in case.

Life definitely seemed to get more and more fun with every passing year, and not just because of my mom. Getting older meant us kids had more freedom to do all kinds of things. And even the little things, like getting to ride our bikes a little further out in our neighborhood, meant a lot.

Of course, Hunter always pushed those freedoms to the extreme. Like the time he built a giant ramp by the pond in our neighborhood, right at the bottom of a ginormous hill. He went riding down the hill full blast and launched himself off that ramp into the air and right into the water, bike and all.

A bunch of the neighborhood kids stood there watching in awe from the shore, but it was honestly too much for me. I was worried he was gonna hurt himself.

"You are a moron!" I yelled at him, as Kamron came flying down the hill and flew up and landed in the water right next to him. "What are you gonna do if that bike lands on you in the water and you, like, break a rib? Good luck swimming back!" I yelled.

"Aww, come on!" he yelled back, flipping his wet hair out of his eyes with a shake of his head. "Who's next?"

"Not me," I replied. Nobody else wanted to go, either. Even Kamron

Hunter (left) and Kamron, being Hunter and Kamron, in our kitchen

realized it was a pretty dumb thing to do and decided not to take another run at it.

"Well, fine," Hunter yelled back. "I guess I'll go do it again by myself." And he did. And we all watched him in awe, knowing nothing we said was gonna stop him from having his fun.

I can't remember how old we were when Hunter found one of those big M-80 firecrackers in one of our dad's dresser drawers. We were definitely too young to be playing with fireworks by ourselves, that's for sure. Our families were always getting together and shooting fireworks off at one of the neighborhood houses during the holidays or one of our birthdays. And we'd been warned about a million times not to ever play with them without adult supervision. But Hunter, he got it into his head that it would be *really cool* to see what happened if we set off that M-80 inside a glass bottle.

Actually, I think it was my idea to try that, but he's the one who decided to run with it.

We did it over at his house, on his back porch, while his mom was up on a ladder painting the walls of their living room.

"You ready?" he whispered.

"Yeah!" I said.

Hunter lit that M-80 and dropped it into a bottle, and I was just gonna stand there right next to it and watch it explode. I don't know what we were thinking. Thankfully Hunter was smart enough to whisper, "Hide behind the chair! Quick!" So we did. We hid behind an Adirondack chair on his porch and looked at it through the slots in the wood, and when that M-80 blew up, it was like a bomb. We stood up all wide-eyed with our ears ringing, and we looked around, and the whole back of the chair was full of shards of glass. The explosion made Laurie fall off the ladder inside, and she came running out of the house, kind of limping a little bit, scared to death at what she was about to find.

"What happened?!" she yelled.

We told her, and she looked at all the shards of glass in the back of the chair and all the color drained from her face.

"And neither one of you got hurt?" she asked, looking us all over for shards and blood.

We both shook our heads.

"We're fine," Hunter said.

That's when Laurie got mad. And I mean *mad*. I got sent right back to my house and I could hear her yelling at Hunter from all the way across the street.

The two of us weren't allowed to play together out of our parents' sight for a good while after that.

Even when there were plenty of eyes on us, though, Hunter and I could still manage to get into trouble. And it wasn't just me. He had that effect on everybody. His enthusiasm for testing life's limits was almost as infectious as my mom's enthusiasm for wanting us all to have fun.

That kind of enthusiasm in life, for anything, tends to draw people in like a magnet.

Spending all those years keeping up with Hunter and Kamron and the other boys in my neighborhood definitely put me in the tomboy category for most of my childhood. Hanging out with the guys was just something I was used to. Kamron and Hunter were like my brothers. I just did so much with them. I mean, when the girls would start playing with dolls or fixing their hair, I'd be like, "I'm gonna go see what *they're* doing."

It toughened me up, too. I played defense in soccer 'cause I wasn't afraid to just totally stop a girl with my body. If somebody from the other team was coming down toward our goal, I barely even looked at the ball she was dribbling. I just got in there and body-checked her. That was definitely because of all the time spent going toe-to-toe with the boys in my neighborhood.

As we headed into middle school, though, the fact that so many of my best friends were boys caused some awkward moments. I just didn't know how to adjust. It all happened so quickly, the way boys and girls started looking at each other and talking about each other and their priorities started changing almost as fast as our bodies were changing.

I mean, why is it that some boys felt like brothers to me while others . . . didn't?

The first place I ever had a huge crush on a boy was at church camp, of all places.

It was the summer heading into sixth grade, and a bunch of us were at this camp for a whole week—including one talented, dark-haired boy I mentioned earlier, Thomas Rhett Akins. I don't know what it was about him, but I liked him, and I couldn't understand why I'd never really hung out with him before that summer, because he and I got along like we'd known each other our whole lives. He was different from a lot of guys. Even though he played football, he was super comfortable getting up and doing skits, and he was a musician. We just started talking, and laughing, and I swear he fit right in like he'd always been a part of the Crew.

Which is why I'm gonna ask him to tell this story from his point of view here:

TR: That church camp was definitely the first place where Lauren and I started to really hang out. I remember I dyed my hair black that summer. I was the drummer in a band called the High Heel Flip-flops. We were a punk rock band, and that was when my obsession with Lauren began. So standing next to Lauren, we looked like night and day. She was like a foot and a half taller than me, and blond as blond can be. I'd never met a girl who could keep up with the boys the way she did, *and* she was so pretty—I was just hooked. I wanted to be around her as much as possible.

But at this church camp, the girls stayed at one side of the camp and the guys stayed at the other side of the camp. We'd get up and sing camp songs in the morning in the woods and then have morning

Thomas Rhett and me when we first started hanging out, at Madison Church of Christ camp, in middle school

meetings. In the afternoon and evening we'd do sports and swim, rope course and zip line, all that stuff that you'd do at any summer camp but with prayer and some Bible study, too. We had games and dress-up nights, competitions between the cabins, and at the end of it all there was this banquet. And even though we were all just kids still, it was a really big deal to ask a girl to go to the banquet with you.

I had never asked a girl out at that age, but after staying up late and talking to all the dudes in the cabin, basically obsessing over her, saying, "Yo, this *girl.* I really *like* this girl," I think somebody just finally up and told me: "Just walk up and ask her!" So I did. I got up my courage and I walked up to Lauren that morning and I asked her if she would go to the banquet with me that night. And she said, "Oh. I'm waiting on someone *else* to ask me."

"What?" I said. "Who?"

"Tyler Ricker."

Tyler Ricker. She was waiting on *Tyler Ricker* to ask her to the banquet.

Lauren: My girlfriends all told me that Tyler was gonna ask me! And I had a *really* big crush on him. But Tyler was gone at a golf tournament or something that day, and he wasn't gonna come back until late. So when Thomas Rhett asked me I was like, "I think I can go with you, but I think that there's someone who's gonna ask me who's coming late. So I can be your date until he shows up!"

TR: Can you imagine?

Lauren: I was trying to be nice by saying yes to both of them. They were both really, really nice guys, and I felt so bad saying "no." So I thought, "Well, we could at least go for a little bit together."

TR: It was probably the most degrading moment of my whole life.

Lauren: Oh, honey.

TR: It was! You think there's nothing worse than rejection, but *this* was worse. Her saying, "Someone else is going to ask me, and if he doesn't show up then I'll go with you until he gets there?" That's *way* worse than just saying "no."

Lauren: I'm so sorry, honey.

What can I say? I was young and didn't know how to handle any of this stuff yet. I thought I was being nice! I liked Thomas Rhett. I really did. He was sweet, and funny, and so much fun to be around. But I thought we were just friends, like I was with Hunter and Kamron and most other guys.

Tyler Ricker, on the other hand, he was tall, and athletic, and older, and he just had that certain something that made me crush on him, *hard*, the way girls do when they're going into sixth grade. I got all giddy just thinking about him.

It was all sort of meaningless at that point. I mean, all the talk about "dates" and "dating" didn't add up to very much. Everybody pretty much showed up to the banquet and hung out together like they did on any other day, and it wasn't a big deal. I did end up seeing Tyler at the banquet that night, but we talked and laughed like anyone would, and I talked to Thomas Rhett, too.

Tyler Ricker was just a little summer crush—one that I went home and told my mom all about. And she clearly must've gone and told my dad, because it was right around that time when he started paying attention to what I was wearing. "Lauren," he'd say, "you can't keep wearing these short-shorts and shirts that show off your stomach."

"Why?" I'd argue. "They're comfortable. It's hot outside!"

"Because I'm a guy and I know what guys your age think, and you're not wearing that out of the house," he'd say.

From that summer on, if I tried to leave the house in shorts that were too short, or the cheerleader shorts with the writing across the butt that were so popular at the time, he'd tell me to turn around and change. And every time it was, "Trust me. I've been there. I know how boys think."

"Ew. Dad," I'd say. "Can you just not?"

After a while I stopped even trying to wear those sorts of clothes, not so much because he told me to, but mostly just to avoid the awkward conversations.

But those conversations didn't stop. It seemed like every few days my dad kept mentioning something new about how important it was to make good decisions, and to focus on who I wanted to be, and letting me know that "I didn't need to be like anybody else," that I shouldn't give in to peer pressure, or pressure from boys, and that I had to set my own standards because "one day, you won't have to answer to me. You'll have to answer to God."

He often had these conversations and gave these little sermons in front of my friends, and Macy's friends, when we had friends over for dinner or to sleep over. He didn't hold *anything* back. And if Kamron, or Hunter, or anyone else asked him questions—about sex, or girls, or dating, or how their bodies were changing—he would answer them as bluntly as he would if the question had come from one of his own kids.

I would cover my ears sometimes and go completely red-faced at the stories and lessons Dad would tell my friends. But there was nothing I could do to stop him, and all my friends seemed to love him all the more for his honesty.

I guess Thomas Rhett recovered from my banquet rejection just fine, because he started showing up in my life a lot more after that. He got to be good friends with Hunter and Hailey, which meant he was around the neighborhood. And then his mom would come to pick him up and get to talking with my mom, and soon they became friends.

I wouldn't learn all of this until later, but Thomas Rhett's mom, Paige, had been a single mom for quite a while at that point. She and Thomas Rhett's dad, Rhett Akins, had married right out of high school. Rhett was in the music industry and was quickly becoming a country star who went out on big tours a lot of the time. Unfortunately their marriage didn't last. They were married for ten years before they divorced, and as a single mom part of every week, Paige told my mom what a gift it was just to drop Thomas Rhett off to have dinner at our house, or to have other kids come to dinner at hers, because all the kids would play together and it would take some of the pressure off her to do everything herself, even if it was just for one night.

In the late 1990s and early 2000s, it seemed everywhere you turned people were using the phrase *It takes a village to raise a child*, but from what I'd seen in my early life, it seemed to me that it mostly took a couple of neighbors or friends with kids of their own who could give a mom a break once in a while!

It wasn't long after our families started hanging out together that Paige met a guy named Tim Lankford, and they started to get really close. They eventually decided to get married, and we all were so excited. Everybody loved Tim.

Tim and my dad got along really well, so after Tim became Thomas Rhett's and Kasey's stepdad, we all got even closer. Instead of just saying "hi" outside after church, we'd meet up in the parking lot and all go out to eat, usually at our favorite Mexican restaurant just up the street. And by the time Thomas Rhett and I were in eighth grade, it seemed like us two were joined at the hip. We did just about everything together. We were as comfortable at each other's houses and with each other's parents as we were with our own. Maybe even more so.

Like this one time, we were at a church lock-in and we weren't supposed to have our cellphones with us. But somehow, Thomas Rhett—who tended to push boundaries a little bit, although not as much as Hunter—snuck his phone in, and without even telling me about it he called my mom.

"Lisa," he said, "come pick us up. We don't want to stay here anymore. It's lame."

Sitting at Chili's (like always) with Kasey, Thomas Rhett, and Macy

And Mom was like, "Okay, I'll come pick y'all up!"

All of a sudden Thomas Rhett told me, "Hey, your mom's coming to get us," and I was like, "What?"

Some of our other friends overheard him and they said, "We want to go, too! We want pizza!" So all it took was one phone call from Thomas Rhett and my mom came and picked us all up from church and took us out for pizza.

Another time we were coming back from somewhere and when we

got close to the neighborhood, Thomas Rhett said, "Can I drive the car?" and my mom said, "Sure." So Thomas Rhett drove our car. This was years before he was old enough to have a license. We were out in the country and there was no one else on the roads, so it wasn't all that risky, I don't think, but that boy could convince anybody to do anything. And when it came to my parents, it didn't even take much effort.

Thomas Rhett was right there listening to my dad's dinner-table sermons, and asking him all kinds of questions about life—just like Hunter, and Kamron, and everybody else. And both of my parents treated him like he was one of their own kids.

I just treated him the same way I treated my other guy friends: like a *friend*. Because that's what he was. It never occurred to me that we might be anything else. Not in middle school, anyway.

At that age, in middle school, to be honest, it felt like my dad's warnings were premature, because I was more interested in riding dirt bikes than I was in dating.

Hunter's dad, John, was the first person to have a dirt bike on our street. He's a mechanic, so he was always fixing things up, and he had a yellow Suzuki that he let us ride sometimes. My dad used to race motocross when he was younger, and he was *good*. So he showed me what to do, and he always insisted that dirt bikes were safer than four-wheelers, "because if a four-wheeler rolls over on you it's heavy enough to kill you." They're both dangerous vehicles, but just like with anything else, Dad insisted he wanted us to learn how to ride the right way so we would know how to do it, respect the bike, and be safe.

When John bought Hunter a red Honda dirt bike of his own, and then Kamron got a Yamaha the next summer, I started begging my parents, "Okay. Can I *please* get a dirt bike? All my friends have dirt bikes!"

That's when they made me a deal: If I saved up half of what it cost to buy one, they'd chip in the other half. So I started doing extra chores for money, and instead of spending all the money I got for Christmas or birthdays or anything else, I started saving it. And once I had something like $800 saved up, my dad said he'd start looking around to see what he could find.

One day, just before seventh grade started, I came home after soccer practice and my mom said, "Hey, Dad wants you in the back yard," and I remember looking out our back window and seeing Dad in his business suit, riding on a dirt bike, doing a wheelie all the way up the back yard.

I lost it. I was like, "Oh my gosh. This is the best day of my life!"

I went running out of the house as my dad pulled up.

"Is this for me?" I asked.

"Yup!"

"Why are you riding in a suit?" I asked him.

"'Cause I picked it up on the way home from work and couldn't wait to try it out!" he said. "Want to ride?"

It was a blue Yamaha TTR125, and I *loved* it.

I hopped on and rode it from my yard to Hunter's yard, then around Kamron's back yard, back to my yard, then back up to Hunter's, then down

After riding my dirt bike

to Mimi's driveway where I hit the corner of the drive and caught some air before riding back down the street. It was awesome!

Hunter and Kamron and I would ride everywhere together after that, and Thomas Rhett and some of our other friends would come with us all the time, too. Not just in summertime. When it snowed and there was ice, we would drag people behind us on sleds. Or when it would rain a lot and our ditches would fill up with water—it would be muddy, first of all, and it's so much more fun to ride in the mud—we would jump down in the ditches and ride, and the water would just shoot out from behind us.

Having all of that added freedom brought plenty of added responsibilities. My dad set boundaries on certain streets in the neighborhood he didn't want me to cross. But riding around, doing donuts in muddy fields (and getting yelled at by the property owner for messing up his land), or jumping over the road's edge while making sure no cars were coming—

all of that was on *us*. And I knew it. I never even *wanted* to do anything I thought was too risky or dangerous on a dirt bike, because I knew that all of my dad's lessons on safety and trust were made with love, and with my best interest at heart.

So I'm not sure why I went and broke my parents' trust over something as trivial as my growing interest in boys. I really wasn't all that boy crazy. But there were some older boys, high school boys, who lived over the far side of our neighborhood, in an area that was well beyond the boundaries my dad had set for us to ride to on our bicycles. (We weren't too cool to ride bicycles even after we had dirt bikes.) And these boys just fascinated me. I could hear 'em throwing parties sometimes, and I knew they had girls over, and every time we were driving with my parents in or out of the neighborhood I'd look over at the houses where they lived and wonder what they were up to.

Well, this one night, right around dusk, I noticed a light come on in the back of one of their properties. It was back where I'd heard them hanging out and talking late at night once or twice before, and so I decided to ride my bicycle up close to see if I could hear anything.

"Where are you going?" Macy said.

"Just up here a little bit. I thought I heard something," I told her, and she followed along right behind me.

"We're not supposed to be up this far," Macy said.

The Crew on one of our many snow days

"I know, I know, it's okay. No one will know. I just thought I heard something," I said.

We stayed there for a few minutes, and I didn't hear anything. I'm not even sure if the boys were home. By the time we turned around and rode back to our house, though, it was dark. It felt like it got dark so fast. And we weren't supposed to be out riding bikes after dark.

When we walked back in the house, my parents were like, "Where did you just go?"

"I just rode up the street a little bit," I said.

Macy stayed quiet.

"How far up the street?" they asked me.

I'm not a liar. It's just not in me. So if my parents point-blank asked me something, I'd just come out and say it. And I did. I told 'em where we'd gone, and the two of us got in huge trouble. We were grounded. No bikes. No friends over. No going to any friends' houses. For *days*.

Looking back, it was such a tiny thing that I did. Nothing happened! I rode my bike maybe a quarter of a mile up one street beyond where I was supposed to go. And yet, because my parents always trusted me and I'd gone and done what they told me not to do, I felt like I'd broken their trust. I told on myself, I fessed up, which made me feel better in a sense because at least I was honest with them, but at the same time I was *dishonest* going where I knew I wasn't supposed to go.

Laying in bed that night with tears in my eyes, I kept asking myself, "Why did I do that?"

It was late when I stepped foot out of my little bedroom jail and found my dad sitting in the living room.

"Hey, Dad," I said, sitting down next to him. "I just wanted to say I'm sorry again."

"I know you're sorry," he said. "We all make mistakes. What's important is that we learn from them and make better decisions the next time. And I guarantee you there will be times when you'll make more."

I nodded.

"You're older now. I won't be there with you all the time, and I can't make up your mind for you. I'm just here to guide you, and I just hope that you make the easier choices. Well, maybe the *harder* choices at the time, but the choices that will make your *life* easier."

"I'll try," I said.

"I know you'll try. You're way better at trying than I ever was. But you're getting to an age now where you don't have to answer to *me*. The only one you have to answer to is yourself, and you're ultimately answering to God."

My dad looked up at the clock and said it was late, and that I needed to get in bed. He gave me a big hug and I went back to my bedroom, and I thought about what he'd said.

In just a few weeks I'd be in seventh grade. And at Goodpasture, that meant I'd start taking classes at the high school building. In just two years, I'd *be* in high school. I could hardly believe it. I was so excited for everything I imagined high school would be. Formals and football games, and dating, and all kinds of things I was sure I hadn't even thought of yet. And I just hoped I was ready for it.

I remember thinking it was a good thing that I messed up that summer. (*Messed up* being a pretty relative term, since what I did wasn't really so bad.) It meant that I was starting the new school year with a clear head, thinking, "This is on *me* now. My decisions are mine. And those decisions I make, they're between me and God."

Honestly, that made me kind of nervous. This wasn't kid stuff anymore.

Still, I tried to look at the positive: I already knew that God was listening. I knew that He answered prayers. I just had to remember that I needed to be ready to answer to Him, too.

4

First Everythings

Going to high school was everything I dreamed it would be. And a whole lot of the sense of togetherness, and school spirit, and excitement that I wanted out of my high school experience built up in the fall semester around football.

We were a small school, but our football team was mighty. We went to State almost every single year—and every single year, we got beat by Alcoa. To this day when somebody mentions Alcoa it makes my blood boil. I don't know what was going on over there, but it seemed like every boy on that team was big enough to be a college player. Even the freshmen. Still, every year, the Goodpasture community rebuilt a belief that *this* was gonna be the year we beat Alcoa at State. "We can do it, we can do it! This year's gonna be the year!"

That hope and excitement and anticipation filtered into everything we did during the first part of my freshman year. (Spoiler alert:

One of the first pics of me and my friend Lindsey, at church camp

We went to State that year, and it was a complete bloodbath. It wasn't even a competition. Alcoa mopped the floor with us.)

Getting ready for those games was *fun*. My girlfriends and I—including my new friend Lindsey, a tall blond classmate who was even more of a tomboy than I was (if that's possible)—would buy blank T-shirts from Walmart and paint our favorite players' names on the back. We would deck ourselves out in face paint and glitter and go cheer 'em on from the stands as if every game was our own personal Super Bowl. The players were our friends, so we knew how hard they were working and how badly they wanted to win. We wanted to do everything we could to support them.

After Thomas Rhett's Friday night football game

Me and Lindsey made shirts and I painted Thomas Rhett's number and name on the back of mine ☺

Thomas Rhett was one of those players, a receiver, and he and his buddies all used to come up to our house to hang out after practice, sometimes three days a week. Sometimes they'd stay for dinner before heading home to do homework and get some sleep before doing it all over again the next day. Dinner was usually leftovers from the steak and potatoes Mom made for us on Sundays. She grew up on a cattle ranch in Texas, so steak and potatoes was her number one meal, for sure. And that was just fine with all those hungry football players. Then after the games, on weekends, my family and Thomas Rhett's family would go out to eat together, usually at Chili's, with some of our other friends, too.

All in all, the whole tradition of having all kinds of friends come up to our house and our neighborhood didn't change one bit once I was in high school.

It seemed like everybody wanted to come to our neighborhood for Halloween. It became such a destination for trick-or-treaters and so many of our neighbors got so into it that we couldn't even fit all the candy we got into grocery bags anymore. We had to carry pillowcases to hold it all. I weighed mine one year when I got home and, no joke, it was eight pounds! We didn't think about quitting trick-or-treating because we were older, either. We just designed more elaborate costumes and helped out with the decorating more than we had when we were young. Why would anybody want to give that up?

The moment there was a hint that we might get a snowstorm early in the season, a whole bunch of kids asked if they could sleep over, just in case school got out. Which meant we had a whole bunch of football players locked in at Camp Gregory after practice one night.

It was that age where a lot of the moms were like, "Is it weird if the boys spend the night?" And my parents would tell 'em, "No." They'd ask my parents for advice about it, too, like, "What do you do?" And my dad was always matter-of-fact about it, like, "Well, I mean . . . As long as you make a place on the floor and keep 'em in separate rooms, I don't see any issue. Rules are rules."

Macy and I knew the rules. Boys were not allowed in our rooms with the door shut, ever. And Mom didn't like us hanging out in the bedrooms anyway, even with our girlfriends. She was always like, "You don't need to be back in your bedroom, just, you know, hang out *here.*" The kitchen and living room and dining room were just fine, and we were so open about everything, it didn't matter to us that our conversations were happening within earshot of our parents. We didn't have anything to hide, so there was never anything uncomfortable about it.

And honestly, the sleepover thing was just practical. We lived pretty far out, and some of our friends from school lived equally far out to the west or south of Goodpasture. It could be thirty minutes or more between houses. So it was just easier, and safer, to let friends spend the night, especially as kids got older and started to drive.

We worked together, too. Not at jobs, really, since most of us were still too young to drive and couldn't get back and forth to any sort of a real paying job, but a whole bunch of us started to do volunteer work. I was mentoring middle school kids through my church, which I loved. I adored working with kids, and it felt so good to think that I'd learned enough in my own life already to be able to share it with these kids coming up.

We all also volunteered to work on floats for homecoming. One of our friends' dads was a contractor, so he would build the frames, and then our whole class would build them out and decorate them with paper-mache

*Building floats with friends from my class
at Goodpasture*

and paint. We'd spend every night of the two weeks leading up to home-coming in the fire hall, building those floats until late at night. It might seem kinda dumb to some people, but to us, this was serious stuff. It mattered. If we messed with any of these traditions, it might mess up the season. Plus, it was so much fun. So we stuck with it and gave it our all, just like every class before us, and hopefully every class after us.

And even though all of our Goodpasture activities kept us extra busy, we still made plenty of time to get together with our neighborhood friends, including Hunter and Kamron and *their* friends, who all went to Davidson Academy. I was thankful for our traditions: Thanksgiving and Christmas, going to Opryland, bringing more and more friends and families along whenever and wherever we went—I lived for the familiarity of all of those things.

The only ritual that changed even a little bit in those years was deciding where we went for spring break. For years, our springtime week off from school marked the first time each year when Dad would take us camping. But by the time I was in high school, my mom and I managed to convince my dad to take us someplace a lot warmer and a little more fun: Key West, Florida.

The first time we convinced him was in the spring of my eighth-grade year, and he insisted that the only way we could afford it was if we drove.

"That's fine with us," we said. "We don't care. We're going to Key West!"

So we made the almost seventeen-hour drive straight through the night, and as soon as we got there, we knew we'd be back. In my freshman year, Hailey, Hunter, and Hannah came down with their parents, too, and before we knew it, spring break trips to Key West became a new tradition. We vowed to invite even more friends to come with us the next year.

I didn't date anyone seriously during my freshman year. I had my first older "boyfriend" for a little while, a senior, but when we went on dates it was mostly with groups. And when we broke up, I flirted with some other guys—also in groups. And I definitely felt like some of my guy friends were thinking differently about me, just like I was thinking differently about them. We were all still hanging out with a lot of friends everywhere we went, though, and our parents still had to drive us around, so not a whole lot changed. We still went to church on Sundays, and youth group on Wednesday nights, and I was still in the mindset that the guys I knew and grew up with were always going to be my friends. I didn't want any of that to change.

Thomas Rhett and I had gotten closer and closer as our families got closer, to the point where he really was my best friend. I always got the

feeling that he still liked me the way he liked me way back at church camp in the sixth grade, but I also felt like he gave mixed signals about what he wanted to do about it. Like the time at the beginning of our sophomore year when my cousin, Allie Brooke, got her driver's license. She was a year older than me, and she was al-

Just two close friends in an after-banquet selfie

ways a super responsible kid, so my parents trusted her to drive with us kids in her car from the start. That brought us all a whole new level of freedom. And one day, she and I and Thomas Rhett and a couple of our other friends all got tickets to see Green Day in concert—our very first concert without parents. We were so excited! We drove into downtown Nashville for the show on a school night, and the band was awesome. We sang every word and had so much fun, and on the way out of the arena, Thomas Rhett grabbed my hand in the plaza, right in the middle of a whole crowd of people, and shouted at the top of his lungs, "I love this girl!"

Everybody looked, and I was *super* embarrassed. I did not like being the center of attention. *At all.* And I really didn't think he meant anything by it. It's not like he'd ever said anything directly or tried to kiss me or anything. We were all just laughing and pumped full of energy after that concert, and I was sure he did it for fun, just to embarrass me. We were always messing with each other.

Even when we got home after the show, he still didn't make it clear that he wanted to date me. His parents lived close to Allie Brooke, in a neighborhood that was a little closer to Goodpasture than mine, and since it was a school night, the plan was for me to spend the night at his house; that way we'd both get a good night's sleep and then Tim, his stepdad, could drive us to school in the morning.

When I think about it now, I guess that shows just how much trust my parents had in me, *and* in Thomas Rhett. His parents must've had a lot of trust in us, too, because no one was awake when we got home. We went inside, and we sat and talked for a little while. And at one point, Thomas Rhett leaned in close to me. For a moment I thought, "Is he gonna try and kiss me?" But instead, he took his thumb and he wiped away my eyeliner and mascara, which I had put on pretty thick for the concert.

"You don't need to wear makeup," he said. "You're so pretty without it."

I thought that was kinda sweet. But still, he didn't try to kiss me. He just showed me to the guest room, and he went to his room, and we both went to sleep and woke up and went to school the next morning, where we told everyone all about the concert because there wasn't anything to say about what happened between us.

Not that anything *major* would've happened. Thomas Rhett and I both believed in the values we'd been raised to believe in. I was sure of that.

I don't think it was more than a week or two later when Thomas Rhett finally did try to kiss me. We were sitting out on the trampoline in his back yard, behind the fence where no one could see us, waiting for my mom to come pick me up. And we were talking and laughing like we always did. And the sun went down, and the sky was all pretty, and it felt like the stars just aligned in that moment. We looked at each other, and got real quiet. And he smiled a funny smile, and I definitely smiled back. And then he leaned in, and the trampoline kind of sunk down under us, so I sat up quickly and we slammed our teeth into each other.

"Ow!" I said.

It was bad.

"Aw, man," Thomas Rhett moaned.

Paige popped her head out the back door and said, "What are y'all doing?"

"Nothing," Thomas Rhett said.

She went back inside and we both looked at each other and laughed so hard. A few minutes later my mom pulled into the driveway and we climbed down, and as we walked through the back gate he held my arm and stopped me.

"What are we doing?" he said. "Like, are you *not* gonna date me? Are you *not* gonna be my girlfriend?"

I didn't know what to say.

TR: Lauren was my best friend. She really was. She knew me better than any of my guy friends. And when you're attracted to your best friend, I don't know, it just feels like everything kinda adds up, you know? I know I was all awkward about it, but I thought for sure we were meant to be together.

Here I'd been making any excuse I could to spend time with her, showing her every day how much I wanted to be around her. Even when I knew how to do my math homework, I'd say I was having trouble and ask her if I could come over to her house to get help. I mean, I wanted to be around her *all the time.* I would've put anything in my life on hold for this girl.

"I'm sorry," I said to him. "Let's just give it a little time, alright?"

"Yeah," Thomas Rhett said. "Sure."

He looked so discouraged. I felt horrible.

A few weeks later, Thomas Rhett tried again. He leaned in and kissed me—this time while we were standing on solid ground.

I'll admit, it was a little weird at first. We were so close as friends, it was almost like that scene from the movie *Back to the Future,* where the mom character in the 1950s doesn't realize she's kissing the boy that's really her future son: "This is all wrong," she says. "I don't know what it is. But when I kiss you, it's like I'm kissing . . . *my brother.*"

Thomas Rhett *wasn't* my brother, though. He wrapped his arms around me and we kissed again, and it turned out that he was a pretty good kisser. Suddenly it all felt really *right.* Next thing I knew he started holding my hand in front of other people, and not in a way that was meant to embarrass me. And instead of just hanging out with each other, we started hanging *on* each other everywhere we went. I liked the way it felt when I held on to his arm as we walked, and when I put my head on his shoulder during a movie. He felt safe, and warm, and it was definitely kind of exciting, and next thing I knew, we were a couple.

Our parents were actually pretty happy about it. They always thought we were meant to be together, and everyone said we were just too cute together. But honestly, even in the first few weeks of our new relationship, I had doubts.

Thomas Rhett was kind of following in his dad's footsteps as a musician. He would play guitar and sing for our friends, and that wasn't really appealing to me. He was always the center of attention, and I never wanted to be even *close* to the center of attention.

For those who don't know, Thomas Rhett's dad, Rhett Akins, was a huge country star in the 1990s. His first album, *A Thousand Memories,* came out in 1995, and his first #1 hit, "That Ain't My Truck," was one of my staple childhood country music songs. That song was on the radio all the time, and it seemed like every kid I grew up with knew every word. He went on to write something like twenty-nine #1 singles for and with other big country artists, including Blake Shelton and Jason Aldean and Luke Bryan, which makes him a total legend in the country music industry.

There is one story that really puts into perspective just how well known and well respected Rhett is in the country music world. Thomas Rhett and I were out with his dad one time when we were in high school, and we ran into Taylor Swift in the parking lot outside of Keva Juice in Hendersonville. This was right after she blew up into a teenaged superstar, and yet *Taylor* was the one who walked over so excited to meet *Rhett*.

I just kind of shrugged at all of that, because despite being so close to Nashville, fame and stardom wasn't anything I was ever drawn to. I had friends of friends who went to high school with Taylor, so I didn't see her as any different from other talented kids I knew, and I only ever saw Rhett as Thomas Rhett's and Kasey's dad.

Not that I didn't respect their accomplishments and their talents. I mean, Thomas Rhett most definitely inherited his dad's musical genes. By the time we were in high school, he'd traded the punk rock look and the drum kit for an acoustic guitar, and he could *play*. I mean, he was way beyond his years. He was already writing songs, and he could sing, too, and he had this knack for sounding things out and playing just about any kind of music anyone ever wanted to hear, by ear. He carried that guitar with him everywhere, to every party, and he'd bring it out and start entertaining the crowd.

I know some girls might love that, but something about it bothered me.

I kept thinking, "Why does he always have to pull out his guitar?" He was good. Real good. And the girls loved to watch him sing. They would say "Play this song" and "Play that song," and I would leave the room every time. He got upset one time and asked me, "Why don't you stay? Like, why can't you sit in a room and listen to me play?" And I'd say, "Because I don't want to listen to you play. I want to hang out with you!"

I truly loved to hang out with him, but watching him as if I was some kind of spectator or fan? That just didn't do it for me. That's not how I wanted to spend my time.

At fifteen, I have to say, Thomas Rhett was also pretty clingy. He acted jealous whenever I talked to my guy friends, or the other football players, or the other guys who lived in my neighborhood. I couldn't understand what in the world he was jealous about. I wasn't jealous of the girls who sat at his feet and stared at him while he played his guitar. I trusted him, and I never gave him a reason not to trust me at all. Plus, we were all still friends. We were like family. We hung out. Nothing had changed. Still, it got awkward between Thomas Rhett and me on more than a few occasions. Whenever I felt that jealousy come out of him, I'd ask if maybe we should quit this whole thing and just be friends again.

"No! How could we do that? Not with the way I feel about you," he would say. "Don't you feel the same way about me?"

I did. Sometimes. But most of the time I didn't know what I felt. When I was honest with myself, I wasn't really sure that I wanted to be in a relationship as a sophomore in high school. We were young! Why not try new things, with new people, and date different guys with different interests, who maybe I *hadn't* known for my whole life, but who might be fun to get to know?

"I don't know if I want to be in a serious relationship with anybody," I'd tell him.

He'd immediately back down and say, "Well, that's okay. We'll just keep it casual, then." But he clearly didn't want to keep it casual. His jealousy and possessiveness kept showing itself again and again. He wanted to be with me *all the time.*

I'm making it sound like it was all bad, and it wasn't. Not at all. Being with Thomas Rhett made me feel so good. He wasn't somebody I felt like I had to try to impress. I didn't have any fear that he might reject me, which is the way I felt around some other boys. Plus, I could 100 percent be myself with him. I could joke around the same way I would with my girlfriends. And I never had to worry he might do something to make me look bad. I just felt safe. I think that's it: Thomas Rhett was a safe place for me.

He also treated me so well. We had so much fun together, and I kept thinking, "How lucky am I to be dating my best friend?" Just the fact that he liked me so much and wore his heart on his sleeve about how much he liked me was endearing. The two of us could lay out under the stars and talk for hours, just the easiest conversations that wandered around all over the place, dreaming of our futures, and talking about everything under the sun or the moon without it ever getting awkward: without there ever being a moment where it felt uncomfortable, or like we didn't know what to say, or where I thought for one second that he might judge me for something I was saying.

Talking with Thomas Rhett, one-on-one, hanging out with him, was as simple as simple could be.

I just wished it would stay that way when we were around our friends.

I turned sixteen that November, and got my driver's license, and my parents bought me a used Jeep Grand Cherokee. That changed everything. All of a sudden, Thomas Rhett and I had the freedom to go anywhere we wanted. He's four months younger than me, so I was always the one behind the wheel, picking him up in the morning so we could go get Starbucks or Krispy Kreme on the way to school, or picking him and his friends up after football practice to come back to our house for dinner. We went to the movies together, all on our own. We took drives just for the sake of driving around, while we listened to music and talked and talked some more. We'd run out and rent movies together, and go to friends' houses, and stop for smoothies.

We drove to youth group together on Wednesday nights, too. That's just what we always did. It's funny, but church was a huge part of our lives. All of our lives. At school, kids would carry Bibles in their backpacks and even their back pockets. We all would underline verses that were important to us, and it almost felt like a competition to see whose Bible could be more marked-up and ragged from all the use we gave 'em. I'm sure for some people it was just for show, but doing all that reading, going to church on Sundays, going to youth group—you couldn't help but absorb the lessons even if you tried to fight it. And yet, at Madison Church of Christ, it seemed to us like it was getting harder and harder to sit still and listen.

We didn't have any instrumental music in our church. No organ. No gospel choirs. No guitar playing while they passed the offering basket. It was quiet. The sermons were good and we loved the people, but it was still pretty conservative.

The reason we went to a church camp "banquet" and not a church camp "dance" is because dancing wasn't allowed in our church. We didn't have dances at Goodpasture, either. We didn't have a prom: The Junior/Senior Banquet was the big event that we looked forward to, the one everyone got dressed up for and dreamed of going to with the perfect date.

It wasn't a dance, though. No band, no DJ, no dancing. Just dates color-coordinating their outfits and eating a fancy dinner together.

That style of worship might have been fine for my parents, but I was sixteen now, and dating, and driving, and starting to set my own priorities in life—and I realized it wasn't fine with me. It wasn't fine with Thomas Rhett, either. Music was such a big part of our lives, and especially his; we thought, "Why is it disconnected from our connection to God?"

That's when fate stepped in and helped to steer us in a new direction.

My cousin Allie Brooke went to a different church, with a very different youth group.

"We have a band every Wednesday. You'd love it. You have to come!" Allie Brooke begged me. "It's so much fun."

"Fun?" I said. "I don't know. I don't think my parents are gonna go for it. Especially Dad."

"Just try one night, and if you like it, then we'll cross that bridge and tell your parents afterward," she said. "I'll help you tell 'em if you want me to. They trust me. They'll listen to me!"

Even though I was a rule-follower, I did the calculations in my heart and decided not to tell my dad before I went. I figured it was better to check it out and see if I was really interested before I got him all upset over nothing. It was just one night. Plus, he always told me to follow my heart, and going to that new youth group did *not* feel wrong where it counted: between me and God.

I knew I'd better tell at least one of my parents where I was going, so I told my mom, and she was surprisingly okay with it. "I'm just happy you're telling me you'd rather go to church than go do something that could get y'all in trouble," she said. "I don't care where you go. Just the fact that you want to go to youth group is enough for me."

So one night, I drove over to Long Hollow Baptist Church—and that one night was all it took. I was hooked! It wasn't a party or a concert or something. They talked about all kinds of serious stuff. But through the music and the joy everybody shared in that room, I really felt more spiritually alive than I'd felt in years.

"You have to come," I told Thomas Rhett. "They have a band!"

He was pretty hesitant. He knew that his mom (like my dad) was a strong believer in the more conservative ways of the Church of Christ.

"Just try. Just come one night, and then if you like it, we'll talk to your mom together," I said.

He looked in my eyes and shook his head and said, "You know I can't say no to you."

I was so happy. I gave him a big hug, and the next week we went together. Thomas Rhett was blown away. Honestly, at that age, I don't think he believed in God the same way I did. He needed something to lift him up and remind him that going to church could be a good thing, and what better way to do that than with music?

After that, we both made up our minds to go to Long Hollow.

Telling his mom and my dad wasn't easy, though.

Thomas Rhett's mom got pretty upset at him. Man, it is not fun for anybody to have that kind of a confrontation, for a mom with her teenage son, or for a teenager with his mom, that's for sure. Thomas Rhett was upset by it. Still, he wasn't going to back down, and he had a feeling that eventually she would forgive him.

As for my dad? "No, no, no!" he said. "Madison is where you've grown up, and it's where you should keep going."

This was not a comfortable conversation.

"Church isn't supposed to be fun," he said. "It's supposed to be *real.*"

"I mean, I get that," I said, "but it *is* real. It's real, too. Like, you have *both* things."

"It sounds like it's just a concert, Lauren. You can't pay attention in that kind of environment. You can't focus on what you're supposed to be focusing on."

"Well, I don't agree, because some of the lessons I learned there already I will never forget. The fact that it was fun and the music was good made me want to focus even more on listening to what they had to say, and to pay attention even more to what I ought to be paying attention to."

"Well, I don't think you should go," he said.

To which I said, "Well . . . I'm going."

Given all the talks we'd had, he knew it was my right to follow my heart, and he knew that I was too old to try to punish over defying his word. So he ended the conversation right there, saying, "I just hope you know what you're doing."

And the amazing thing was, *I did.*

His one request was that I continue to go to Madison Church of Christ on Sundays, so we could all be together as a family, and I agreed. Madison still felt like home to me, and I loved my family, so that didn't feel like much of a sacrifice on my part. It felt more like a win-win for everybody.

Thomas Rhett and I started going to Long Hollow Baptist on Wednesday nights and raving about it to everyone we knew. Pretty soon half our Crew decided they wanted to come see what it was all about.

So I ended up driving Hunter and Hailey, and Thomas Rhett's sister, Kasey, and even my own sister, Macy, to Long Hollow every Wednesday night from then on. A few months later, when Thomas Rhett started driving, he'd take Kasey and maybe Hunter and Hailey on his own, so I'd grab a couple more friends instead—whoever could fit in my car. And because our Crew was so confident and sure of ourselves in this new choice we'd made, it inspired a whole

A typical night crammed into the back of a car on the way to church, this time in Hailey's car with Kamron, Kasey, and Hunter

bunch of other kids from school and even a few from church to come over to Long Hollow, too.

Paige eventually forgave Thomas Rhett and came around. And my dad eventually forgave me, too.

I felt bad for parents who didn't get it, or didn't allow it, or stayed mad about it. I mean, we could have been doing much worse things on our Wednesday nights than listening to music and talking about God. The values and morals they were talking about at Long Hollow were the same values and morals we heard about at Madison: respecting each other, giving, loving, being kind, "saving yourself" for marriage, all the things.

Only at Long Hollow, I felt it had a way better chance of sinking in with almost every kid because it became the "cool" place to be on Wednesday nights, for every school around—even for kids who didn't grow up in church. And the messages were presented in a way that made us *want* to be there, to be a part of a community of faith-based kids.

Sharing that new journey in faith definitely brought me and Thomas Rhett closer together as we headed into the holiday season that sophomore year. And I have to say, holding Thomas Rhett's hand as we walked under the Christmas lights at Opryland brought a whole new level of romance to our annual tradition. We snuck away from my parents at one point and ran outside and spun around together under the giant tree of lights, and then fell to the ground, laughing so hard, and it felt like it was straight out of the best romance movie either of us had ever seen. (That would be *The Notebook,* by the way. We're both still obsessed with that movie.)

I didn't think I could feel more alive and in love than I did in that moment.

I *loved* him, and he loved me. There was no doubt about it. I'd loved him for a long time already, as a friend. Our families loved each other. And this? This was just a fun new layer to put on top of it all.

Honestly, it all seemed perfect when it was just the two of us, one-on-one.

In fact, we were so close and having so much fun together that season that my parents invited Thomas Rhett and his mom and sister and Tim to go with us on a Caribbean cruise in January. (By that time, Thomas Rhett had a six-month-old little brother, Tyler, too, but he was too young to come with us on the cruise.)

We had so much fun, lounging in the sun, and filling up our plates at the all-you-can-eat buffet, and watching from way up on a balcony while the cruise director led a bunch of half-drunk adults through a "best legs" contest by the pool, with music pumping through the speakers and people dancing in their bikinis and Speedos in front of a panel of judges. Honestly, it was kind of jaw-dropping, and hilariously entertaining to watch.

When we stopped in Cozumel, though, my dad struck up a conversation with a Hispanic man at the market, and my dad being my dad, he somehow ended up getting an invitation from that man to follow him back to his neighborhood, to his home, where he lived. Next thing I knew, in the middle of our vacation, Tim, Dad, and Grayson piled into a van and went way out of town, far from any place tourists gathered, where they couldn't even see the cruise ship anymore. Dad brought his camera with him and documented the whole thing, and he showed it to us when they got back.

On the cruise, dating—for the first time

It was beautiful the whole way. They were still close to the beach, and the scenery was stunning, but when they got out and walked up to a group of tented, blanketed little homes, the man took them right into his house to show them some of the handmade items he was hoping my dad might purchase. The house was basically one room built from cement blocks. I don't even think it had doors on it. It was just open to the wind. And they had orange-colored hammocks hanging, stacked tall, strung up right on top of each other. That's where they all slept.

They met the man's wife, and his children, and they all spoke Spanish, so my dad couldn't really communicate very well. Still, everyone smiled and laughed as they tried to introduce themselves.

Dad kept asking questions and commenting on everything, like, "Oh, cool. So this is where you cook?" The man kept laughing as he showed them around.

The thing that struck me the most, I think, is that even though these people were clearly very poor, they were surrounded by family. There were kids playing soccer together, and moms hanging laundry, and grand-mothers fanning themselves in the shade while they watched the kids play and cared for the little ones. I realized that although their home was so different from my own, the way they lived—surrounded by family and love—was exactly the same.

My dad was clearly struck by that, too. This man's generosity and spirit and clear love for his family moved him.

Dad always carries cash with him, and just before they left to go back to the ship, he pulled out every dollar he had and handed it to that man, saying, "Thank you for welcoming my family to your home. Please use this to do something nice for your family."

"No, no, no!" the man said. Then he went inside and came out with some of the handmade goods he sold at market and tried to sell them a whole bunch of things instead, and my dad said, "No. You keep that so you can sell it and keep making money. I just want to thank you for being so nice to us today."

My dad put the money in the man's hand. It couldn't have been more than a hundred dollars or so, but from the look on the man's face—it seemed like it was life-changing for him.

Seeing the way that man and his family lived was life-changing for us, too. For all the mission trips I'd heard about and this vague dream I had that someday I'd love to go to far-off places and help other people, espe-cially children, I'd never seen poverty quite so up-close before that day. Even though I was only seeing it through my dad's camera lens, it hit me in a different way than it might have if I'd seen it on TV or anywhere else. I mean, there are homeless people right in Nashville, and some of them panhandle at streetlights, and my mom and dad would always pull over and hand them some cash or food out the window, saying, "Have a good day!"

Now that I was driving, I did that, too.

This was different. It made me want to lend a hand in some way be-sides giving them money. It reminded me how important my dream was, deep down in my heart, to go and do mission work someday. Not mission work in terms of converting anybody to my religion, but simply doing good works in the name of Jesus. Helping people. Supporting people. Loving people. In any way I could.

Back out at sea, I got tired early that night. Everyone else was out catching a show or having a drink, but I went back to our cabin just to get some sleep. The air was so beautiful out on the open sea that I fell asleep on the balcony.

I have no idea how long I was asleep before I felt someone gently touching my cheek, and I opened my eyes, and Thomas Rhett was sitting right there beside me.

"What?" I said. "How did you get in here?"

"I climbed over," he said.

I sat up straight like I'd woken from a bad dream. "You what?!"

Thomas Rhett's cabin was next door. Apparently he had knocked on my door and when I didn't answer, he went into his room, went out to the balcony, looked over and saw me laying there, and decided it would be a good idea to climb over to my balcony, on the outside of the ship, in the middle of the night, over the *open sea* just to get to me!

TR: If I had fallen, I would've been in the middle of the ocean.

Lauren: And our families were gone. They were all out doing things.

TR: I mean, no one would have even heard me.

Lauren: No one would've known.

TR: Yeah.

Lauren: It makes me sick to think about it. His mom still can't talk about that story without feeling sick.

TR: I guess it was a little crazy. But I was crazy about her! I know she kept saying she didn't want to be serious, but I wanted to be serious, and I saw a chance for us to be alone together on that balcony, under that beautiful sky, and I wasn't gonna miss it.

We ended up propping our elbows up on the railing and looking out at the ocean and the wide-open sky, and talking for what seemed like forever before our parents came back—and freaked out when they heard what happened.

Thomas Rhett was definitely full of adventure and romance. I mean, climbing a balcony to get to your girl is straight out of Shakespeare. I'm just glad it didn't end up being a tragedy.

The adventures continued at another stop in Mexico, where apparently there's no drinking age. So at dinner, with both of our families, Thomas Rhett just straight-up ordered a beer without asking anyone for permission. The waiter just took the order like everyone else's. Everyone laughed as he walked away and Tim said, "Fine, you can taste it, but then I'll finish it." So the waiter brought Thomas Rhett a beer, and he took a big drink of it and he turned to me and said, "Here, do you want some?"

I looked around the table and nobody objected, so I said, "Okay, sure!" So we split a beer in Mexico. I felt like such a rebel, even though it was, like, completely legal where we were.

I think I mentioned early on that Thomas Rhett was a bit of a boundary pusher, and in the weeks and months to come, he would not only be responsible for giving me my first sip of beer, but my first chew, my first dip, and my first cigarette. Neither of us smoke now, but I swear Thomas Rhett could talk me into doing just about anything, good or bad—and honestly, it's still the same today.

TR: I got a little wild in high school. Like, after football games I would go over to my friends' houses and we'd drink beer in their parents' basements. Lauren wasn't into any of that, but when I wasn't around her, I was just a redneck hanging out with redneck people. We'd smoke cigarettes, and dip, and drink. I guess that made me sort of a rebel.

He never pushed me to do anything I didn't want to do. I was a teenager. Teens *try* things. That's how we learn. I just refused to do anything that I didn't feel was safe. That "stay safe" lesson had been drilled into me about a million times, and if anything made me feel less than safe, I'd hear my dad's voice booming in my head. But with Thomas Rhett, I didn't *want* to steer clear of everything. He made me feel safe. I *liked* being adventurous with him. And with those big brown eyes begging, how could I say no? How could anybody say no to him? There was just something about him.

I'll never forget when we wandered into an empty ballroom on the cruise ship. There were hundreds of people walking and swimming and lounging around outside in the sunshine; it was almost impossible to find anywhere to be alone. When we walked into the ballroom, though, there was not a soul but us in that red-velvet-lined space, with a little stage, and floor-to-ceiling windows. Thomas Rhett walked up to the baby grand piano on that stage and he found that it was unlocked. So he sat down, and he started playing, and I sat down right next to him on the piano bench.

"What's a good song for the middle of the ocean?" he asked me.

"What's that Celine Dion song?" I asked back. "You know—"

"The *Titanic* song?" he said with a laugh.

"Yes!" I said.

"Hold on," he said, and he started playing around on the keys, and just like that, although he'd clearly never played that song before, he started figuring it out—and, not that I'm shocked, it sounded really good!

It was super romantic, and it sounded so pretty.

Having him play just for me was a whole lot different from sitting there watching him entertain a room full of people. This was just the two of us. Hanging out.

Then again, the *Titanic* was a big cruise ship that sank, and Rose and Jack never saw each other again after that cruise ship met its demise. So maybe one of us should have thought that that particular theme song might be a bit of a bad omen. Not about the cruise we were on, thank goodness. But maybe, just maybe, about *us*.

Once we were back in school, Thomas Rhett's high school jealousy started showing up again. A couple of rocky months later, spring break came around, and just as we'd promised, the Gregorys went back to Key West. And we brought a *crowd*. Thomas Rhett's dad, Rhett, and his girlfriend came along instead of Paige and Tim on this trip. We'd seen a lot more of Rhett as his kids had gotten older and he wasn't out on the road quite as much. We'd gotten to know him pretty well by then, and he was so much fun to be around. He was into hunting and fishing, a real country boy at heart—to the point where you wouldn't even know he was famous if you didn't know who he was. And of course, Thomas Rhett and Kasey were

My dad walked in and took a video of Thomas Rhett on the piano, serenading me (naturally) with "My Heart Will Go On"

right there with us, along with their grandmother, Rhett's mom, Mammy. Hailey and Hunter and their little sister, Hannah, came down with Laurie and John again, too. (Key West became Hunter's favorite place in the whole world after our first trip.) So did my dad's sister, and my uncle, and my cousin Allie Brooke. And so did our mutual friend Mitch Barnes and the whole Barnes family, including his parents, who were friends with my parents, and his three brothers and their sister.

All of this meant that Thomas Rhett and I were anything *but* alone with each other on that trip. And on top of that, the truth was, Mitch Barnes was an older boy I'd always had a crush on.

A crush that seemed to turn mutual that spring.

Which meant that things were about to get a little tense in the otherwise laid-back world of Key West, Florida.

5

Breaking Up

That spring break trip with our big Crew was one of the most fun trips any of us had ever been on in our whole lives, and it wasn't till right toward the end of it all that emotions started running high.

One day, Mitch and I were hanging out on the beach like the friends we'd always been, but I guess we got a little bit too high school flirty, and Thomas Rhett wasn't having it.

The two of them were actually friends, but after watching Mitch spending so much time with me, and getting kinda close to me, and putting his hand on my back or my shoulder, Thomas Rhett couldn't take it anymore.

"Hey, Lauren!" he said from behind us. I hadn't even realized he'd been watching us. "Can you come over here?"

I walked over to him and he said, "Can y'all stop flirting?!"

"Whoa, whoa, whoa," I said.

I grabbed Thomas Rhett's hand and took him for a walk down the beach.

"Look," I said. "I'm not *yours*. I'm not a possession. I have guy friends. I have *always* had guy friends. I *will* always have guy friends. That is not gonna change. Our friends are just way too close and intertwined to have this kind of emotion threaten to push anyone away. I love you, and I care

The Crew in Key West on spring break

A post-snorkeling and (I'm pretty sure) post-breakup picture, in Key West (L to R): Jackson, Mitch, Allie Brooke, me, Hunter, and Thomas Rhett

about you, I will always be your friend and I hope you're always mine, but this relationship isn't working anymore. We are just way better off as friends, I think."

"Lauren, he was—"

"I don't care what he was doing. This isn't about some other boy. This is about *us*. You and me. And this possessive, jealous thing just doesn't fly with me. So I'm sorry, but I just want to be friends again."

"So that's it?" Thomas Rhett said.

"That's it."

"For real? We're breaking up?" he said.

"For real."

I was really upset that night, and my friends told me that Thomas Rhett was, too. I wouldn't have blamed him if he never wanted to talk to me again.

I suppose that could have been it for Thomas Rhett and me. Someone else might have taken that heartbreak and stayed mad about it forever. It crushes me to think about it, but if that breakup had gone the way some people's breakups do, it might have split our two families apart. My dad might have lost a friend in Tim, and my mom would've lost Paige, who'd become such a close friend to her by then. My sister, Macy, and Thomas Rhett's little sister, Kasey, were side by side in almost every family photo and video we had from the last two years. Our breakup could have ruined *all* of that.

But so could the fact that our relationship had gotten so *serious*. As a high school girl, I didn't want to feel suffocated, or like someone was always watching me like a hawk. It was causing too much tension, and it needed to end.

When it did, our families were right there to support us. Both of us. My parents loved Thomas Rhett, and they felt bad for him because he was so upset. They talked to us both about it, together and separately, and tried to assure us that it wasn't the end of the world. They were like, "Listen, you are only sophomores in high school. You both are going to learn so much more and change so much in the next few years." They could see the bigger picture. "It's not like y'all were engaged and about to be married. You're friends. You've *always* been friends. You can get through this and still be great friends, like always."

I believed them. I was pretty sure Thomas Rhett did, too.

We lived in a community where we were all so close, it was almost necessary to get along after you broke up with somebody. I mean, yeah, it might have been awkward for a while, but there was no chance we weren't going to see each other at school, at games, and around town. We all went to the same events, functions, and church activities, and the same movie theater and Starbucks and Dairy Queen. We were going to see each other. So we either get over it and deal with it like grown-ups or end up miserable and alone all the time.

Way before this breakup, my parents told both of us that not wanting things "to seem awkward" was never a reason to stay with somebody. "Don't date someone if you're not happy. Don't stay in a relationship for somebody else. You've got to be true to who you are," my parents always said.

Breaking up kindly was just the way we were raised. We knew that to stay mad at someone for a breakup wouldn't be right. It isn't the loving thing to do.

To truly love someone sometimes means giving them the benefit of the doubt; the grace to allow them to have and express and live out what may be a very different perspective from yours, simply because it's *theirs*.

That wasn't easy. Especially because we were so young.

Thomas Rhett took the breakup harder than I did, obviously. He didn't want to break up. He came around more than once asking me, "Are you sure? Can't we try again? Please?" We even sort of got back together one time for a hot minute, but it didn't work out.

As if to put the nail in the coffin, Mitch ended up asking me to his Junior/Senior Banquet—and I said "yes."

Thomas Rhett drove up to my house after that and practically begged me to take him back. "Don't go out with Mitch. Of all people. Please!" he begged. And I put my foot down and told him we were done, once and for all.

"I'll go out with whoever I want, and who I choose to go out with is none of your business!" I told him.

He jumped back in his truck and squealed the tires and kicked up gravel all over the front yard as he tore off down the road in frustration and anger.

That was a pretty immature thing to do, I thought. Then again, we were both pretty immature at the time. We were just figuring this stuff out. I

Friends forever, no matter what; this was taken after watching fireworks at our house on the Fourth of July

just hoped he didn't hurt himself or anybody else as he peeled out and sped away from the neighborhood on those winding back roads.

I don't know why teenage emotions run so high.

There was no part of me that wanted to hurt Thomas Rhett. *None.* I was sure we'd be able to be friends again. It would just take some time.

Thomas Rhett and I were friends. *Best* friends. We'd *been* friends for nearly a third of our lives at that point. We weren't going to throw that away. We weren't going to break our families apart. That just wasn't going to happen.

I was right.

Mitch and I didn't last very long as a couple, and it wasn't long before Thomas Rhett and I started hanging out again as friends. Actually, it wasn't long before Thomas Rhett had a new girlfriend.

Kacy—not to be confused with Thomas Rhett's sister, Kasey—was a grade above us. She was beautiful. A cheerleader. She played tennis, which I had started to play in high school, too, and I only wished I could be as good as she was.

Kacy was a super sweet girl, and Thomas Rhett seemed to really like her. I was glad to see him happy. And I was even more glad to find that I could talk with the two of them and we could get along just fine.

I didn't see a whole lot of Thomas Rhett that summer. I got a job at Sonic, and we both just got to doing our own things—with other people.

Over the course of that summer, I started to hang out a lot more with a new friend group I made through my cousin Allie Brooke and the youth group at Long Hollow Baptist.

As a high schooler, I think it's only natural that whenever you meet and spend time with new people—no matter what the circumstances—you end up thinking, "Dang, I think he's cute," or, "He's really awesome," or, "Well, he seems like he might kinda like me."

That is exactly what happened in this new friend group—especially with a boy named Michael. Michael, a star basketball player from nearby Beech High School who was tall, and blond, and *so* cute.

Once it became clear that he was as interested in me as I was in him, Michael and I started dating. And once we started dating, we were inseparable.

Michael was a good human, with a good heart. He was good to every-

one he knew. He was respectful. He was full of love, and faith, and he was so much *fun*. I mean, like the most fun—and it didn't even matter if what we did was something super exciting or not, he would *make* it fun, no matter what it was.

He also never showed any jealousy toward any of my guy friends. He trusted that I would stay true to him, and I did the same for him.

It seems like in no time at all I got close with Michael's family. And he and his friends became friends with mine—including Thomas Rhett. Just as I'd hoped, and my parents had prom-

Michael and me on a trip to the beach with friends

ised, the two of us started hanging out again after we were back
in school and with other people.
I felt a little anxious about hanging out together at first, but as
soon as we settled into it, we were
good. He came up to the house
and brought Kacy with him. And
we ended up at the same parties
together, where Thomas Rhett
would still sing and play guitar
like he always did. Michael and I
even went on a couple of double
dates with Thomas Rhett and
Kacy.

*Michael and me with
Kacy and Thomas Rhett at
Goodpasture's banquet junior year*

We were friends again. And it
was so nice.

Compared to our crazy sophomore year, our junior and senior
years of high school were smooth sailing. Through football games and
homecomings and formals, and all of the traditions that mark time and
make high school so memorable, our overlapping friend groups stayed
together. And we found and made rituals of our own.

Sometimes groups of kids would go to a place we called The Middle, a
fenced-in grassy area off Center Point Road that just seemed to be in the
middle of where everyone lived. Guys would park their trucks there and
drink a beer or two, and smoke cigarettes, and couples would cozy up and
hang out far from any parents' view. And other times we'd go up to The
Spot, an undeveloped area way up at the top of Thomas Rhett's neighborhood. You needed four-wheel drive to get up that hill, which was out of
sight from any of the houses that were under construction in the neighborhood just below, and once you were there, there were views in just
about every direction, for miles and miles, with nothing above us but the
stars. We hung out there a lot, just talking and laughing and enjoying the

view. Sometimes you'd see fireworks off in the distance. Sometimes we'd bring some fireworks up there ourselves. But no one ever got too crazy, and I don't think a single one of us doesn't dream about taking a drive back up there today, just to sit under the stars and remember when.

I say "no one ever got too crazy," but that statement does not include Hunter.

One night, we were out rolling with him, and it turns out that the person who owned the house we were rolling was a cop—the parent of a guy we knew who was not one of our favorite people. It may be the only time we rolled someone to purposefully annoy them or get them in trouble. And of course, Hunter was right there leading the charge. It was all going smoothly until he tripped over something and made a big noise, and all of a sudden all the lights turned on in the house.

"Let's go, let's go!" we whisper-yelled, all jumping in my Jeep. But Hunter said, "I'm not done yet!" and ran around to the back of the house. "Go, go, go," he said; "I'll meet you on the other side."

What he meant was the other side of the neighborhood, and to this day we don't know what it was that Hunter did in the back of that house. He was gone for what seemed like a really long time, and we thought for sure he'd gotten caught. Then all of a sudden, he came bolting out of the woods yelling, "Go, go, go!" and he jumped in the back of the truck.

The fact that we made it out left Hunter's mischievous side beaming with pride.

Hunter kept playing soccer as he got into high school, and he became a star player almost instantly. It's amazing how much he grew up between eighth and ninth grade. He was muscular, and tall, and he had this gorgeous long hair that was his mother's pride and joy. (Did I mention that Laurie was a hairdresser?) Every time Hunter walked into our house he would ask, "Can I borrow a ponytail holder?" His hair just kept getting in his face all the time, and it was always sweaty on the soccer field. It drove him crazy.

"Why don't you just cut it?" I said to him one afternoon.

And then Macy said, "Yeah, you should do a Mohawk."

You should have seen Hunter's face light up at that idea. He loved it! He then proceeded to beg my mom to cut off his beautiful locks. She and Laurie were like sisters by now, and the idea of taking the hairdresser's son and shaving his mane of hair off wasn't something even my mom thought would be a good idea. But who could say "no" to Hunter? She held the clippers and we all watched in awe as big patches of his long hair fell to the floor.

Laurie was so stunned by the sight of her Mohawked son, I'm pretty sure she shed tears, and I'm sure that she found some way to get my mom back a few weeks later.

There was plenty of laughter and forgiveness to go around.

Always.

I had some pretty big decisions to make toward the end of high school, like all kids do. When it came to thinking about where I wanted to go to college, and what I wanted to pursue as a career, growing up in a family and community full of kindness, love, and grace had a huge influence on the goals I set for myself.

First: I wanted to go to a school where some of my good friends were going. I didn't want to get away from everyone and "start fresh" the way some kids do. I wanted to stay connected, even as I took the leap and went somewhere outside my community and away from home.

Second: I wanted to help people. I was hoping to start that during some of my summer breaks by going on mission trips. Social media was becoming more popular at this point, and I watched on Facebook as some of the girls I knew from school went to places like Africa and Central America on mission trips, and I hated to admit it, but I was *jealous*. I wanted to go and help so much. "We just can't afford to send you on a mission trip, Lauren. I'm sorry," my dad told me. "Not with college coming up. We need to save." So I started to think, "How can I help people right here? What's a way to help, and especially to help children, as a career, every day?"

I decided I wanted to become a nurse. I always admired the work that nurses do, and I was pretty sure that all the scrapes and bumps and bruises and gushing blood I'd encountered as a kid had toughened me up enough to do the job.

Actually, my scrapes, bumps, and bruises were still happening.

Me and Michael went four-wheeling right before homecoming my senior year, and we flipped the four-wheeler.

"I told you those things were dangerous, Lauren!" my dad scolded.

We had gotten ourselves into a pretty bad accident. I sometimes wonder how we didn't break our necks. I ended up with a black eye, and Michael messed up his shoulder. That put a major wrench in his senior basketball season at Beech High. We should have been a lot more careful, but once that four-wheeler started to tip, there was just no stopping it.

Dad had been right, as always, but I had to learn my lesson the hard way.

Funny enough, I ended up being voted homecoming queen, and my mom always says that I was the only homecoming queen in history with a black eye.

Homecoming our senior year with Thomas Rhett watching me being escorted onto the football field. Kinda sweet. ☺

By the time graduation came around, I was not only black-eye-free, but all my plans were in place. After an incredibly tense wait, I was accepted into the University of Tennessee, Knoxville (Go, Vols!), which is where Michael and my best friend Lindsey and a whole bunch of other kids I knew were going, too. I would have to work hard my freshman and sophomore years to pass all kinds of tests to make it into the nursing program at UT, but I was ready for the challenge.

I went to prom at Michael's high school, where there was music and dancing and just so much fun. It was pretty dreamy. And we went to my own Senior Banquet at Goodpasture, too. I couldn't believe how quickly those four years had flown by, or that me and Thomas Rhett and so many of our group of close-knit friends were now the graduating seniors. How did we even get here?

We all took pictures together in our caps and gowns and felt so lucky to get to walk across that stage to receive our diplomas while surrounded by everyone we loved.

There was never any question in our minds that this tight-knit Crew would stay tight. Our foundation was just too solid to be shaken. I was sure of it.

6

Moving On

The University of Tennessee is a pretty big party school. But partying, in terms of drinking, just wasn't my thing, and it wasn't my friends' thing, either.

I went into school still very much in a relationship with Michael, the same tall, blond, super nice guy I'd been dating for the last two years. I was happy. I wasn't interested in looking for anyone new, and maybe that's part of the reason why the party scene just didn't draw me in.

We formed a tight-knit group with friends from both Goodpasture and Beech High School, who we got even closer to at UT than we did back home. It was a core group that didn't leave us, and who, for the most part, were raised with the same kind of values we all shared.

Our weekend partying consisted of going to an eighteen-and-up restaurant/bar to dance, and then me and Lindsey sneaking in the back stairwell late at night to the guys' dorms in

This pic was actually taken after college, but it's one of my favorites ever of me and my bestie, Lindsey

North Carrick to watch DVDs on our friend Eric's massive seventy-five-inch TV, which barely fit in his room.

That was about it.

I know there were people who laughed at us, who thought we were all goody two-shoes or something, but I had the best childhood, high school, and college experience ever. We always had *so* much fun. We just stuck to what we believed, and a huge part of being able to keep out of trouble was having a friend group that did, too. We weren't saints. We were still kids. I mean, I'm sure some of us might have stashed a couple of beers in the back of a fridge in a dorm room, but we weren't interested in "getting wasted" all the time. That was not our priority, and we all were cool with that. It's just so much easier to make safe choices when your friends are like, "Yeah, I don't think we're gonna go to that party, either. Let's just do what *we* wanna do."

I suppose part of my attitude toward partying and drinking—and other things college kids tend to do—also came from my dad's voice being in my ear all the time.

It was pretty early on in my freshman year when Dad took the whole "open-book parenting" thing to a whole other level.

It happened out of the blue one day, and it started with the same kind of talk he'd been giving me for as long as I can remember: "It doesn't matter what you do, ever. I will always love you. But at the end of the day, I was given to you as your boss on Earth to help instruct you," he said.

"I know," I said.

But he reiterated, "Try to learn from me and do as I say, not as I do."

"Okay," I said.

And then he said: "Please, just try not to have sex before you find your husband."

My jaw just about hit the kitchen floor. I didn't even have a response to that.

"I just think it complicates things," he said.

What? Dad?!

I started to put two and two together, and I awkwardly asked him, "Like, what do you *mean?*"

And that's when my dad told us that he hadn't been a virgin when he married my mom.

"What?!" I said.

"And neither was she," he said, just as my mom walked into the kitchen.

"Neither was I what?" she said.

"A virgin," Dad said.

"I—Steve! What in the world?" she hollered. Her face turned beet red.

"She needs to know these things before it's too late!" he told her.

Oh, yeah, and did I mention that Macy was in the room? She was a sophomore in high school at the time.

I was shocked. Mainly because we'd grown up going to Madison Church of Christ, where clearly *no one* had sex before they were married. (Or so I thought!) Especially not my seemingly perfect, "make right choices" parents.

"When I've told you that we *all* mess up, I mean all of us," Dad said. "And you'll mess up, too. We're all human. I want to challenge you to be better than me. All I'm saying is I hope y'all choose to make your lives easier by waiting to have sex until you get married."

The fact that this conversation happened out of the blue, in our kitchen, wasn't even a little bit surprising to me. But the *topic* of that conversation was definitely surprising.

Maybe it's no big deal to kids in other families, but I was in absolute shock that my parents weren't virgins when they married. Like I said earlier, I grew up thinking that my parents *always* made good decisions. They *always* had it together. So it was kind of mind-blowing to realize that just wasn't the case.

What I was quickly learning is that nobody *always* makes the right decisions, and that the so-called right decisions aren't necessarily right for everybody anyway. My dad owning his truth and being so transparent with me in hopes I would learn from all of his life lessons was really impactful to me. I was starting to realize that none of us know all the answers, and none of us get it all right. Not even our parents.

And honestly? That's freeing.

Dad admitting that he and Mom had messed up something that I had always believed was *that* big, which was *that* important—at least to my young, still-pretty-green ears—it definitely made me feel like I was on a more even playing field with them. It let me know that when and if I had *my* big mess-ups in life, I didn't need to feel so much shame about them. It allowed me to have way more grace for myself, as well as grace for other people when *they* didn't get it all right, either.

This wasn't the last time he talked to us about sex, either. Those talks of his sunk in with me and would stay on my mind just about any time a thought of sex came up from that day forward. It made me think about the personal choices I wanted to make.

Let's be honest: It's not like I never thought about it. Michael and I had been dating for a long time. Plus, I didn't live in a bubble, and I wasn't naïve. I had friends who were having sex. It just makes such a huge difference who you surround yourself with in life, and the person I was closest with—my boyfriend—had the same values and beliefs that I did.

I'm glad we kept things as uncomplicated as possible, too, because for the first time in my life, I was facing some challenges unlike anything I'd ever faced before.

First of all, I was struggling to get good grades. I'd always done really well in high school. I'd worked hard in school, but I never realized how difficult school could be until I tried to succeed in all the classes I needed to pass in order to get into the nursing program at UT.

I also didn't get into the sorority I wanted to get into, the one I had my heart set on and the one most of my friends got into. I got *rejected*. And I know that doesn't seem like an earth-shattering problem, but it hurt. I felt like I got left behind.

Alpha Delta Pi (ADPi) is the sorority that the older sister of one of my girlfriends (through Michael), Gillian, was in at UT. It was the only sorority I ever envisioned myself being a part of, and I'd been told by Gillian's older sister that I was absolutely someone they wanted, even before I rushed. And they really did want me! It's just that, for some reason, another sorority placed me higher on their bid list, which overruled the

ADPi bid. I watched as all my friends walked through the front door of the sorority I really wanted to be in, the one I knew I was meant for, and I felt as if I'd been cut from the basketball team or the cheerleading squad. As if I was the *only one* who got cut.

I know there are much bigger problems in the world. I get it. But at the time this felt really big to me. I'd never lived away from home. My mom was upset by the news about ADPi when I called her, which made me even *more* upset. And honestly, it felt like the first time in my whole life that I hadn't achieved a goal of mine.

It *hurt*.

I tried to look on the bright side. I tried to make friends in this other sorority, and I did make a few. But whenever I saw girls wearing ADPi sweatshirts around campus, my heart sank.

A few weeks in, I decided to drop the sorority I'd gotten into. Some of the girls in it didn't like me for that. But I knew where I belonged, and I was determined to take the unusual step of rushing again during my sophomore year.

Michael, my blue-eyed, steady boyfriend, was there to let me cry on his shoulder and to put it all in perspective.

"Look, it's not the end of the world," he told me. "There's always next year. You have us. And maybe it's a good thing, like your dad always says. Maybe this bad thing is just God leading you in a better direction."

Did I mention how much my dad loved Michael? He adored him. Michael was kind, and he took such

A typical Camp Gregory Halloween

good care of me. Later in the semester I got real sick, and Michael brought me soup and made sure I was okay. He slept on my floor, in case I woke up and needed anything. I mean, he's exactly the kind of guy you want to bring home to your parents.

And I did. I brought him and my other college friends home. Often.

For Halloween, instead of staying on campus, we drove the nearly three hours to get to my neighborhood so that we could go trick-or-treating. On random weekends, a bunch of us would show up out of the blue and Mom would throw hamburgers on the grill and make it just as warm and welcoming as their home had been my whole life.

At Christmas, we decided to throw an ugly Christmas sweater party, and we must have had sixty people show up—in our tiny little house—wearing the funniest, gaudiest sweaters they could find. It wasn't just college friends. It was old friends. Thomas Rhett and Kacy were there, and Kamron, and Hunter, and all the old Crew. Thomas Rhett was going to Lipscomb University, right in Nashville, where my mom had finished her social work degree, and he and Kacy were still going strong. It was so good to see them. To see *everyone*. We were all growing and changing and exploring new careers and new lives, and yet, we were never disconnected from each other for more than a couple of months at a time. Any of us.

Our friendships were sacred.

Around that time, it started to seem that Thomas Rhett was more serious about his music career than he was about going to college. He'd started a cover band and he was playing at small bars around town. Granted, most of these bars were so small they didn't even have a stage. Thomas Rhett and his band would just set up in the corner and do their thing, most of the time while half the audience kept talking and eating and drinking without even listening. But he loved it. He loved that he was getting paid to go play music, even if it wasn't very much money, and even though he insisted that he and the band were terrible.

"The way I see it, I'm getting paid to practice," he said to me one time.

"That's cool. There aren't many careers where you can say that!" I said.

* * *

On the night of the ugly sweater party, we talked and laughed like we'd always done. It felt good to have my best friend back in my life, and I could tell he felt the same. He promised to come out and visit me on campus during the spring semester, and he did. He and a friend of his even crashed on the floor in my dorm room, since it was too far to drive all the way back to Nashville in just one day.

In fact, I ended up having more time to hang out with Thomas Rhett than I'd ever planned on that spring semester, because at one point, just

The first annual ugly Christmas sweater party

before spring break, Michael and I broke up. It all started because of some really immature fight, over what I can't even remember. Maybe it was just a symptom of our eyes being opened to a whole new world. We'd both made new friends beyond our Crew, and I think we were going through some growing pains, just figuring out how we wanted to do college life. I think both of us were like, "Dang, look at this new world. Do we really want to be dating the same person we've been dating for the past two years? Or do we want to explore a little?"

The breakup wasn't pretty, though. It made us cancel our spring break trip that year, which meant everyone's plans were changed to accommodate our sudden separation.

I ended up going on a spring break trip with Thomas Rhett and all of his friends, at his grandmother's beach house on Amelia Island.

College dating certainly takes some weird twists and turns. One day that week, a group of us decided to drive all the way to Panama City, Florida, where we met up with Michael and all of my college guy friends and hung out for a day. Just seeing Michael for a few hours made me rethink the breakup. I realized then that I didn't want to be a college girl just dating for the fun of it. I wanted something real. I missed Michael.

I started asking myself, "What am I looking for?" and I quickly realized that everything I was looking for was so much of what I had with Michael. He was safe. He was good. So I told him that. "I hate not being with you," I said, and we got back together right after that trip.

Michael was, and is to this day, a gentleman. He's so much fun, but he'll also do whatever is best for a relationship. He's strong in his faith, and knows what he believes, but he was always willing to hear me out. He wouldn't shut me down for having a different opinion. He was truly a good listener, and that was so important to me. He was spontaneous and just wanted to go and live life. He was funny. He was loud—*so* loud, to the point where I'd get embarrassed sometimes. But I always felt so safe with him. He's a good friend to his friends, and the best brother to his sister, and son to his mom. He *never* spoke against his mom or his dad. He was never disrespectful to them. He truly had everything that a girl would hope to marry one day. He was that guy who girls wait their whole lives for, and I couldn't understand why any part of me would ever even think of walking away from that.

It wouldn't be the last time Michael and I would break up for a short period, though.

Thomas Rhett and I ended up talking a lot through these relationship ups and downs. We leaned on each other. He drove all the way out to visit me a whole bunch of times that year. He and Kacy broke up and got back together, too, and he dated some other girls at Lipscomb as well. None of those relationships were serious, though. In fact, we talked about how hard it was to find someone compatible.

"Even when I like someone, there are all these little things that seem to get in the way," he told me in my dorm room one time.

"Right?" I said. "Like, I think someone's a nice guy, and then I can't believe how rude they are to some stranger. It's such a turnoff."

"Yeah," Thomas Rhett said. "The more I look around, the more I realize there just aren't really many girls I would want to be around all the time, the way you and I can just hang, you know?"

Waiting for the elevator in my dorm on one of the weekends
Thomas Rhett came to visit at UT

"Yeah," I said. "I'm so glad you're my friend."

I liked having guy friends, and they seemed to like having me to consult with about their girl problems.

At one point that year, our friend Eric went through a breakup that he never saw coming—and he came over and told me it was all my fault.

"What?" I said.

"Yeah," he said. "She was convinced that you and I had something going on, and she just wouldn't let it go. So she broke up with me."

"That's crazy!" I said.

"I know," he said.

Eric had been with his girlfriend for longer than I'd been with Michael, and he was devastated. He truly didn't know what to do with himself after that.

Every Wednesday since we'd been at school, I'd knocked on Eric's door and asked him to please come to church with us. Eric wasn't a believer, and I just thought maybe it would be good for him. On the Wednesday after his breakup, he finally said, "F—it. I'm coming. Hold on!"

Eric went to church with us that Wednesday night, and the next, and the next, and he started asking questions, trying to make sense of everything he'd heard all his life but had tried so hard not to believe. At one point he asked me how I could believe in God when there's so much bad stuff in the world, and there's no proof of His existence—the kind of thing that people who struggle with faith always ask. I ended up answering with an analogy my dad used to tell us when we were younger.

"If you were to walk out into the woods—"

"What woods?" Eric said.

"Any woods. A forest. Just listen," I said. "If you were to walk in a forest and all of a sudden you came to a clearing that's perfectly square. There are no trees, no weeds, but there's woods all around, and there's a garden there. You've got radishes in one row, you've got pumpkins in another, and corn in another, and sunflowers, and tomatoes. So what would your first thought be? Like, 'Oh. That's funny, the wind must have blown just perfectly enough so there are randomly no weeds here, and the perfect rows of corn, perfect rows of tomatoes. It just happened by chance!'"

"No, obviously," Eric said.

"Right. That would be crazy. No one in their right mind would go, 'Yeah, that's exactly what happened. It just naturally happened, randomly, over time!' Every person I know would say, 'No. Clearly somebody planted it.'"

"Somebody was here."

"Somebody was here," I said. "Now, think about the complexity of all the perfection that it takes to make the human eye be able to see. Or a woman having a baby and what her body can do. Just the mind, what *we* can do. It's like, 'How can you think that this was all an accident?'"

"Yeah, but, what's—how do you know it's 'God,' like, what *is* that? Like, what—"

"So, slow down. I think at that point you go, 'Okay. Well, there's *something*. There's *something* that did this. There's someone or some *thing* to attribute it to. Let's figure that out.' And I think if you're willing to search and figure out what that looks like, you'll find what you're looking for. You'll find it. And God's not gonna leave you hanging. I mean, if you ask for Him to help you where you're at, that's what He does. He will find you where you're at. And I think you just have to be open to it and He'll give you an opportunity."

"So I just have to trust that He's going to make it clearer?"

"You just have to be open to it, yes," I told him. "And so much of that openness is just praying. I mean—"

"Praying how?"

"Just pray," I said. "Just talk to Him. Whatever you picture, or even if you don't know what to picture, just start praying and I'm telling you, answers will come. I'm not telling you that you have to think exactly the way I do, or pray like I do, or believe like I do. But once you start getting answers, once you open your eyes to it and realize that there's no way we're all just here by accident, you'll get it."

Since Thomas Rhett was on the road, Eric took me to ADPi formal

I don't think it was two months later when Eric pulled me aside one night and said, "I can't believe I'm gonna say this, but all that stuff you talked about, I get it. I've been praying, and I believe in it, Lauren. All that stuff in church that I fought for so long—it's the one thing that was missing in my life. Like, this big hole in my life feels gone now. Like, it's full!"

He seemed so relieved. So happy. So much less broken, less devastated by his breakup, and suddenly not struggling so much.

I can't even explain how good it felt to see him find his way like that. And he wouldn't be the last friend I'd talk to with that very same analogy my dad used to use, and I swear, those words helped so many people find their way when they were wrestling with their faith.

My own faith seemed stronger than ever as my freshman year ended, and I found that the more I trusted God to take me down new and unforeseen paths, the better things turned out for me. Like when I interviewed for a job as a counselor at a summer camp in Texas, where I didn't know a soul. And they offered me the job. And I *took it*. It was so unlike me. The only person at the camp who I knew even slightly was a guy named Stephen, who had dated a friend of mine back at UT.

There was one other guy there my age, though. A guy named Landon, and it was also his first time at camp. He was the only other person from UT who was assigned to counsel the high school camp—everyone else I knew was working at the middle school camp. So he and I connected on Facebook, and we started hanging out, and we became really close friends that summer.

When camp was over, Landon came to my parents' house, and I went to his house, and I met his family. We hung out a bunch, and then we went back to school and stayed really close friends. And the more we got to know each other, and the closer we got, he would always say to me, "You remind me so much of my aunt. You've got to meet my aunt." And I would always think, "That's such a weird thing to say." Like, what friend of yours goes, "Hey, you've gotta meet my *aunt*?"

Still, I'd say to him, "Cool. Yeah. You'll have to introduce me some time."

Landon never did introduce me, though. He just kept mentioning it, and I'd always wonder, "Why?"

The reason wouldn't become clear for years.

I guess that's just how God works.

At the start of sophomore year at UT, I rushed again. I was one of just a handful of sophomores in the bunch—and I decided to do what they call a *suicide bid*. You're supposed to write three sororities on your bid card at the end of the week, but I wrote *ADPi* on all three lines. Which meant if I didn't make it, I wouldn't get into any sorority at all.

The adult in charge of the whole process pulled me aside and said, "You can't do this."

I explained to her that I was willing to live with the consequences if I didn't get in, and she went and found her supervisor to try to talk me out of it.

"I hear what you're advising," I said, "but respectfully, I need to do this."

The woman shook her head and dismissively told me, "I hope you know what you're doing."

In my heart, I knew I did.

I'm pretty sure it was the first time in my life I ever stood up to an authority figure, other than my dad. But the next day, I received an email inviting me back for bid day, which, because I'd made a suicide bid, meant that I got into ADPi!

What's the old saying? "If at first you don't succeed, try, try again." I would add, "Even when certain authority figures advise you otherwise!"

And here's the most amazing part: During that first week, when I was a sophomore and everyone else was a freshman, I met three new members who would become three of my very best friends in the world. Like, lifelong friends.

First off, I got closer to Gillian, the friend I knew through Michael, and whose older sister was already in ADPi. But then I met Amber, and Adeline, and Dee—a girl who'd gone to Goodpasture in the class behind mine. And the four of us would grow so close, we knew we'd never be apart.

Once I was a part of ADPi, everything once again felt right in my world. I was surrounded by friends, all the time, and I felt like I truly had a home away from home on the UT campus. And that felt *good*.

School was still super hard for me, though. Harder than I ever anticipated. I nearly failed statistics, which pulled my GPA down so low it hurt my chances to get into the nursing school. And my dad told me that if I didn't get into nursing school at UT, I would have to switch to a new school completely. It terrified me. He insisted he couldn't pay for another year at UT just to get my grades back up, not when Macy was applying to colleges, too. I just felt so much pressure. The application to nursing school was due toward the end of the year, and as if that pressure wasn't enough, Michael and I got into a stupid fight and broke up again that summer.

That's when my faith came into play again. The entire time I was working at the camp in Texas that summer, I found myself praying not only to get

A Nashville night out with some of my best girlfriends: Amber, Adeline, and Dee

into nursing school, but for me and Michael to get back together. I told God that I couldn't take switching schools: "Not now. Not after getting into ADPi. Not after how hard I've worked." I also told God I wanted to be in a relationship again. "I don't like being single. I don't like not having a partner to share things with."

As soon as I got back from Texas, I asked Michael if I could see him—and we got back together that very day.

It happened so fast, I didn't even have a chance to tell Thomas Rhett about it until he showed up out of the blue. He drove out from Nashville to my parents' house, and I was so surprised to see him.

"Your timing could not be any more perfect, because I have some really good news: Michael and I are getting back together!" I said. "Actually, he's on his way over right now. So you'll get to see Michael, too!"

"Oh, wow!" Thomas Rhett said. He seemed really surprised. "I'm happy for you, Lauren. You two are great together. You really are."

"Thank you!" I said. "It's so good to see you. What's up?"

"Oh, nothing," he said. "I just missed seeing you since you've been counseling at camp this summer."

TR: I was lying. I only drove out to her house that night for one reason: to tell Lauren that I loved her. To tell her that every other girl I'd ever been with wasn't good enough, because all I did was compare them to her. I wanted to tell her that I'd changed. That I'd grown up. That I wasn't the jealous type anymore. I was ready to lay it all on the line. I knew what we had, and I didn't want to lose that ever again.

When she told me Michael was on his way over, I just about died. I mean, how many near misses could I have with this girl? My heart just broke. I did my best to hide it and be supportive, and I must've done a pretty good job, 'cause she never knew.

When it came to getting news about the nursing program, though, the drama got all drawn out. A few of my friends received letters from the nursing school before I did. Some got in. Some didn't. Not knowing my fate made me feel sick to my stomach.

I was sure I had a good interview. My dad had coached me. I walked in confident that I had the sort of people skills they looked for in new nursing students. But I also knew I probably had the lowest GPA of any of my classmates, and the nursing program was extremely strict about its academic standards.

I could hardly sleep at night. I worried myself sick that I wasn't going to get in.

When a letter finally arrived, I took it to my car so I could be alone. I opened it, and I looked at the first line. I saw the word, "Congratulations," and I just started bawling. I was so overwhelmed with gratitude, to God, and to my dad's coaching.

One of my friends with a higher GPA than mine didn't get in, and it pretty much broke our friendship. She ended up transferring to a different school.

The pressure was high, and it would only get higher.

Thankfully in my junior year, things in my social and personal life seemed to go right back to the way they'd been. I got busy juggling my sorority life with the difficult task of keeping my grades up in nursing school. I moved into an off-campus apartment in a house I shared with some of my very best friends. And Michael and I stayed on track without a breakup for pretty much the whole year.

Thomas Rhett came up to play his first big bar gig in Knoxville that year, at a place with an actual stage—even if it was just a few inches off the ground—and Michael and I went to see him. We were surprised to see that he had a new girlfriend with him, and things got kinda weird. When I was talking to Thomas Rhett, she would grab on to him and pull

It was hard trying to balance the workload of nursing school . . .

. . . with the nonstop social activities of sorority life

him in close, as if she didn't want him to talk to me. It kinda felt to me like she was claiming ownership over my best friend.

When I finally got a minute alone with him, I said, "Is this your new girlfriend?"

"I'm sorry," he said. "I told her you and I were real close. It probably makes her uncomfortable with you being my best friend and all. It's not normal for a guy's best friend to be another girl."

A few weeks later, Thomas Rhett sent me a text that I didn't quite understand. He said something about not being able to be best friends with me anymore, because it was causing too many problems whenever he dated someone. I mean, I had heard my whole life that guys and girls can't be friends; that eventually the friendship will get in the way of love. I just never believed it was true. And I don't think he thought it was true, either. But he clearly needed to get that off his chest, and I texted him back, saying, "I get it."

Thomas Rhett was riding high in every other area of his life. He wasn't even finished with college yet and his dream was already becoming reality. He'd been signed as a song-writer by a Nashville publishing company, which meant he was getting paid to go in and write

At Puckett's Grocery and Restaurant in Nashville, one of the first times I ever got to see Thomas Rhett play in public

songs for a living. Jason Aldean actually recorded one of Thomas Rhett's songs while Thomas Rhett was still a junior in college. It was so cool, and we were all so proud of him. And then he got to play some acoustic sets for all the record labels in town, and more than one of those labels offered Thomas Rhett a record deal! It was crazy. He didn't have to put in half as many years as his dad did before he was on his way.

Thomas Rhett's Big Machine signing party

"Lauren," he said. "I can't even explain it. There is no other explanation than this was all God, because I have not worked hard enough and I am just not good enough for all of this to be happening right now."

"Yes you are! You *are* that good," I told him. "I'm so proud of you!"

That very year, Thomas Rhett signed with the Big Machine Label Group—the same record label that Taylor Swift was on—and they had a big signing party and everything. I texted him that day, apologizing that I couldn't be there, and wishing him all the best. I felt so sad that I wasn't there.

That spring, just before the end of our junior year, Michael and I went to the ADPi spring formal together, and it was perfect. He looked so good dressed up in a suit and tie, I thought I would die. The fact that we were back together, that we knew we wanted to be together even after spending some time apart the previous summer, made everything feel right in the world.

The very next night, we were holding hands when he stopped me on the sidewalk outside my apartment. He turned me around, and he looked in my eyes, and he said, "Lauren. Where do you see yourself in five years?"

"I dunno," I said. "I mean, I'll be working as a nurse by then, and—"

"No, I mean . . . Do you see us getting married?" he said.

I hesitated.

I looked at him, trying to grasp some kind of answer to a question that for some reason, in all that time, I hadn't really thought about that much.

"I, um," I said. "I mean, do you see yourself married to *me*?"

Michael looked down at the ground. He seemed really sad all of a sudden.

"We can't do this," he said.

"Do what?"

"We'll be graduating next year, and if you don't know that you want to be married to me by now, I don't even—honestly, I don't want to say this, but—"

"No!" I said. "We can get married. I mean . . . Let's do it!" I said.

I could feel myself panicking.

"No, Lauren. You know it, just like I know it. It's just not right. We should know by now. It's been a long time, and—we just can't date anymore."

"Oh, no, no, no," I said. "Michael, where is this coming from? I can't be without you. I don't even know what life *is* without you."

"I'm sorry," he said. He squeezed my hands, and I could see he had tears in his eyes as he turned and walked away.

"Michael," I said. "Michael!"

He just kept walking.

All of a sudden, I could barely breathe. I ran up to my apartment and my heart kept racing. I could feel it pounding in my chest. I felt dizzy. I worried I was having some kind of a panic attack. I didn't know what to do.

I called my dad.

"Hello?"

I was crying so hard I couldn't speak.

"Lauren? Lauren, what is it?" he said. "Take a breath. Please. Tell me what's wrong."

My dad was normally cool as could be. He kept his head on straight in any situation, but the longer I went without saying a word, the more I could hear the alarm in his voice. He thought for sure I'd been in a car wreck or that somebody had died. "Lauren, I need you to calm down," he said. "Please."

My crying only got worse.

"Lauren. Please tell me what is wrong. Calm down. *Talk to me!*"

I stopped my cries just long enough to get the words out: "Michael broke up with me."

"Oh no," my dad said. I could hear the panic disappear from his voice, and instead, as he tried to console me, I could hear his heart breaking for me.

He knew from the sound of my shaking voice that this was not a temporary thing. This was not some silly breakup that wouldn't last for more than a few days.

He knew, I think, because I knew it, too—somewhere deep down inside where I tried to hide things I didn't want to admit could possibly be true.

In that moment, to me, it felt like everything I knew, everything I relied upon, everything I'd dreamed of and imagined my life was all about—as if my whole *world* was over.

7

The Front Porch

Macy's high school graduation party was on Friday the 13th of May, 2011.

My year had already wrapped up by then. I'd packed up and moved home—and been missing Michael the whole time. I was just so depressed, and I could not believe it was really the end.

It couldn't be.

I couldn't let it be.

I knew Michael was coming to Macy's graduation party. We'd all gotten too close over the last five years for him to miss something that big in her life, no matter what had happened between us. And I kept getting my hopes up: *Friday will be the night. We'll see each other and everyone we know will be here, everyone we love, and we'll talk, and it'll all get worked out.*

When the night of the party came, though, I hardly got a chance to talk to Michael at all. He said "Hi," and we made a little small talk. That was it.

I tried to stay in a good mood for the sake of my sister. The next day she'd be walking onstage to receive her diploma, and this night was all about her. Everyone we knew came by to congratulate her and wish her well. And the best part of all is her graduation wasn't the precursor to a big goodbye. She'd made up her mind to follow in my footsteps and come to UT in the fall, and I was so excited at the thought of her being there.

Me and Hunter cracking up at who-knows-what at Macy's graduation party. He was always making me laugh!

Dad and Thomas Rhett at Macy's graduation party

Michael and I were both excited to welcome her into our group of UT friends.

I couldn't help but wonder how that was all going to work now.

Hunter was at Macy's party, and it was so good to see him.

He seemed really happy that night. He was out of school now, and seemed to really be working hard on living his best life. I was proud of him.

As the party started to wind down before midnight, I noticed Thomas Rhett was still there. He was talking with my dad. He had hardly spoken to me all night, and I wasn't sure why. It wasn't like him. He knew all about me and Michael. Maybe he was just giving us space or something, I don't know. But now that Michael was gone, I was really hoping to talk with him. Mostly because he always made me feel better.

TR: Lauren's dad knew everything. He knew I'd driven to the neighborhood that last summer to tell Lauren that I loved her and wanted to be with her. He knew I'd failed. He'd always been someone I could talk to about anything, and he'd been giving it to me straight ever since we were little. So I told him everything I was feeling, and he encouraged me to talk to Lauren. "Just go on and tell her. Be honest with her. Don't hold anything back and you'll see where the chips fall," he said. He's just a big believer in being open and honest about everything. So when he saw that Lauren and Michael weren't getting back together at the party that night, he pulled me aside in the kitchen and said, flat-out, "If you don't tell her how you feel tonight, I'm gonna tell her myself."

Thomas Rhett finally stopped talking to my dad and made his way over to me. He asked me if I wanted to go out on the front porch so we could talk.

"Sure," I said.

It was a beautiful night. The moon was full. And the two of us sat down on the little bench out there and caught up about everything. Our breakups, of course, but more about school, and what was happening with his career, and Macy, and my parents, and how glad we were that they were still in this same home that we could always come back to.

The air was getting a little chilly, and the two of us kept getting closer and closer until we were pressed up right next to each other, keeping each other warm on the bench in the light of the full moon. It was one of those perfect conversations under the stars, except for one thing: Thomas Rhett kept looking away like he had something on his mind. It was almost like he was nervous or something. I could just tell something was up with him.

"Are you sure you're okay?" I said, more than once.

"Yeah. I'm fine. Really," he insisted.

Around two in the morning I heard my mom up walking around the house.

"Lauren?" she whispered, turning lights on and off. "Lauren?"

She finally opened the front door and turned on the porch light, and caught a glimpse of us squinting at her from the bench.

"Oh!" she said. "Sorry. Go back to what you were doing. Good night!"

She shut the light off and closed the door and we both laughed.

"That was weird," I said.

Thomas Rhett circled the conversation back around to my breakup with Michael, and he wondered out loud if there might be a deeper reason why the two of us broke up.

"What do you mean?" I asked him.

"Like, I was with Kacy off and on for almost five years, too. We broke up more than you and Michael did, but we kept coming back together. Even this last time, after you and Michael got back together, she and I started hanging out again, and there is nothing I didn't like about her. She's great. And I really thought that after all that time, I thought I ought to marry her."

"Really?"

"Yeah. Just like you thought you were gonna marry Michael, right?"

"I guess."

"And then I just had this revelation one day. Like, 'Why do I feel like there's something missing?' I was like, 'There's a reason that I don't have a peace about marrying this girl,' and now that we're broken up, I wonder if it's because deep down in my subconscious somewhere, I really wanted to be with *you*."

"What?"

"Like, I think maybe it's a good thing me and Kacy broke up," he said.

"Wait, is that why y'all broke up? Because—wait, what are you saying?"

"Lauren, I've been in love with you since I was fifteen years old."

I could not believe he was doing this.

"It didn't matter that we broke up, or we were with other people. Like, no matter what happened, you never left the back of my mind. Do you get what I'm saying? Even when we went on double dates, I was thinking,

'How great is it that I get to be around *you*.' Which probably wasn't a healthy mindset, but, you know, it's just how I always felt."

I was having a hard time processing everything Thomas Rhett was saying. I was still upset about my breakup with Michael and I kept thinking, "Why is Thomas Rhett telling me all of this?" My mind was racing. Was he telling me he couldn't be my friend anymore?

I needed him to be my friend right now. I couldn't understand why he was doing this. I couldn't lose him, too.

"I love you, Lauren. And I know you don't want to hear this, but I've dated other people, and it's just not the same. They're not *you*. And I can't be 'just friends' with you anymore. I *love* you."

"No," I said. "Thomas Rhett, no! Why are you doing this? You're my best friend, like my brother, and you've kind of just ruined our relationship!"

"Please don't say that. Don't you see how lucky we are? To *be* best friends? To love each other, and to love each other's families like we do?"

"No. Uh-uh. I needed my friend tonight," I said. "I thought that was why we came out here, because you always know how to make me feel better. Every time. You make me laugh."

"Right?" he said, with a big grin. "See! That's what I mean. You do the same for me. Who gets that lucky?"

"No. I just—I can't believe this is happening."

"I'm sorry, but I can't pretend anymore. And I understand if you don't want to talk to me for a while."

He put his head down and I hugged him, mostly because I wanted him to shut up. But he wouldn't. He kept on talking over my shoulder. He kept explaining how he'd tried to tell me, so many times. He said he'd tried to tell me on the very night that Michael and I got back together. That was the reason he drove all the way to my parents' house that night last summer. Not for something else. For *me*.

"But," I said, "you know as well as I do that we've already tried. We weren't good together as boyfriend and girlfriend. We didn't work. We were awful together," I said.

"We were fifteen! You're not the same as you were then, and I'm definitely not the same. I stopped being jealous a long time ago. It finally settled in with me that if somebody doesn't want to be with you, then they just don't want to be with you, so I'd be better off letting it go."

He started talking about the plans he had for his future, and he asked me whether I'd even be interested in being with a musician who'd be on the road all the time. But the truth was, I didn't even consider that a real possibility. This was Nashville. People get signed to labels and never become "stars," all the time. I thought he was being delusional—about *everything.*

"It's late," I said. I stood up. "I need to be up in like three hours to get ready for Macy. I just need to go to bed."

Thomas Rhett stood up, and on that tiny little porch, I couldn't get by him.

"Just kiss me," he said.

"What?"

"One kiss," he said. "Just one kiss, and if you don't feel anything, if you honestly don't feel anything, then we'll walk away and I'll never talk about it again."

He stood there with the moonlight on his face, and this look in his eyes like I'd never seen before. As if this really was it for him. As if this moment, right here, mattered more than anything else in the whole world.

"Come on," he said. "I dare you."

He looked down at my lips, and I looked at his, and he pulled me in and kissed me—and my whole world split wide open.

I can't explain it. I could not understand what was happening. As our lips pressed together, I felt it all the way down to my toes. I realized that Thomas Rhett wasn't the same fifteen-year-old I'd dated at all. He was my best friend, but he was all grown up now and so much more confident and . . . I *loved* him. Not like a friend. Not like a best friend. I *loved* him, like I'd never loved anybody else.

With one kiss, I realized that I'd been overlooking the greatest relationship in my life, and it had been right in front of me the whole time.

We pulled our lips apart for a few seconds, almost dizzy from the way it felt, and we looked at each other, and Thomas Rhett started to talk again: "Was that just my imagination or did you fe—" and I kissed him again, this time with my whole body.

We hugged for what felt like forever, almost shaking a little bit with this giddiness every once in a while, like, "I just can't believe this!"

I felt the love of this man so deep into my heart, my whole body had chills, like nothing I'd ever felt before. I had been in a good relationship. A solid relationship. With a good man. Then Thomas Rhett came along and filled my heart with something I didn't even know I was missing.

The sky was starting to lighten up on the horizon, and the early-morning birds started singing.

"I've got to go to bed," I said.

"Alright," he said.

"And you've got to go *home*. Are you coming? To graduation? Will you be there?"

"Oh, definitely. I wouldn't miss it. I'll see you in the morning."

"So," I said, "I guess we'll talk more tomorrow?"

"Definitely," he said with the cutest smile.

We kissed again, and he hopped off the porch as I opened the front door.

I was still starry-eyed and in shock as I turned and whispered, "Good night, Thomas Rhett."

"Good night," he said.

I watched him drive away, and then I barely slept. I laid in my bed and just couldn't quit smiling. I kept thinking, "What just *happened*?"

That one moment, that one kiss on my parents' front porch, changed everything.

I didn't say anything to anybody when we first got up. There was just too much to do, and I didn't want to take away from Macy's big day. But once Thomas Rhett and I were in the auditorium at Goodpasture, sitting near the front next to my parents, looking up at Macy as she sat in her cap and gown on the stage, Macy and I started communicating with our eyes.

She knew something was up. So I looked over at Thomas Rhett and then back at her, as if to tell her, "Something big happened last night. With *him*." And once she realized what I was saying, her eyes got big as saucers. When the ceremony was over, she came running up to me and pulled me aside and made me tell her everything. She was so excited for both of us.

So were my parents. So were Thomas Rhett's parents. Our families were thrilled.

Our friends? Well, that was a different story. As the reality of our new situation set in, so did the realization of what it looked like from the outside: Michael and I had *just* broken up. It was so new that some of our friends were just hearing about it. Because Thomas Rhett and I were so close, and how quickly things moved—it looked bad. Some people jumped to conclusions, like, "I bet things were happening with them before she and Michael broke up." And that hurt so much. I hoped they would've known me well enough to know I wouldn't do that to Michael.

Beyond that, though, some of my close girlfriends who were with me through the breakup just couldn't get on board with me moving on so fast. They assumed this was some sort of a rebound, and that hurt, too. I hoped they would've known that I would never do that to Thomas Rhett. I tried to tell them, "I need you to trust me. This is real."

With every day that went by, I realized more and more how right it felt for Thomas Rhett and me to be together.

He was driving me home in his truck one night, it couldn't have been more than a week after our kiss on the front porch, and he said, "Wow. Look at that."

"Look at what?" I said, and all of a sudden he pulled the truck off into a big open hayfield just outside my neighborhood. He turned the headlights off, and there must've been a million lightning bugs in that field. They kept flickering everywhere we looked.

"Come on," he said.

We went and climbed into the bed of his truck, and once we were laying down with each other, the stars seemed even brighter than the bugs. We stayed in the back of his truck and just hung out there and talked for hours under the big starry sky. It was so magical, to both of us, that Thomas Rhett pulled out his phone and took a selfie, just to remember the moment. He keeps that picture on his phone to this day.

The bed of his truck became our personal little getaway that whole summer.

One night, we were laying in the truck bed when a storm came out of nowhere. We were caught in the middle of a torrential downpour, and instead of running for cover, we

In the bed of Thomas Rhett's truck, watching lightning bugs in the field on a summer night

just stayed there wrapped up in each other. It was pretty romantic—this crazy, amazing moment in the back of his truck. It was warm outside, and everything was so new and exciting. The only thing a downpour did was make us even closer.

Sometimes we'd go hang out in the bed of his truck right in front of my parents' house, just so we could be alone. We didn't need anything but each other. Just the two of us and a playlist of old Frank Sinatra songs, and it felt like the whole world was perfect.

8

Love . . .

It was hard going back to school. Thomas Rhett and I wanted to be with each other all the time, and the distance between Knoxville and Nashville never seemed longer.

He decided to quit school so he could dedicate himself full-time to his music career, which disappointed his mom so much. Paige just wanted him to get his degree. To have a fallback. To play it safe. "What's one more year?" she said. "It's so important." But Thomas Rhett had his mind made up and he wasn't budging. He was in love with music, following his heart, following his dream, and he had good reason to believe that dream was worth pursuing. That fall, his career started to heat up just the way he'd talked about with me. The record company sent him out on radio tours, going door to door, basically, to radio stations all across the country, meeting with program directors and influential radio personalities. He'd be gone for days on end. And when he wasn't gone, he'd be in Nashville, writing and recording. There was even talk of him going on tour in the new year, just to get his feet wet—possibly as an opening act for a major artist who played in front of tens of thousands of people.

I knew enough about the music business to know that even then, he might not ever make a solid living as a musician. Truly. Making it in music is like making it in sports. It's like winning the lottery. The odds are like one in a million. Maybe worse. But I knew if it didn't work out the way he dreamed, I would be his fallback. After all, I would be working as a nurse. Nurses make a pretty good living. So we'd be fine.

When Thomas Rhett was gone, I found myself on the phone quite a bit, trying to do what I could to help Hunter. He had struggled a lot during his high school years. His tendency to get into trouble wasn't laughed off as easily as it had been when he was young, and he was having a hard time finding a balance between having fun like he always did and taking responsibility for things the way you're expected to as you get older.

That summer, not long after he graduated, he called on me to ask if I would be an accountability partner for him. It was more of an encouragement thing, to be someone he could call whenever he needed help or advice. And of course I said "yes." But I didn't think I would be enough. "I can be here for you, like your big sister, like I always have been," I told him. "But there are gonna be things that you're gonna need a guy to talk to. Why don't you talk to Thomas Rhett?"

Thomas Rhett had been hanging out more than ever with Hunter that year, anyway. So this just made the two of them get a lot closer as the year went on. Hunter talked to him about girl trouble, and called on him when he wanted to steer clear of any "bad influences" he didn't want in his life. Hunter really wanted to set his life right, and I saw Thomas Rhett stepping up and giving him such good advice.

Honestly, watching him be such a good friend to Hunter made me love Thomas Rhett even more than I already did.

Hunter was still as thrill-seeking as ever. That summer, he and a few friends I didn't really know discovered a whole new version of The Pit a little outside our old neighborhood. It was a long hike out into the woods on Smody's Farm, right where two big hills came together and formed a deep, rocky valley. Those boys built a platform and a rope swing way up at the top of it, with a skateboard tied onto the bottom of the rope so you could use it to swing standing up.

"That thing is insane," Thomas Rhett said. "I would never!"

"And of course Hunter was the first one on it, I'm sure," I said.

"He is *always* first," Thomas Rhett said.

★ ★ ★

Being in Knoxville for my senior year was hard. Thomas Rhett and I had such a magical summer together that being apart was difficult. But whenever he had a break, he drove straight to Knoxville to see me. And whenever we had something big to celebrate—a new step in his career, an A on a big paper of mine—we'd celebrate by sharing a bottle of wine. Something about having a little wine felt a lot more grown-up than drinking beer. Thomas Rhett had met some people in the music industry who were pretty sophisticated wine drinkers, and we enjoyed learning a little bit about the different vineyards and labels and types of grapes that existed in the world. Whenever we finished off a bottle, we'd write the date and a note about what we were doing that day on the label and then save the bottle, kind of like a wine-bottle journal. It was so much fun to look back over them and remember the exciting and random moments that happened that year.

At ADPi's Barn Party at UT

Every day we couldn't be together was a day we wished was different, and recognizing how much we missed each other was a big part of what got us talking about getting married sooner rather than later. If Thomas Rhett were to go on tour, he said, he wanted me to go with him—working around my schedule at UT as best we could. And I absolutely wanted to go! There was just no way to do that if we weren't married. It wouldn't feel right. Not with the way we'd been raised, and the way we wanted to be together as a couple.

We loved each other. We were attracted to each other. We wanted desperately to be together as husband and wife. And it was getting harder and harder to wait.

See, for as long as we'd been dating other people, even through all the growing up and experimenting we'd done as we both went off to college, we'd both stayed true to our values.

We were both virgins.

We'd taken our parents' words and our youth leaders' words to heart, and there was something so special about knowing we were starting from the same place as we thought about getting married. We talked about it a lot, and we were both so grateful to Michael, and to Kacy, that they were raised the same way we were, to value how sacred the bond of two people can be. If either of us had dated people who didn't have the same values, who knows what might have happened?

I mean, don't get me wrong, it's not like we didn't kiss a ton or get a *little* too close a few times. We just always made a choice to stop short of breaking the promise we'd made: to save ourselves for marriage.

TR: It really is some kind of a miracle, isn't it? I mean, I dated Kacy off and on for five whole years, and we never had sex. I broke a lot of rules in high school. I followed rules, too, but I mean, I drank some. I never followed the dress code. I grew my hair long. I got Heelys banned from our school, the sneakers with the wheels in them, because I kept wearing them and grinding the wheels on the floor. But this rule? This rule that was based so strongly in our faith? Even through college and the start of my career, that never got broken.

I know it seems hard to believe in this day and age. To look around at what's on TV, you'd think that everyone was having sex before marriage. But that's just not the reality. I talked about this with kids I mentored through church, and at summer camp, and I talked about it with friends

in college, too, and the vast majority of people I knew found it such a relief that they weren't worrying about getting pregnant, or STDs, or the
emotional strain that comes with having sex as a teenager. They were
happy about not doing it. They were happy about not sneaking around,
and not having to lie to their parents. Some of them just realized that they
weren't mature enough yet to handle the consequences of it all.

I had friends who had sex young, and Thomas Rhett definitely knew
people in the music industry who had lots of sex outside of marriage. I'm
not naïve, I was not sheltered, and I don't judge anyone. But both of us
had friends who regretted some of the decisions they made when they

were teens, or even as adults. My dad
was one of them. He was so open about
the choices he made before he met my
mom, and so honest with us about everything, that it was pretty hard to ignore.

Neither one of us wanted to live with
those kinds of regrets, and I'm really
thankful for that decision.

For me and Thomas Rhett, knowing
that we were going to experience our
first time *with each other*—it was beyond
exciting. It just made it so much more
meaningful than it might have been otherwise. We didn't realize what we were

*Tailgating at a
Tennessee football game*

doing at the time, but we had saved ourselves for each other. And now
that we knew we were together, and we felt more and more like this was
forever, the anticipation was killing us! When you love someone so much
that you just want to be with them all the time, the idea of giving your
whole self to that person and sharing that physical bond after you're married is Just. So. Good.

Having patience and control and self-discipline was another story,
though. It was *not* easy. I honestly hoped Thomas Rhett would hurry up

with the engagement so we could get started on planning our wedding, in part because I wanted to hurry up and get to our wedding night. For some reason, though, he seemed to be dragging his feet.

"I just don't have the money right now," he'd say.

"Well, it doesn't need to be anything fancy. I don't care about a ring. I just want to be married to you!" I'd tell him.

It was true. But it was almost Christmas and I still didn't have a ring on my finger. I couldn't understand why.

TR: I had the ring. I bought a ring way back before we even started talking about getting engaged. It was burning a hole in my pocket. I was just waiting for the right time. I wanted her family to be a part of it. I wanted us to be surrounded by the people we loved. I thought it might be romantic to do it at her favorite time of year, and I also wanted it to be a surprise. I didn't want her to help plan it, or to be in on it. I wanted to make it a moment she'd never forget.

I didn't want to turn into a bridezilla and make Thomas Rhett "put a ring on it," or hound him to the point where it annoyed him and pushed him away, though. I was sure that he wasn't getting cold feet or anything like that, so I knew I needed to be patient. If I didn't back off and give him the space to ask me in his own time, I might have smothered him the way he smothered me when we were first dating back in high school. So I just did my best to forget about it and enjoy the holiday season, which for me was always easy.

We threw our fourth annual ugly Christmas sweater party on December 14, and it was *huge*. There were so many people there I couldn't even count, all packed into my parents' house just like they had been for the past four years, and we had so much fun.

Four *years*. How had another four years flown by already?

A week later, our family and Thomas Rhett's family made our annual pilgrimage to Opryland. Walking hand in hand in the romance of all the twinkling lights was even better than it had been back when Thomas Rhett and I did it the first time around, as teenagers. My dad was real playful about the two of us being together now, too. He found some mistletoe and held it above our heads, making us kiss as everyone, almost on cue, went, "Awww." It was funny.

Just as we were wrapping things up, my dad ran into a co-worker of his. "Hey," he said. "What's going on?"

The man gave my dad a hug, and then he looked at me and said, "Where's the guy? Is this the guy?" and he looked at Thomas Rhett and then pointed to his ring finger. I was like, "What?" I figured Dad probably told him that I was gonna marry this guy, or something, but I was a little confused by how forward he was about the whole marriage idea.

Before I could even ask Dad about it, though, everybody started talking about what we should do for dinner. I was starving, so I suggested we just eat at one of the restaurants right there at Opryland.

"Nah," my mom said. "The wait for a table will be way too long."

"Well, I don't mind waitin' with y'all," I said. "The wait might be shorter than driving somewhere else."

That magical night at Opryland: all the kids in
our families sitting on a tree, youngest to oldest
(except, technically, I'm four months older than Thomas Rhett)

Macy agreed and backed me up, and Thomas Rhett shot her a weird look.

"I don't want to wait. It's too crowded here. Why don't we go to Giovanni's?" he said. "I'm sure Steve can get us a table."

He looked at my dad.

"Oh yeah," Dad said. "Let me call Giovanni," and he walked away dialing his cellphone.

Giovanni Ristorante-Bar was my parents' favorite Italian restaurant. The owner used to run an Italian restaurant in midtown Manhattan, but he closed up and moved to Nashville years ago and brought all of that amazing big-city food and wine knowledge with him. We loved it.

"He can squeeze us in!" Dad said.

We said goodbye to another year at Opryland and piled into our cars and headed across town.

The whole staff at Giovanni's was welcoming as always, but the place was packed. I was surprised they were able to clear a table for all eleven of us, and we didn't even have to wait when we got there.

We sat down and ordered drinks, and almost immediately Thomas Rhett stood up.

"Hey," he said, "I want to see the new cigar room. Will you show it to me?"

Thomas Rhett liked to smoke the occasional cigar. And I love the smell of a cigar because it reminds me of my granddaddy and my dad.

"Yeah, it's right upstairs. Go see it!" I said.

"No, I really want you to show it to me," he said.

Giovanni had just built a cigar room on the second floor, and he'd shown it to me and my parents the last time we were in. I'd told Thomas Rhett all about it. But I didn't understand why he couldn't go take a look at it himself.

"It's right there. Go look! I'm starving," I said.

"Please," he said. He was all excited like a kid on Christmas Eve. "Please, please show me the cigar room?"

"We just ordered drinks," I said. "Babe, can't you wait until after dinner?"

After listening to her son keep begging me to go upstairs, Paige finally turned around in her chair and pleaded, "Oh, Lauren, just show him the room!"

I was kind of annoyed. I wanted to sit with our families and enjoy this moment, not go look at a cigar room I'd already seen. "Okay," I said. "Geez."

I led Thomas Rhett up the big wooden staircase and around to the glass-door entryway to the cigar room. There was no one up there. The lights were off.

"I don't know if we should be up here," I said.

"It's alright," he said, and he went ahead and opened the door. He reached right in and flicked the light on. There was a bottle of wine in there, sitting on a little table next to a vase of beautiful flowers in that tiny private room with the high-vaulted ceiling. It was Cakebread wine. A really nice wine. I recognized the label from when Thomas Rhett showed it to me in a liquor store one time, and said he hoped to be able to afford a bottle one day.

"Oh," I said. "I really don't think we're supposed to be in here. Looks like somebody is already using the room or something. We can come back another time."

"It's alright," Thomas Rhett said, pulling me into the room and closing the door behind us.

"What are you doing?" I said.

All of a sudden Frank Sinatra's "The Way You Look Tonight" started playing through the speakers, and Thomas Rhett took my hands, and looked into my eyes with his big brown eyes, and said, "You know I love you so much, and I can't imagine doing any of this without you."

Suddenly I realized what was happening. My dad's goofiness with the mistletoe, the way his friend acted toward us at Opryland, the table at Giovanni's being ready for all of us so quickly, Paige basically *scolding* me to go show her son this cigar room—I was the only one that whole night who had no idea what was going on.

Oh my gosh, I thought. *This is happening!*

Thomas Rhett let go of my hands and picked up the bottle of wine, and he picked up a silver Sharpie that was on the table next to it, and he wrote something on the label. Then he turned back to me and got down on one knee.

"I've loved you since I was fifteen years old," he said, "and I want to spend the rest of my life with you."

He held up the bottle with the label pointed toward me, and I read his words:

Marry Me?

I lost it. I started crying. My stomach started doing backflips and my smile was so big it hurt my cheeks as I grabbed the bottle and the Sharpie and wrote my response on the label:

Well . . . Duh, Yes! with a big heart next to it.

I turned it back toward him and that's when he pulled out the most beautiful diamond engagement ring I'd ever seen—a ring that was just way beyond my expectations. It looked like one I'd shown him one time that was nothing but a fantasy.

TR: It *was* that ring. I mean, what other ring could I get for her after she'd shown me the one she wanted the most?

He slid the ring onto my finger, and I felt like I was gonna pass out. I was just so overwhelmed.

We kissed and hugged, and the first thing I said was, "We need to go tell everyone!"

That's when I turned and saw that our moms and sisters were already standing right outside the room, peering in through a little window on the side. "Wooo-hooo!" they yelled as I pushed the door open and they wrapped their arms around the two of us.

We made our way back down the staircase to the applause of the whole entire restaurant full of people, and into the arms of my dad, and big hugs from my brother, and Rhett, and Tim, and Thomas Rhett's little brother, Tyler. The waiter came over and popped open the bottle of Cakebread, and we shared it with everybody. It was by far the best wine I'd ever tasted.

I couldn't wait to tell all of our friends that we were engaged. I knew it was rude to take my phone out at the dinner table, but this was defi-

We got engaged!!

nitely an I'll-make-an-exception kind of night. The first call I made was to my best friend Lindsey. Just a week earlier, at our ugly sweater party, I'd talked to her all about how much I couldn't wait for Thomas Rhett to propose.

"You're never gonna believe this," I said, "but Thomas Rhett proposed!"

"Oh my gosh!" she said. "That's amazing!"

I told her I really wished I could see her tonight but she kind of rushed me off the phone real quick, saying she was busy with something and I should call her tomorrow.

"Yeah, okay," I said. It was a little weird. It wasn't like her. But I had other calls to make, so I did, and then I got back to celebrating with our families.

On the way out of the restaurant, Thomas Rhett said, "I have one more surprise for you."

I thought, "What on earth could it be?" I mean, what else did this guy have up his sleeve? And what could possibly top this night?

Instead of driving me back to my parents', he pointed his truck toward his mom's house, and as we drove up, I noticed there were cars parked all up and down both sides of their street.

"Oh my gosh. What did you do?" I asked him.

"You'll see," he said with a big grin on his face.

When the two of us opened the front door to his mom's, my ears got blasted with shouts of congratulations and the sight of a crowd full of just about everybody I ever knew—including Lindsey! Not only did she know about the engagement, she'd been at Paige's house the whole afternoon setting up for the party.

I looked up at the banner they had made that said, *Congratulations on Your Engagement, Thomas Rhett and Lauren!* and it dawned on me that it took time and planning to get this many people together in one place at one time, and a whole bunch of people in that house had been at our ugly sweater party.

"Wait," I shouted, "did all y'all know this was gonna happen? At my parents' house? A whole week ago?"

"Yup!" everyone said, nodding and laughing.

"And none of y'all said anything?"

"Nope!"

"Wow," I said. "Y'all are *good!*"

What was already the best night of my life became even better, because we got to share it with all of our closest friends and family.

I felt a tap on my shoulder and turned around. "Hunter!" I said, and I threw my arms around him.

"Congratulations," he said, shaking Thomas Rhett's hand behind me as we hugged.

"Oh my gosh, I'm so happy you're here. And Kamron!"

My neighbors and lifelong brothers from across the street in either direction were right there

With my boys, Hunter and Kamron, at our surprise engagement party

with us, together for one of the biggest nights of our lives, and I was just so happy to see them both.

"Babe," I said, "take my phone. Take a picture of the three of us!"

We posed together as Thomas Rhett took our pic, and we all laughed and caught up on everything like we were twelve years old all over again.

I felt like we hadn't seen enough of Hunter in recent months. He didn't seem to call on us quite as much as he did over the summer and fall. He was still dealing with a lot, and we were worried about him, but seeing him so happy and healthy that night, laughing with us in the glow of the Christmas lights on this amazing night—it meant the world to me.

"Thomas Rhett did all of this," I thought. He pulled all of these people together. For *us*.

I pulled him into a slightly private corner and gave him a big kiss, and pulled my face back just enough to look in his eyes, thinking, "How on earth did you pull this off?"

"I love you so much," he said.

He smiled, and held me tight, and I said, "I love you, too."

9

. . . and Loss

As we turned the corner into 2012, it became clear that Thomas Rhett and I wouldn't be able to get to our wedding night as fast as we might have hoped. Thomas Rhett went right back out on radio tour, and I went back to school for my final semester, thinking maybe we'd get married in early summer, as soon as I graduated. But in March, Thomas Rhett got some really big news. His manager confirmed that he was gonna go on the road as an opening act on Toby Keith's summer tour. Thomas Rhett would be playing major amphitheaters. And on top of that, the tour was going to lead up to the release of Thomas Rhett's very first EP that August.

It was all happening so fast. There was just no way to plan the kind of wedding we wanted with everyone we loved around that schedule, so we put our wedding on hold and decided we'd get married at the first opportunity we saw for a significant break in Thomas Rhett's calendar: in *October.*

We couldn't help but laugh.

"I guess if there's any excuse a guy could come up with to have to postpone a wedding, going on tour with Toby Keith's a pretty good one," I said.

One night, when he managed to get out to my apartment in Knoxville, after what felt like the longest two weeks ever of not being able to see each other, we celebrated his tour news with a bottle of Cakebread that we didn't have to share.

"Are you sure you can afford this?" I said.

"Not really, but it's worth it," he told me.

We'd been missing each other so much, and after sharing that bottle of really good wine, the two of us couldn't keep our hands off each other. Missing him made it harder to hold back. We were alone. We were engaged! There was no reason for us to wait any more—except for the promises we'd made to ourselves.

So even then, even when we both felt *more* than ready, we cooled things down and took a few steps back.

"We've been patient this long," Thomas Rhett said. "I guess a few months longer won't kill us."

"You sure about that?" I asked him.

"No!" he said, which made us both laugh some more.

Staying true to who we were meant everything to us. I just hoped that the added temptations that would come with his chosen career wouldn't mess things up. I'd certainly heard some stories. As a charter pilot, my dad had flown all kinds of music stars and sports stars in and out of Nashville, and he'd told me some of what he'd witnessed firsthand. Without going into detail, some of those stars made choices that were sure to jeopardize and in some cases completely wreck a marriage.

Thomas Rhett wasn't like that. I knew that. But a part of me also knew that when everything feels right, when you're making faith-filled life choices, that's when Satan tends to work the hardest—doing anything he can to try and mess things up.

So I prayed. I prayed that everything we'd been given in our lives so far would survive whatever darkness or temptation might come our way as all of these opportunities opened up in front of us.

The things you worry about, the things you think might be a problem, the things you focus on and stress over—sometimes those aren't the things that wind up hurting you at all. Sometimes, things come at you out of the blue. Things you never imagined.

Like the phone call I received after 11 p.m. on April 14, 2012.

A cryptic, out-of-breath phone call in a panicked voice from my friend Cody.

"Lauren!" he yelled. "Where are you? I—"

"You what? Cody? You're breaking up."

I was on campus, walking back from Carnicus, this crazy annual fraternity/sorority carnival-circus-competition that was a big tradition at UT. ADPi won! First place. We were so excited. My mom was there. She drove out to see us all at Carnicus. So was Macy, who was now an ADPi, too, and my close friend Dee. Kamron and his fraternity had competed as well. There were a bunch of us, all celebrating and laughing, wearing makeup and face paint and crazy costumes.

"Hold on, guys. Shhh," I said. "Cody? Are you okay?"

"Yeah . . . we—don't—"

He was out of breath, like he was running with the phone in his hand, and the phone just kept cutting out.

"Cody, I can't hear you."

"Sorry. Gotta go."

"Cody?"

He hung up on me.

"What in the world?" I said.

"What's going on?" Dee asked.

"I don't know," I said. "That was Cody." Dee knew Cody. Cody was one of Hunter's good friends, and Dee had actually dated Hunter over the summer. "He seemed really out of breath and it was breaking up, but it sounded like something was wrong."

I tried Cody back, but it wouldn't go through. We got into my car, and were just about to drop Dee off when Hunter's sister Hailey called. "Hunter fell," she said. "From the swing. The rope swing. In the woods on Smody's Farm."

"Oh my gosh. Is he okay?"

"I don't know. It sounded bad. Like, Mom and Dad are on the way to the hospital. They're taking him to Vanderbilt."

Vanderbilt is the biggest hospital in Nashville, and the only hospital in the whole region that operates a level 1 trauma center.

This wasn't something minor.

"Vanderbilt's the best. They'll take good care of him. But what happened? What were they doing out there in the middle of the night? I swear, if Hunter did something stupid and hurt himself, I'll kill him. He can't keep doing this!"

"I don't know. They were out there, and the guys he was with said they begged him not to get up on the swing, but you know him."

"Of course he did," I said. "But, how bad is he hurt?"

"No one will tell me, Lauren. Hold on," she said. "Mom's calling me. I'll call you back."

We dropped Macy off at her dorm and made it back to my place just off campus. As Dee got out of the car to head to her place, she said, "Please let me know as soon as you find out more. No matter how late it is. Please call me."

"We will," I promised.

Kamron had gone back to his dorm, so I called him, and he had gotten word from someone in the neighborhood, too, but apparently nobody knew what was going on. Nobody had answers. Kamron's mom walked up to Hunter's house as soon as she heard that John and Laurie were on their way to the hospital, just so she could stay with Hailey and Hannah until they knew more, and she said she'd call us if she found anything out.

I walked into the bathroom at my apartment and stood there in front of the mirror, washing makeup off my face, coming down from this incredible high of such a fun night, just thinking about Hunter and worrying how bad this might be.

Then Hailey called me again. "I'm driving to Vanderbilt right now," she said. She sounded so upset and angry. "No one will tell me what's happening, and they keep telling me not to go. They can't stop me from seeing my brother. Me and Hannah are going."

My mom called Edwina, Kamron's mom, who was right there with Hailey and Hannah. She had just gotten off the phone with Laurie.

"My mom's on the phone with Kamron's mom right now," I told Hailey. "Just hold on a minute."

"Kamron's mom doesn't know anything I don't already know," Hailey said.

"Hailey, just hold on, okay? I'll talk to Mom and I'll call you back."

As soon as Mom got off the phone, I saw her body language change in an instant. She was calm. Almost too calm, like she was in some kind of a daze as we sat on my bed and she started telling me what she'd heard.

"I guess Hailey kept calling them nonstop, saying she was gonna drive to the hospital," she said.

"I know."

"So Laurie called Edwina and told her to keep Hailey at home. She said it's because by the time Hailey got there, they wouldn't be there. You've got to tell Hailey to stay at home."

"Mom," I said. "Why?"

"Honey," she said, as tears started streaming down her cheeks. "Hunter is dead."

I just stared at her, like I couldn't believe what just came out of her mouth.

"He fell off the swing, into the valley. Hit his head on the rocks. He didn't have a chance. The paramedics pronounced him dead at the scene. They weren't ever driving him to the hospital, honey. He was already gone."

"What?" I asked.

"Hunter's gone."

"No," I whispered. "No. No, no, no."

I fell to the ground and just started weeping. My mom knelt down and put her arms around me, and my phone started ringing. Again and again. I looked at the screen and it was Hailey.

"No," I cried.

"You have to tell her to stay home," my mom said through tears. "She's gonna get to the hospital and nobody's gonna be there. John and Laurie are already on their way home."

"Okay," I said, sucking whatever air I could gather and stopping myself from crying.

"Hailey?" I said.

I could hear background noise. She was in her car, on the road.

"I'm going to the hospital," she said.

"Please don't go to the hospital," I said. My voice was breaking. I couldn't hide my emotions.

"Why?" she said.

"Just please listen to me. Please go home."

She started crying, really hard. "If you know something, you need to tell me," she said. "If you know something, you have to *tell me,* Lauren. You can't not tell me."

"I can't," I cried. "I can't, I can't. Just wait for your mom to get home," I said.

I couldn't hold myself together. This was my childhood best friend, she was like a second sister to me, and she was begging me to give her the worst news she could ever hear. "You know something. I know you know, Lauren. What happened?" she wailed.

"Your mom and dad are on their way home. Right now. Just go home. Please. Please," I said, and I couldn't take it anymore. She knew me so well, she knew the second I started talking that I had more information than she did. So I did the only thing I could, out of respect for her parents' wishes: I hung up the phone and prayed that she listened. I prayed that she turned around and went home.

I left Mom in my room and went upstairs to wake up my friend Gillian. I walked straight into her bedroom saying, "I need you. Gillian, I need you," and I just started crying. She woke up confused and said, "What's wrong? What's wrong?" and I said, "He's dead, he's dead."

"What? Who is? What's happening?" she said.

"Hunter. Hunter died. He had an accident, and he's not okay. He's not okay."

Mary, one of our other roommates, heard what was going on, and she woke up and she came out. And I ran back down the stairs to go back to my room, and at the bottom of the stairs, my body gave out again. I collapsed to my hands and knees, just bawling, and my two friends sat next to me, holding on to me. "I don't think I can do this," I cried. "I don't think his family can deal with this. I don't know how they're gonna make it through this." And immediately both of them just started praying. They were praying over me and praying for Hunter, and praying for his family, and my family.

They prayed until I was able to get back on my feet.

Back in my room, my mom wrapped her arms around me and I collapsed onto her shoulder for I don't know how long.

"Mom," I said. "We need to tell Macy."

"I called her while you were upstairs," she said.

I started crying all over again just thinking how Macy must've taken the news.

"Is she okay?" I asked.

"Not really, no. We need to go pick her up."

"And Dad?"

My mom was silent.

"I'll call him," I said.

I woke him from a sound sleep, and it took him a minute to understand what I was saying.

"He hit his head?" Dad said. "How bad is it?"

"No. He's not . . ." I couldn't say the words out loud. "He's . . ."

I started crying.

"Hunter's dead, Dad. He's dead."

"What? Oh, no," he said. His voice trailed off and I could tell he was just trying to process what I'd told him.

"I just can't—we need to go. Mom?" I said. She was on the phone with Macy again, telling her we were coming to get her. "We need to go. We need to go to their house. Hailey, and Hannah, we need to be there—"

"Let's go," Mom said, standing up and grabbing her purse.

"No, now wait," Dad said to me. "I don't want you driving through the night. Y'all go to sleep and we'll figure out what you need to do in the morning, when it's light."

"Dad, there's no way I'm going to sleep."

"But you have school—"

"I'm not going to class either way, Dad. I can't," I said, and my mom motioned for me to hand her my phone.

"Steve, we'll be fine. We'll see you in a couple hours. Just please, go to Laurie and John. They need you. They need all of us."

"I will," he said.

My parents said goodbye to each other and we packed up and headed for the car.

I called Dee as we walked, and broke the news to her. She was a wreck. She just couldn't believe it. Then we went to pick up my sister, pulling up to the breezeway of North and South Carrick, the big dorms where I lived in my freshman year, and seeing my sister come down with tears in her eyes, more broken than I'd ever seen her. And it wasn't just her. There was a whole group of neighborhood kids from our hometown, who all knew Hunter, who were all his age, who had all gone on to UT, and they all came downstairs, and they were all there waiting for cars. Every one of 'em was planning to caravan back to Hunter's house, and hardly any of them said a word. I got out and we all saw each other and just kinda hugged for a second, and then Macy got in the car and we left.

"I need to call Thomas Rhett," I said.

I wiped my tears a little bit and called him. It was 1:30 in the morning at that point. I knew he was over at his friend Drew's house, in Nashville.

I had to call twice before he picked up the phone.

Just like my dad, he had a hard time understanding what I was saying 'cause I'd woken him up from a sound sleep.

"No," he said. "Lauren, no. This cannot be happening."

We talked through it for a few minutes, and I gave him all the details I knew, and I said, "I don't think I can tell anyone else. I can't do it. Can you call Kasey, and your parents, and . . ."

"Yeah," he said. "I'll call 'em. You just get back safe."

"You have to go to Hunter's house," I said. "I don't know how they're going to make it through this."

My tears started flowing again.

"I don't know, either. I'm sorry, baby. I'll go right now," Thomas Rhett said. "I'll see you when you get there."

"Okay. I love you."

"I love you, too."

For the rest of the car ride, two hours and forty-five minutes all the way back home, my mom and sister and I didn't say a word.

I kept thinking, "This doesn't happen. How can we have this beautiful life where we're all best friends, and then *this*? I mean, *Hunter*? He's too *good*. He's *too good* to go. God, he cannot be the one to go."

The only sound besides the wind and the road and the thoughts in my head was my sister's hopeless, quiet crying in the back seat. She just kept crying and crying and crying. She never stopped.

As we finally pulled into our neighborhood, I felt this fear and this sadness and this desire to get to Hunter's family all rise up in me, from the pit in my stomach right up to my eyeballs. The car wasn't even in park yet when I opened the door and jumped out and slammed it shut and went running up the hill toward Hunter's front steps—the hill I'd run up a million times in my life—thinking, "Nothing is ever gonna be the same."

Crossing his front porch, walking through his front door, and rounding the corner by the fireplace, where pictures of Hunter and Hannah and Hailey were hung above the mantel, I saw Laurie standing there all by herself. I ran to her and hugged her, and we didn't say a word. I just hugged her for the longest time, and I felt this woman—my second mom,

Hunter's *mom,* who had been there for me and my family for my whole entire life—I felt her collapse in my arms.

At some point, she gathered herself just a little, and stood up tall and wiped her tears, and nodded at me, because there didn't seem to be any words that any of us could say to make sense of any of this, and I nodded back, and I turned to the right and looked into the kitchen, where all the men were standing up against the sink, leaning against the countertop. And then I saw Thomas Rhett. He was standing next to my dad, and I went and fell straight into Thomas Rhett's arms. I sobbed. I didn't say a thing, and he didn't say one thing, either.

It struck me that this was the first time I'd ever fallen into his arms first, before I fell into my dad's.

I let go, and Thomas Rhett looked at me to make sure I was okay, and I nodded, and I went to my dad, and I cried again as he held me for the longest time.

Seeing Hailey and Hannah hurt more than I can possibly put into words. They were just inconsolable.

And John? I will never get over what it was like to see a grown man, a father figure like him, so broken. I'll never get over any of it. I don't think time heals losses like this one. The sharpness may fade, eventually, but the scar is permanent.

I knew it was permanent that very night.

By morning, it seemed like everybody we ever knew was there. Everybody you could dream of. People just kept showing up from all over. And I am positive that Hunter's family needed every bit of support that walked through their front door. I don't know how they would have survived without it.

No one left, either. I don't think I even went across the street to change my clothes. For days. I just stayed right there, in that house. I laid on Hunter's bed, alternating with Kamron, and his sisters, and anyone who could fit in his room. Then we all spread out on their living room floor and anywhere else in the house we could fit.

We all needed each other in order to make it. Our friendships, our families, our circles of support that grew and extended and overlapped in every direction from this neighborhood we all shared—this was the power, the strength of all of that, in action.

TR: In a way, Hunter was the glue. Even for me, personally. Not that I wasn't good friends with Hailey or Hannah or Laurie or John, but the reason I came around, the reason so many people came around all the time, was to see Hunter. Just to be around him. Wherever he was, that's where the party was. He was the wrangler of groups, the one who everyone was drawn to, from ten different families, to high school friends, and college friends—Hunter was always in the middle of it. It was such a crushing loss, for so many people, from so many walks of life, who'd all been brought together by this one wild kid.

One of the men who helped put together Hunter's celebration of life—we refused to call it a funeral—had helped to organize Johnny Cash's funeral. *The* Johnny Cash, one of the biggest country stars of all time. And he told us that Hunter's celebration of life drew more people than Johnny Cash's funeral.

We had it at the Jacksons' house, which was right next door to where Mitch and his brothers and sister lived, on a piece of land that sloped down to the Cumberland River. It was beautiful. But there were people there who none of us even knew. We were his best friends. We thought we knew *everybody* he knew, but that day we kept asking people, "How do you know him?" and the answers surprised us every time.

Hunter's influence on the world extended way wider than any of us had even imagined. It's like everyone he ever met was his best friend. Honestly, he never met a stranger. He treated everyone as an equal, and he brought so much life to so many. He truly loved people the way Jesus tells us to. He loved people *so well*. He just loved on everyone he met. He was passionate about everything, and everyone. And the love he gave showed in the love he and his family received at that beautiful ceremony, on that day by the river.

TR: Hunter's and my absolute favorite artist was Eric Church. Still, to this day. And I like him so much probably because of the bond we shared. And when Hunter's mom asked me to sing Eric Church's song "Sinners Like Me" at Hunter's funeral, I've never wanted to *not* sing somewhere so bad. I mean, hand me a guitar and I'll sing anywhere, anytime. But that? First of all, that song—I tear up on that song regardless. But knowing that it was one of Hunter's favorite songs ever was, like, almost impossible. I don't even remember actually singing it. I ended up doing it as a duet with our friend Haley Hamilton, and I know we sang it, because everyone said they were moved by the song. But I just don't know how I got through it. It's almost like I blacked out, and somehow my body just kept singing.

Hunter's mom had bracelets made, custom camouflage bracelets with Hunter's initials and a fishhook on them—since Hunter loved to fish—and she gave them to all of his closest childhood friends, just to remind us of Hunter every single time we looked at them. And, not to jump ahead too much, but to this day, Thomas Rhett never takes his off. You see that bracelet in photos in magazines, and when he's walking the red carpet in a suit and tie, and on his wrist at his concerts.

So does Kamron.

I keep mine on my keys, in my purse, right there with me everywhere I go. So does Macy. All of us.

Those bracelets are a constant reminder of our friend—a constant reminder that friendship is sacred, and that Hunter's spirit is always with us.

But a bracelet can't replace the presence of a person. A memory can't replace the presence of a friend. I didn't understand it when people said

Hunter
and me . . .

. . . and Hunter with his family

things like "He'll always be with you in spirit." I didn't want him with me "in spirit." I wanted my friend back. My brother. By my side.

How was I supposed to finish classes and final exams with that big of a broken heart?

Honestly, it was so hard to get back to life after that. In some ways, none of our lives have ever been the same.

When the celebration of life was over, there were a few friends of Hunter's who stayed at his house for weeks and even months on end. To this day, when Kamron goes back home to our neighborhood, he sometimes goes and sleeps in Hunter's bed instead of his own.

And Hunter's parents, his sisters—I don't think any of them have ever been the same.

None of us have.

We all just loved him so much.

TR: It's like when a block gets pulled out of a house, the house doesn't sit the same. You know what I mean?

10

Our Day

When I went back to school, I fell apart.

Not a day went by, not an hour, when a vision of Hunter's smile and a shimmer of his spirit didn't cross my mind—and stop me in my tracks.

In the mornings, when I woke up, I thought of him. At night, when I tried to sleep, I couldn't close my eyes without picturing him.

The knot in my stomach and the weight in my chest made it feel like someone was crushing me, all the time.

I tried to get back to my normal routines, but everything I did felt foggy. Walking on campus, sitting in classes—it all felt unreal to me. As if I was disconnected from everything, and everyone.

I found myself close to failing one of my nursing classes, Pharmacology 2. A class I needed to pass before I'd be allowed to take the NCLEX, the test to determine if a person is ready to become a licensed nurse. I had to pass another test before I could graduate, too, the HESI exam, which was like a pre-NCLEX. And I'm someone who suffered from horrible test anxiety anyway.

Moving back to Knoxville made home seem so far away. I missed my parents. I missed Thomas Rhett. I found myself alone with my thoughts all the time, and my thoughts were all depressing. I was just too heartbroken over Hunter to think straight.

When I went to make up an exam I had missed, I had a full-blown panic attack. I started crying and hyperventilating. I went to my professor, and my words didn't even make sense. She got real worried about how I was acting. She said I needed to go to the counseling center on campus.

"The what?" I said.

I didn't even know there *was* a counseling center on campus. I'd never been to a counselor before, and I was nervous, but I ended up meeting some of the nicest people, and they helped me walk through everything, including finishing up nursing school. I had to retake a class in the summer, and I had to retake the HESI exam until I passed it. My counselor served as a psychological outlet and gave me a place to process and address all of my heartbreaking thoughts and serious anxiety. And I wouldn't have known there was help there waiting for me if my professor hadn't pointed me in the right direction.

As long as I had a plan in place, they would let me walk with my class at the graduation ceremony in May, and I would technically graduate in August. So it was all good. I just needed to take a breath and not worry about finishing on such a strict four-year timeline.

"So you'll be okay?" Thomas Rhett asked me on the phone.

"I'll be okay," I said.

"Thank the Lord," he said. "I've been worried about you."

I knew he was worried. Even as Thomas Rhett dealt with his own grief and loss, he always let me know he was there for me. Really *there,* when I needed him most.

We couldn't be together in person as much as we would've liked, but we made the best of things. We talked on the phone. A lot. He had an album to finish and a tour to get ready for. We also had a wedding and marriage to get ready for, and with all the grieving we were doing, and all the pressure we were feeling, there were just so many challenges all at once. We needed help, and the thought of finding a third party to help us navigate this stuff all at once suddenly seemed like a really good idea.

We contacted an old preacher of mine who was a family friend and asked if he would give us premarital counseling. We didn't see any harm or shame in doing something like that. The opposite, actually. Especially after the experience I'd had at the counseling center at UT.

We wanted our marriage to go right, right from the start. We weren't experts on marriage. We'd never been married! I mean, you wouldn't go try to fly a plane without some instruction. So why would you enter into a lifelong commitment to someone without getting some training on how to stay lifetime-committed? Why not get some expert advice on how to do this? And yeah, we got advice from our parents, and our friends' parents. But just like a college professor might offer a more research-based approach to something you want to study, or a professional business mentor might offer a more objective, long-term view of the career you're pursuing, we thought that a marriage counselor might offer advice that our own personal friends and family just couldn't when it comes to one of the most important steps of our lives. A decision that's going to affect everything from that day forward, not just in terms of your love life and romance, but in terms of the children you raise, and the family you're connected to, and your personal finances, and legal obligations, and your career, and the decisions about where you live—absolutely everything. Whether you get it right or not, you're going to have to live with the consequences of that one decision for the rest of your life. So why not do what you can to make it right?

Plus, we were facing some pretty big challenges. The fact that Thomas Rhett was getting ready to go on the road, and (hopefully) he'd pick up another tour after that, and another, and another, building his reputation to a point where he could headline at major venues himself, meant we would be starting off our lives together by being apart a whole lot of the time. On top of that, once I passed the boards I would start on the ground level as a nurse, which would inevitably mean that I'd be working night shifts. If I was working the night shift and Thomas Rhett was out playing shows, and both of us were trying to get some sleep in between, that pretty much meant that we were never going to see each other.

"Hmmm," our counselor said at our very first visit. "The first year of marriage lays the foundation for everything that happens in the years that follow," he said. "You need to be *together*. Every day, if you can."

"Well, what if we don't have a choice?" Thomas Rhett asked him.

"You *always* a have a choice. There are cases where the choices are extremely limited. And that's okay. But you still have choices to make. I mean, if a couple isn't going to be spending any time together, getting to know each other, making adjustments, learning to live with each other, then maybe you ought to consider that it just isn't the right time to get married."

It was shocking. If he hadn't been my former preacher, I'm not sure if we would have trusted him saying something so blunt like that.

"Are you serious?" Thomas Rhett asked him. "I mean, that's just not an option. We want to be married. We *know* we want to be married."

"Okay then," he said. "What is marriage if it's not working together as a team? A partnership? If it's not building a safe and comforting home for each other, and I'm not talking about physically where you live, but *how* you live: the kind of safe space you make and build and create for each other, just the two of you. And if one of you is simply gone, just missing from the equation, that's going to be awfully tough. It's doable. I've seen plenty of military families make it in the long run after an early deployment of one partner or the other. But if *both* of you are gone, if both of you are fully invested in careers that keep you from being with each other, I mean, how is that a partnership? How is there a chance of you building a home of your own? How is that even a marriage?"

His words hit us hard.

We prayed about it, together and separately, and in the end, the choice we had to make was difficult, but clear: Because Thomas Rhett's career was already moving so fast, and he was already so far ahead of where I was, it just made sense to put his career first. Which meant we needed to put my career on hold.

I knew I could come back to nursing at some point in the future. I knew there are always nursing jobs opening up since it's such an in-demand career. The opportunities that Thomas Rhett had, though? If he turned his back on those now, there was a very good chance they would never come back. *Ever.*

So we made up our minds: Once we were married, wherever Thomas

Rhett went, I would be with him. We would spend as much time as possible together, sharing our lives in every way, for at least the first year. After that, we agreed—and our counselor agreed—we could reassess our situation and figure out what works best for us. Because only after that first year of getting to know each other as husband and wife would there truly be an "us" to build on.

My first taste of what my new life with Thomas Rhett would be like came early, in July of that year, when he upgraded from a van to a tour bus for the very first time for his tour with Toby Keith.

I was living by myself, going to summer school in Knoxville and studying for exams when his bus swung by to pick me up on the way from Nashville to Raleigh, North Carolina.

"Oh my goodness. This is your bus?" I said.

"Not bad, right?" he said.

I said hey to the guys in the band, and met the driver, and threw a backpack full of clothes up onto the one empty bunk that they saved just for me. I don't even think I told my dad I was going on that trip, just because I didn't want to worry him, and I wasn't sure how he would react since we still weren't married. (Sorry, Dad!)

I was so excited to get on that bus, mostly because I just wanted to be anywhere Thomas Rhett was. And the anticipation of everything was just so new and exciting. To think of my fiancé opening up for a major tour—it was just incredible. The bus was fun, like we were riding in luxury, sitting at a table, watching TV, walking around—doing things you don't get to do when you're on a road trip in a car. And then watching Thomas Rhett get up onstage, in front of all those people, I could not believe how great he was. I'd never seen him perform at a venue bigger than a high school talent show, or the bar in Knoxville. This was the Walnut Creek Amphitheater, a big summer concert stage, and Toby's crowd of more than ten thousand people.

None of it was anything I'd ever imagined doing in my life. But I was all in. This was a new adventure, and I was ready—because I loved Thomas

Rhett. Seeing him smile, seeing how excited he was after that show was over, as I waited right there on the side stage just so proud of him, there was no better feeling in the world.

"Wait till you see where we go from here," he said.

But it didn't matter to me if he became a star, or if that amphitheater was the biggest venue he ever played. As long as we had each other, I knew we'd be good.

What mattered most to me was getting to October 12—our

Backstage before Thomas Rhett played at the Grand Ole Opry

wedding day. And while that was only three months away, it turned out we had some unusual hurdles to clear before our big day came.

First, Thomas Rhett released his first EP that August, and he was nervous about it. Which meant he needed me to be there for him as much as I possibly could. So I showed up. I held his hand and reassured him before he walked into press interviews. Whenever his stomach started doing backflips before he took the stage for an important performance, I reminded him just how much he was meant to do this. I saw how competitive he felt as he watched the charts, and I saw what his singles were doing compared to some of his new-artist peers; I reminded him that his success didn't have to happen all at once. I tried to be a calming voice on his shoulder, reminding him that it was all in God's hands anyway, and that I would be there for him no matter what.

"I'm so glad I asked you to marry me," he'd say.

Which gets us to the second big hurdle we faced: There were forces in the music industry who didn't want him to get married at all. When I started showing up in pictures on Thomas Rhett's social media accounts, before anyone in the public knew we were engaged to be married, some of his female fans made comments, like, "Who is this chick?" and "Hands off my man!" and "Look at this gold-digger of a girl!"

That last one really got me, because Thomas Rhett wasn't making much money, and anyone who knew me knew that was never my motivation. People have no idea what a grind it is for musicians in the early days. I mean, yeah, he had an advance from the record label that helped him make ends meet while he got his band together and went on the road. But after paying for all the expenses of road life, Thomas Rhett was only pulling in about $1,500 a month. That was all he had to live on, and that wouldn't change for a while. The two of us were planning to live in a condo that his dad owned in Nashville, just because it was the only place we knew we would be able to afford once we got married, and we knew how lucky we were to have that. We wouldn't have been able to afford rent and utilities, let alone have much of a life, anywhere in the Nashville metro area on that kind of income.

On a date during my senior year of college, at Market Square in Knoxville, Tennessee

More than hurting me personally, though, the comments fans made about us on Thomas Rhett's social media accounts troubled some people in the industry. There were powerful people in the music business who advised Thomas Rhett that he should wait to get married—otherwise the all-important audience of young women wouldn't buy his records or come to his concerts.

Thomas Rhett did his best not to listen to them. He tried to blow them off. But it kept coming up, and it was hard to ignore. Thomas Rhett was just starting out. How could he *not* want to at least give the benefit of the doubt to people who'd been in the industry for decades? It was easy to think, "Maybe we ought to be listening to them."

We also had a lot of people in our ear saying, "Twenty-one is just too young. Why not wait?" or stealing the old line from that Journey song: "They say that the road ain't no place to start a family."

Thomas Rhett didn't want to jeopardize his career, and I didn't want that, either. And neither of us wanted to jeopardize our relationship. Yet both of us knew in our hearts that this was right for us, and we were willing to work hard to make it work.

At one point early on, Thomas Rhett opened for Luke Bryan, and the two of them became buddies almost instantly. Luke would become somewhat of a mentor to him, and one time when they were hanging out, Thomas Rhett told Luke what was going on.

TR: I told him I was getting married in October whether people liked it or not, and I said, "Hear me out. I love this girl. I've loved her since I was fifteen years old." And once I explained my position, and my history with Lauren, Luke was like, "Buddy, if you love her, then forget everybody else. You do what you want to do. You go marry her! You've gotta be true to yourself or nothing else matters."

Thankfully, Thomas Rhett's manager agreed. She told everyone they encountered that we were meant for this marriage, and that they should support it.

I thank God all the time that Thomas Rhett's manager is who she is. Her name's Virginia Bunetta, and first of all, she's a woman. That shouldn't make a difference, but it does. She just sees the world through a woman's eyes, and that makes every difference in a business that's dominated by men. Second, she has always put Thomas Rhett's best interests first, above profits or acclaim or anything else. And that's the kind of person you want in your life. What was in Thomas Rhett's best interest was to be true to himself, and to be honest about who he is. She knew that in country music, maybe more than in any other genre, being true to who you are, being real, is a strength in the long run, because that's what fans connect with most.

What really mattered in Thomas Rhett's life is what had always mattered: faith, family, our roots, our friends; and although it seemed counterintuitive, the advice Thomas Rhett received from some of his closest allies in life, including my dad, his dad, and his stepdad, Tim, was that putting what matters most *first* will actually do more for your career than putting your career first. In *any* industry. Not that work doesn't take sacrifice and struggle and effort. It does. Your job deserves a lot of time and energy if you want to be successful. But you have to ask yourself why you're doing what you're doing. And if the *why* is to make your life better, and the job—whatever that job is—is hurting your life, keeping you from your faith, your family, your friends, and all the rest of it, then maybe something's wrong.

So we did it.

On October 12, 2012, we got married.

I wasn't one of those girls who'd dreamed about what her wedding would look like ever since she was little. I never really gave it any thought until we got engaged. But then, I set my heart on a few things that had to be just right.

One, we needed to stay close to Nashville so all of our friends and family could be sure to be there. Thomas Rhett's grandmother and some of his dad's family live in Georgia, and it's so dreamy on their farm. We seriously thought about having our wedding there, but the majority of our family and friends were so close to Nashville, we ultimately decided it would be much easier to keep it near town. We were just too worried that any long-distance travel might get in the way of some of our closest friends showing up.

Two, I wanted to get married under a tree. I could just picture the two of us getting married under a big old tree in all the fall colors and I knew it would be absolutely beautiful. Thomas Rhett loved the idea, so we looked around and found the perfect spot at a farm just outside Nashville.

Not only did they have a big, beautiful tree on a gorgeous lawn, but there was also a farmhouse where we could get ready, and a pavilion so we could have a dance floor.

That was the third thing: We had to have dancing. We wanted a live band—not a DJ—and we wanted everyone to dance and have fun.

Lastly, I know some brides like to have rice tossed in the air when they leave at the end of the night. And some people blow bubbles instead, which is really cute, and some people like rose petals. But for me and Thomas Rhett, I just had this vision of us running through all of our friends and family holding sparklers as we left. I just thought that would be so pretty. And I guess that automatically meant that I wanted the wedding to end sometime after dark.

That was about it. I didn't care much about anything else, and I truly wanted other people to go ahead and make the decisions. I didn't want my wedding day to stress me out. I just wanted it to be a day filled with love. And thanks to all the planning my mom and dad and sister and friends did, it was.

We didn't spend a ton of money. We didn't do anything too extravagant. We didn't have money of our own, and my dad kept us on a strict budget, like he did with everything else.

A week before the wedding, some girlfriends and I stayed at the condo Thomas Rhett and I were about to move into, in downtown Nashville— this was a few years before Nashville turned into one of the most popular bachelorette-party destinations in the country—and we ate dinner together and ended up dancing till we shut the bars down. Then the night before the wedding, we had our rehearsal dinner in the space right next to Giovanni's before heading back to Mom and Dad's to get a good night's rest and get ready in the morning.

When Mom woke up, she told me, "I had a dream Hunter was at the wedding."

"*What?*"

"Yeah," she said. "I talked to him. He was wearing all white, like linen, and he was driving around on one of the golf carts, and he said to me,

'Alright, here we go. Are you ready? This is gonna be fun!' and then we hopped on one of the golf carts and he said, 'Let's go!' and he starts driving me around on the golf cart!"

Whatever that dream might have meant, I was glad to hear Hunter was excited about our big day.

Hunter's mom, Laurie, did all of our hair at her house, and Kamron and some of my other friends hung out with us while we got all dolled up. Some of them had gone out so late the night before, and they looked like a wreck. I said, "Y'all are crazy!" But they still got up early just to be there and enjoy this day with us from start to finish, which I thought was so sweet.

There was no way Hunter wasn't going to be right there with me for the biggest adventure of my life. So Hailey, Hannah, Macy, and I came up with the idea to wear his boxers underneath our dresses. It just felt right to do something funny like that in his honor. Then I cut the shape of a heart out of one of his blue shirts, and we sewed that piece of fabric into the back of my dress.

Hunter's blue shirt, cut into a heart and sewn onto the back of my wedding dress

Before we knew it, it was the middle of the afternoon. "We were supposed to leave fifteen minutes ago!" my mom yelled.

"Well, we're not ready yet!" I said.

"We need to get in the car and at least go on to the venue," she said.

So we grabbed everything we thought we needed and loaded up the cars and went.

We all piled into the farmhouse, and our wedding photographer started getting pictures of me putting my dress on and getting last-minute touches to my hair. And she said, "Alright, do you want to get your mom to help you put your wedding jewelry on?"

"Yeah, sure," I said. "Mom, will you grab my jewelry?"

"Okay," she said, "where'd you put it?"

"I don't know. You never gave it to me."

"But you brought it?" she asked.

"No, I thought *you* brought it!" I said.

Now, I've seen situations like this happen where somebody just loses it. You realize you left something important at home, and it's too far and there isn't enough time

Alone for a moment before Dad came to walk me down the aisle

to go get it, and people panic. Somebody starts blaming somebody else and it can ruin half the day.

That just wasn't gonna happen at our wedding.

We just laughed.

All my bridesmaids started taking off their jewelry, handing me earrings and necklaces until we figured out what looked good, and it honestly worked out perfect. It felt really sweet to me to wear borrowed jewelry from my best friends in the world, on top of the borrowed shorts I was wearing under my dress. Old, new, borrowed, blue—I think there's a reason those sayings come along with getting married. A wedding should be fun. It's supposed to be connected to who we are now, and who we were, and the people we love.

If I'd had my heart set on wearing a certain piece of jewelry, I might have ended up in tears or something. But the only thing I had my heart set on that day was marrying my best friend and celebrating our marriage with our friends and family.

There were nearly two hundred people there, and not one of them was a stranger to me or to Thomas Rhett. Not one.

His first EP had dropped less than two months earlier, and his second single, "Beer with Jesus," was certified gold, which meant he was starting to get more and more attention. But we didn't have any unwanted cameras at our wedding. It wasn't a public spectacle. The pressure of all that wasn't on us. (Not yet.)

Right as my bridesmaids were getting ready to walk down the aisle, my mom, who had been so focused on me the whole time, said, "No one fixed my hair yet. Can you just throw it up really fast?"

"Oh my gosh, Mom! I'm so sorry. Yes, of course," I said. I braided my mom's hair and pinned it up, and she checked it quick in the mirror and said, "Thank you."

Then she hugged me and said, "I love you so much."

"I love you too, Mom," I said.

We stepped out of the room we were in and met my dad, and all of a sudden I got really nervous. My bridesmaids and Mom all went outside, and I could hear the music playing, which meant they were heading down the aisle to stand under the tree, and I couldn't even speak. I just clung on to my dad so tight at the top of the stairs, thinking, "Oh my gosh. This is *it*."

I don't think he said anything to try to calm me down. He didn't have to. This strong man who loved and raised me was about to give me away to the love of my life. My husband. The man my dad taught me to pray for ever since I was a little girl. I will never forget that moment I got to have with my dad. It meant everything to me. He just let me hold on to him for a while and he wrapped his arms around me, and it was all I could do not to cry.

It felt like we stood there for a really long time, like the whole world faded away a little bit while my dad held me one last time before walking me down the aisle.

"Okay, we're ready," somebody whisper-shouted up the stairs.

"Okay," he said. "You ready, honey?"

I nodded as I looked at him and smiled, and he grabbed my shaky hand

and held it tight as we stepped down the stairs and out the front door, and I saw everybody I knew standing up on either side of the aisle on that beautiful evening.

"These are all my people," I thought.

And when I looked ahead and saw Thomas Rhett standing under the tree, just like I'd imagined, I knew that right there next to him was exactly where I wanted to be. My nervousness all went away the moment I saw him smile at me.

> **TR:** She had never looked more beautiful, and I swear I almost passed out. It was just so surreal. I mean, I'd told her that I loved her since I was fifteen years old, but I think I loved her from the first time I laid eyes on her, at church camp. How is that even possible? Why was God so good to me? I mean, I was about to marry my dream girl. I could not have been more excited. I just hoped and prayed I could give her everything she deserved.

I desperately wanted to add some Akins-family Southern charm to the surroundings, since we couldn't be at the family farm in Georgia. So Mammy, Thomas Rhett's grandmother, brought big bags full of Spanish moss all the way up from the trees in her yard. We draped the moss all over the branches of the big tree we were about to get married under. It was absolutely beautiful. A stunning backdrop framing all of the people I loved so much.

We even kept the ceremony in the family: Thomas Rhett's granddaddy, his Papaw, got ordained just for our wedding.

It felt like everything in my entire life had led me to that moment, right there, and as I stood next to Thomas Rhett with butterflies in my stomach, listening to Papaw start the ceremony, I thanked God for every bit of it: every twist and turn and lesson we'd learned that brought us to this beautiful day.

Thomas Rhett and I wrote our own vows, separately. I didn't know what he was going to say until he said it, and he didn't know what I was going to say, either. But we ended up writing some of the very same promises to each other, and I thought that was a pretty good sign.

I wrote:

Thomas Rhett
·You have been my best friend for years, & I have loved you since I was 15, but I fell IN LOVE with you at 21. I honestly didn't think it was possible to love someone the way, & how much I love you, BUT thank you for convincing me to kiss you that Friday night - May 13th.
For the rest of our life I promise to:
Dance with you when you ask
Hold your hand whenever possible
Support the bulldogs when the outcome will not negatively affect the VOLS
Laugh a lot with you, pray with you - everyday encourage you, respect you, TRUST you no matter what, make Holiday cookies (slice 'n bake) at every holiday

see the best movies out
in theatres with you
TRY to cook, be the best
mother I can be to our
children, and the most
devoted wife to you for
the rest of our lives.
I promise to always look to God
in all things, thank Him for
all He has done for us and
love Him more than you.

I promise to Give you my whole
heart. You make my life so much
better just by being near me.
You are my favorite - I dont want
to do any part of life without you.
I'm so thankful God has given us
a real life love story. And I VOW to
always remember - you and me
    I love you &   FOREVER

And he wrote:

Lauren,

I vow to love you and only you for the rest of my life. I vow to always be completely honest and open with you no matter how hard it may be. I vow to be a loyal and true husband till the day I die. I vow to be the best father I can be to our kids when that time comes. I vow to always to my very best to lead you spiritually and to encourage you when you are down. I vow to be a good listener and a slow speaker. I vow to get my priorities straight by putting God first in my life and you second. I vow to give you all the love that I have and to continue to grow in love with you every single day of my life. You are my best friend, and the hottest human being that has ever graced my presence. I am the luckiest guy in the world to be able to marry you!

I had to try really hard not to cry as I read my words to him. It all just meant so much to me. Thankfully, when Thomas Rhett read his vows, he made everybody laugh (including me) with his "hottest human being" line. It was just right. He broke the ice and got everyone in just the right mood to party, right before Papaw pronounced us husband and wife and told Thomas Rhett, "You may now kiss the bride."

Finally Mr. and Mrs. Thomas Rhett Akins!

That kiss was as good as the one on my parents' front porch. The one that started everything. I felt it all the way down to my toes, this feeling of love and thankfulness that filled up my entire spirit. We were married now. We were *married*!

It was only after we turned and wiped the tears from our eyes that I noticed that Thomas Rhett's dad, Rhett, had his phone out—and his phone was wrapped in a camo phone case. It stood out like a redneck sore thumb next to all of our pretty dresses and fine suits. I found out later that he'd held that thing in his hand taking video from the moment he walked Kasey down the aisle till the very end of the ceremony, because it showed up in every picture and even in our wedding video. It was just too funny. And you know, honestly, even *that* was perfect.

As long as you have a sense of humor, it's these kinds of ridiculous things that give you a good story to tell and a memory to laugh at way after the day has come and gone. And to me, that's more valuable than any so-called picture-perfect, Pinterest-worthy wedding could ever be.

Plus, once we got to the reception, our wedding turned into a big ol' Southern party anyway. The band started playing, and the caterer served fried tomatoes, and cheeseburgers with the letter *A* branded into the buns, and there was a big mashed potato bar with all the good toppings, and I don't even know what else, because the beer and wine started flowing and somebody just made the two of us a plate as we kept on laughing and talking with everybody. We barely got a chance to sit down to eat!

Thomas Rhett and I danced our first dance to Frank Sinatra's "The Way You Look Tonight," the same song we danced to when we got engaged. Then I danced with my dad at the same time Thomas Rhett danced with his mom to "My Girl" by the Four Tops. There's a picture of my dad spinning me around on that dance floor with all the twinkling lights behind us that's just one of my favorite pictures of the two of us, ever. Then the band played some country, and pop, and rock 'n' roll, and so many classics that kept everybody on their feet all night.

My dad let loose and had such a good time that a few people asked me if he'd had too much to drink. "Nope!" I said. "Not a drop. He's just such a nerd that he did the math and calculated what every minute of this party was costing him, and he decided to live it up and get his money's worth out of every minute!"

I had eleven bridesmaids in my wedding party. More than one person said it was "too many," and that I might look back and not really be friends with some of them years later. All I can say is that so far, so good, because every one of them—including the college friends I got so close to when I

Favorite pic. ☺
Dad spinning me around on the dance floor

pledged ADPi in my sophomore year, Gillian, Dee, Amber, and Adeline—are still some of my closest friends to this day. In fact, I think we could say the same about pretty much everyone who was at our wedding. And that kind of closeness and love and support makes all the difference in the world.

Some of my best girls—and eleven bridesmaids

Fireworks and kissing at our wedding—
doesn't get much better ☺

The night got pretty chilly, and we had to roll down the sides of the pavilion we were under, but by the time we walked outside again, the sky was full of stars.

The owner of the property was a firefighter, and he set off the most beautiful fireworks ever. After all the Fourth of July celebrations we'd had with back yard fireworks in our neighborhood, it felt so good to be outside with everybody, looking up into the night sky together.

Finally, it was time for me and Thomas Rhett to leave all the party people behind—to go back to our condo before heading off on our honeymoon early the next morning.

We left through a glowing human tunnel of smiles and sparklers, just like we'd imagined, and we hopped into Thomas Rhett's truck and sped off to the other side of Nashville feeling more appreciative of our friends and family than ever—at the very same time we were *so* ready to be alone.

Just the beginning of our happily ever after

11

On the Road

In all the times Thomas Rhett had stayed at my dorm, or at my apartment in Knoxville, we were never alone. I had roommates. Even on the tour bus to Raleigh, there were eight dudes in there with us! So this was truly our first night alone together, ever—in the condo we were now going to share. It's amazing how much was happening all at once. It's like we were ushering in the next phase of our lives and becoming independent adults, and doing it all in a twelve-hour span.

It must've been midnight when we got home. We were tired, and we had to be up at 4:30 in the morning to get to the airport for our honeymoon. Not the best planning on our part. (For anyone thinking about getting married, I highly recommend giving yourself at least twenty-four hours after the ceremony before you schedule any flights.)

The time crunch and our overall exhaustion didn't stop us from getting to what we'd been waiting on for so long, though. I don't think anything could've stopped us. Not to mention, we walked into what felt like a romance dream: Allie Brooke had left the reception ahead of us and set out candles and rose petals from the door where we stepped into our condo all the way up the stairs leading into the bedroom. She also put a perfect playlist on the stereo, full of the most clutch wedding-night songs ever. Songs by Dave Matthews, Dave Barnes, Marvin Gaye—the perfect music to set the mood for our very first time.

TR: I won't lie, we struggled at it for a minute.

Lauren: No we didn't!

TR: It was just all brand-new, which meant there was a learning curve—

Lauren: For both of us.

TR: Which was nice.

Lauren: Haha. Yeah . . .

We were nervous. Both of us. How could we not be? But it was the best kind of nervous.

Was it perfect? I don't know how to answer that! We couldn't compare it to anything else, and we didn't have to—because our first time together was just *ours*. It was the start of a whole new adventure for the two of us.

Plus, they say practice makes perfect, right? And our honeymoon in Hawaii was going to be the perfect place to practice. A *lot*.

On the flight to Kauai, we were talking about how much fun we'd had the night before, and how crazy it was that we were married, and then Thomas Rhett looked out the window and got real quiet, and he turned to me and said, "But aren't you kinda a little sad, though?"

I was confused, like, "Sad?"

"Yeah. Like, isn't it kinda sad, still?"

"I'm sorry. Come again? What do you mean 'sad'?"

"Like, you know, you're never gonna go home to your house again. You're never gonna sleep in your parents' house again, as a single kid."

I didn't know what to say. Feeling sad about not being a kid anymore was nowhere near what I was feeling the day after our wedding.

"I mean," he said, "aren't you gonna miss your mom?"

"No! I am not gonna miss my *mom*! And you better not say you're gonna miss *your* mom!" I said. I truly started to panic, thinking, "Holy crap, what did we just do? Maybe he wasn't ready to do this. Maybe we jumped the gun."

Paige was only nineteen years old when she had Thomas Rhett. The two of them were as close as a mom and son could be. He was still bringing his laundry home for her to wash for him, after college, whenever he'd come in off the road. And she didn't mind, because she was happy to see him. But *come on!* Paige had remarried. She had Tim. And Thomas Rhett now had me. I sure hoped he would adjust to our new reality real quick.

Paige—my absolutely incredible mother-in-law—with Thomas Rhett at our wedding

"I'm sorry," he said, kind of giggling. "It's just a big transition."

I convinced myself it was just some kind of day-too-late cold feet or his being overtired after a big emotional day, or something. And I decided to let it go.

I'm glad I did, because we spent the next ten days in a state of total bliss. We rented a Jeep, and took the top off, and drove through the green, green mountains. And every morning at this mountainside resort, right on the water, we had breakfast while looking out on a brand-new rainbow. *Every morning.* It was so lush and green. There were waterfalls everywhere. We felt like we were living in a whole other world. And within one day, Thomas Rhett and I were out surfing. I was getting a chance to live out a childhood fantasy: surfing. Okay, the waves were kind of tiny. Maybe not *Blue Crush*-worthy, but they were good enough for me. I was living a dream, and it was all because I'd married my best friend.

Trusting my heart and marrying the love of my life made all kinds of dreams come true.

Neither of us had ever been to Hawaii, or anywhere really, without our parents or a big group of friends and family. It was so incredible to spend that much time together, without a care in the world, alone. Just hanging out. Me and him.

Kauai is tiny, so we instantly became regulars at a little sushi place down the dirt road, and at the taco stand near the surf shop, where we'd drink a Longboard beer or two before going back to catch a nap, before heading out to lay on the beach till sunset, before grabbing dinner and then climbing into bed together.

It felt more romantic than I'd even dreamed.

Honeymooning at a luau

Our first day trying to catch some waves in Kauai

It was seriously hard to adjust to real life once we got back to Nashville, mostly because we didn't have any time to adjust whatsoever. One day after we got home, Thomas Rhett had to go right back out on the road, which meant I had to load up another big suitcase and climb on the bus and go right back on the road with him.

Honestly, that was kind of great, too. We were newlyweds, twenty-two years old and so in love that absolutely everything seemed fun. Our schedule was packed—and so was the bus. Since Thomas Rhett's career was growing, so was the group that he traveled with. There was a tour manager on the road now plus the band, plus a sound guy, and a merch guy (to sell T-shirts and stuff). There wasn't a lot of storage in the bus, which meant at least one bunk was taken up by gear—they called that the "junk bunk." Which meant there wasn't a free bunk left for me, and I was perfectly happy about it. Snuggling up to Thomas Rhett in a single bunk that was smaller than a twin-size bed, squeezed off to one side of the aisle with nothing but the hum of the highway underneath us, I slept like a baby in his arms.

Even though we were traveling around, we didn't really get to see very much of the country. Being the opener for a famous band doesn't leave much room for flexibility. Thomas Rhett and his band didn't get to choose a time to do sound check. They basically had to stay close to whatever venue we were playing, because sound check would happen as soon as the gear was all set up, and that schedule could vary widely from place to place.

That was okay. Thomas Rhett liked to stay focused. He put a lot of thought and energy and rehearsal into putting on the best show he could play at every single stop, and I didn't have time for sightseeing anyway. I brought all my textbooks with me, and during any free time I sat down and studied for the NCLEX, which I was planning to take in November.

When we did go out to get a bite to eat or something, people started noticing. "Hey! Thomas Rhett! Wow. I'm coming to the show later!" "Wait, aren't you that country singer? 'Beer with Jesus'?" "Oh my gosh! Hi! Can I take a selfie with you?"

Having complete strangers talk this way to my husband was not easy for me to get used to, but he loved it. He was so excited that people recognized him, and even more excited that they knew and loved his music. Everything he'd dreamed about since he was a kid was starting to come true. But it worried me a little bit, like, "What does it mean for us if he gets as famous as he wants to get?"

It didn't make it easier when every bigwig we met in the music industry seemed to say that Thomas Rhett was gonna be the "next big thing." "Just watch!" they'd say. "He reminds me of a young so-and-so," and those so-and-sos were always super well-known names.

Was I excited for Thomas Rhett? Yes! Of course! Who wouldn't be excited to see her husband's dreams come true? It just made me nervous. I mean, if you look at the history of what fame tends to do to most couples, it's not good. Fame doesn't like marriage. I wasn't sure how we'd navigate it all, as a couple.

Whenever I saw him onstage, though, my worries would disappear. He was always nervous ahead of time. He just wanted to be the best he could be, and he felt like his career was on the line at every one of those early shows. Then, even at sound check, he'd step up to that microphone and all of a sudden be in the best mood ever. He was just so happy to hear his band, his songs, his voice coming through those massive speakers and echoing across the stadium, knowing how many people would be there later that night. He loved thinking about and planning how he'd give every single one of them a great night.

I liked to watch from front of house, out where the soundboard and the lightboard sit in the middle of the crowd. Everybody thinks backstage is the place they want to be, but the sound is terrible back there, and you really can't see anything. So I'd go sit out and watch the crew run those complicated boards, and I'd be close enough to see the expression on his face, but far enough back to see the whole show, too. And that spot always had the best sound in the house, no matter how big of a venue we were in.

There was something even better than watching Thomas Rhett's ex-

With Macy, when Thomas Rhett opened at Red Rocks

pressions, though. There were times when I'd turn to the side, or turn right around, and watch the faces of the people in the crowd, and see how they'd light up when he played a song they knew. There were people singing to songs I'd heard him working so hard to write, line by line, or words he'd sung to me in the back of his truck bed when it was just us two. And those songs were giving people such joy. I'd look around and was just in awe of the way my husband was capable of putting smiles on so many faces. It felt so special to be along for this ride, and then to get to hold him close, all squeezed in a little bunk at night, just the two of us tucked behind a curtain in our own little world on a tour bus.

In early November, I went back home for a few days of hard-core studying, and I passed my NCLEX on the very first try. Thomas Rhett was so excited for me, you'd have thought that I'd just won a Grammy Award or something. And I was pretty proud of myself, too. Pulling that off after all the delays and interruptions and heartache, and the wedding and honeymoon and touring—that was not easy. The NCLEX is for nurses kind of what the bar exam is to lawyers. It's *hard*. It felt so good to know that I was free and clear to start my nursing career whenever we decided the time was right.

It also felt really good to know that we were heading into the holiday season, and that Thomas Rhett's schedule was about to be free until the new year.

Heading into Christmas for the first time being married felt like a really big deal to me. I wanted to get it right.

"We're so broke," Thomas Rhett said, "I don't know if we should buy a Christmas tree for the condo. I mean, we're gonna spend Christmas morning at my parents' house anyway, right?"

Merry Christmas!

"What?" I said. "No Christmas tree? I'd rather go without eatin'!"

We got a Christmas tree. Real and beautiful, and ready to fill up with ornaments that we'd collect in the years ahead, just like I'd done with my parents. We couldn't afford the extra $40 to get it flocked, and it looked kind of bare with only the few ornaments we had, so I ran out to the dollar section of Target and found a sale on a big box of precious little gingerbread ornaments in the back of the store—just enough to carry us over until we lived a little more life together.

We still made it to Opryland. There was no way that was gonna change. And we threw our annual ugly sweater party at my parents' house, just like we had for the last five years, only this time with more friends and family than ever.

Some things are sacred. Especially time with family. That was never gonna change.

Best of all, we were able to slow down and spend some time at home. *Our* home. To breathe a little bit at the end of what had easily been the most momentous, memorable, and emotional year either one of us had ever been through.

Taking that break, that moment to get centered in *us,* and what *mattered* to us, *mattered.* Because starting in January, Thomas Rhett's career would shift into overdrive.

* * *

Over the course of the next year, Thomas Rhett played 220 shows (including a long stretch of shows opening for Jason Aldean), finished recording his first album, made music videos, and appeared on national television shows in New York and L.A.—and I was there for just about all of it, as he started to grow the most amazing fan base any musician could ever hope for. We held hands, and I talked him through it when he got nervous. And we both laughed at the crazy opportunities that came his way.

Some of our Crew at our first married ugly Christmas sweater party

The only way we kept grounded through all of that was to stay grounded in who we are.

Thomas Rhett set up some strict rules early on that we both hoped would help keep some of the traps of the music industry at arm's length. For example, he wouldn't allow any girls to come backstage, other than the wives or family of band members. As amazing as most of his fans are, there were some rare cases where people would get a little out of hand in terms of respecting our marriage. So, there were no girls other than wives or girlfriends allowed on the bus, either. Given the way some girls seemed to throw themselves at him from the front row and even tried to hop onstage over the course of that year, I was glad he made those rules. It is not easy to stand there watching girls shamelessly trying to get with your husband.

He took it a step further when it came to making music videos. The record label always hired a model to come in and play "the girl" with him on camera, and after the first or second video, Thomas Rhett put his foot down. First of all, he always tried to get me to be in the videos with him, and I just said "no." I wasn't interested in having anybody watch me. "That's really not me, and definitely not something I want to do," I said.

But then Thomas Rhett told his video director, T.K. McKamy, who also happens to be a good friend of ours, that he didn't want to touch any other girls or let them touch him during the shoots.

"If you want a shot of me holding hands or putting my arm around some other girl, I'm not gonna do it. You're gonna have to use a stand-in," he said.

T.K. thought he was being a bit dramatic. "It's just holding hands," he said. "It's not a big deal."

Even I said, "It's okay. It's just acting. It's like playing a part in a play," but Thomas Rhett wasn't having it.

There's one early video where he's with another girl and there are shots of her holding his hand and leading him to different scenes, and in all those shots, the hand you see holding the girl's hand isn't actually Thomas Rhett's. It's T.K.'s. It makes me laugh every time I see it. T.K. didn't have a stand-in, so he had to go shoot those shots himself, using his own hand to double for Thomas Rhett's.

Our marriage was sacred. So was our physical connection. And although I didn't demand it, it really felt good to know Thomas Rhett cared enough to put that kind of effort into honoring our commitment to each other and keeping it safe.

By setting boundaries and making rules, he made it so I didn't have to wonder and didn't have to worry—and neither did he. 'Cause he and I both knew we didn't want to let the lack of morals that seem to come along with this lifestyle intrude upon the life we were building together.

Our first family photo at Christmas, with Kona

We did our best to stay rooted in the life we'd built around each other at home, in church, and with our families, even as Thomas Rhett kept rushing toward fame and success like a runaway train, traveling from city to city on the tour bus, playing opening shows for Brantley Gilbert and Miranda Lambert and all kinds of big-name artists, while getting more and more confident onstage and getting louder and louder reactions from the crowds every night.

One of the ways we grounded ourselves was with a puppy. The two of us fell in love with a brown, floppy-eared girl who we named Kona (after the region in Hawaii), and we treated her like our very first baby. We trained her in the park down the street from our condo whenever we were home, and took her on the road with us on the bus whenever we could. If she couldn't come with us, my mom would dog-sit, and she seriously treated Kona like her very first grandchild. Somehow, while cleaning up dog messes and putting all of our energy into making sure she grew up right, there didn't seem to be time to let our heads grow too big from all of the excitement in Thomas Rhett's career.

And in March, Thomas Rhett miraculously timed things just right so we could meet my family in Key West for our annual spring break trip, just like we always had—because family seemed more important than ever.

When we came back from that trip, our old friend Kamron decided to come out on the road with us. We'd had just about every one of our friends come to concerts whenever we were close by: sometimes all at the same time. Thomas Rhett would block whole sections of seats just to fit all our family and friends in whenever he could. But this was different. Kamron came with us as we trekked up to Providence, Rhode Island, and the three of us went out together after Thomas Rhett played his first big Cinco de Mayo show.

There was always something about having Kamron in the room with us that put us all in

Kamron sidestage with us on tour with Thomas Rhett, opening for our friends Florida Georgia Line

a Hunter-type mindset, where we just wanted to do something crazy-fun together, and that Cinco de Mayo was no exception.

"We should go get tattoos!" he said.

Thomas Rhett and I looked at each other and said, "You in? Let's do it!"

We'd already been talking about getting a matching tattoo together. We kept thinking about what was important to us, looking back over our history, and we finally agreed that we wanted something to signify the moment that changed everything: our kiss on my parents' front porch.

Just putting the date on our skin didn't seem special enough, though. We wanted something more. I knew I didn't want a big tattoo. I wanted it to be simple. We thought about the porch, and the *location* of the porch, and it finally dawned on us that night: "We should get the coordinates. The exact location on a map."

As a pilot, my dad was an expert in coordinates and map reading, and he'd taught me all about it. So I looked it up and found the latitude and longitude of the exact spot on a map, and we decided to put half of the coordinates on my arm, and the other half on his. So all we had to do to map out that magic spot was to put our arms together.

We marked those coordinates in permanent ink on our skin that night.

A few days later, Thomas Rhett released his third single, "It Goes Like

This," which was written by his dad—and that song went to #1 on the Country Radio and Mediabase charts.

His first #1 single!

This was serious now. This was for *real*. All of a sudden everyone in the music industry was looking at him like, "This kid is one to watch," and more and more people started recognizing him whenever we went to the grocery store, or to dinner, and sometimes they'd stop him when we were walking down the sidewalk, even in places I used to think were far from the center of the country music universe, like up in Boston, Massachusetts.

It was wild. It was fun. And once again, it made me nervous. I rolled with it, though, and rolled with him, as he started doing bigger interviews and radio stops all over the country, as well as playing bigger and bigger shows.

We were out on the road so much, going through the same long days of waiting for sound check, I started to go a little stir-crazy. I know that sounds weird, since we were moving all the time, but that's what it felt like. I didn't have my textbooks with me. I didn't have a job. I didn't have anything to do besides hang out with Thomas Rhett and the band and crew. And all of it was fun. But it started to feel like having fun wasn't really enough of a way to spend my days.

I kept asking the tour manager and the assistant tour manager, anyone who would listen, for a job. "Hey, can you radio me up? Can I, like, *do something*? I'm kind of losing my mind. You don't have to pay me, just give me something to do!"

Rhett and TR at Puckett's

They never actually listened. They just laughed.

As we got closer and closer to his first full album release that October, I was so happy to see Thomas Rhett so excited and engaged and loving what he was doing. But his success also became an obsession for him. Like, "I've gotta be better. I've gotta *do* better. Who's doing better than I am?" It felt like he could hardly ever relax and take a break anymore. We'd go home and hang with family, celebrating birthdays—including Kona's first birthday, complete with a doggie birthday hat and doggie birthday cake—and we'd have a normal moment for maybe an hour at a time, but then he'd get right back to talking about which single should get released next, and texting his manager, or going to work out at the gym, *again,* not only so he'd look the part of a country star, but so he'd maintain the stamina it takes to jump around and give every ounce of energy he had when he played longer sets on bigger and bigger stages.

More and more, it seemed like even when he was "off," he wasn't off. His mind couldn't leave his work behind. His mind just never shut off.

He knew his work had become all-consuming, and he apologized sometimes, but it was clear to me that he was struggling pretty hard with being present. Paige felt it. My parents felt it. Our friends felt it.

We'd be at the dinner table and all he'd want to talk about was how amazing so-and-so's new single was, or how he'd love to have a show that could compare to Bruno Mars's someday, and what he should wear on TV for that appearance coming up, and how the guy doing the mastering on the record was bringing it to a whole new level—and sometimes I didn't even know what he was talking about, because the language of the music business was a language all its own.

To some degree we all stood back a bit and smiled and watched it happen, gladly, because we knew all that thought and effort and time and preparation he was putting in was exactly what it was gonna take to make all his dreams come true.

But for me? His wife? A now twenty-three-year-old woman who'd set her career aside for more than a year and was riding around on a bus without feeling like she had anything worthwhile to contribute except maybe a hand to hold and a shoulder to lean on? It started to feel like I was living in Thomas Rhett's world. Full-time. I knew it was what I'd signed up for. I knew it. I thought I was on board for it. Or at least I kept telling myself that I was.

A part of me was feeling like I didn't know exactly where I fit in anymore, and that was a tough pill to swallow after just one year of marriage.

I missed our family.

I missed staying still.

I missed the back of his pickup truck.

I missed the sweet boy who danced with me under the stars.

More than once, in the dark isolation of our crowded single bunk on the tour bus, I told him, "I just wish you'd come live in my world again, every once in a while, that's all."

He'd tell me it would get better: "Once the album is out, once I'm more established, once I start headlining and can call the shots a little bit more . . ."

And I'd look at him, and I'd say, "Okay," because I desperately wanted to believe him.

Then I'd kiss him good night, and I'd fall asleep to the hum of the highway, feeling pretty sure that he hadn't really heard one word of what I'd just told him.

*Kissing my forever wedding date
at my friend Dee's wedding*

12

Oceans

Thomas Rhett's 2013 touring season was finally ending, and I was just so ready to be done. To be home again. Just me and him.

I felt myself exhale as we got off the bus and drove to our condo, but then Thomas Rhett ended up on the phone half the day. I exhaled again when we were finally on our way to my parents' house for dinner that night, but then his phone rang again. He took the call while I sat in the passenger seat, staring out the window.

"Alright," he said as he hung up. "That was Virginia. We got that interview we'd been talking about. So I've gotta head up to New York City tomorrow night. I'm thinking we make it a long weekend so we can spend an extra day or two, maybe see a show—"

"What?" I said. "No! We just got home!"

"It'll be fun. I promise. I'll only have to work those couple of hours, and we can make it a mini-vacation in the city. You love New York."

"I love *home*. You know how much I've been looking forward to being off the road," I said.

He started the car and started to drive.

"I know. But you know this is huge. I can't turn it down. Plus—"

"Why not? When is enough *enough*? This is insane. It never stops. Just when I think we're finally getting a break, you get another call."

"This *is* getting a break! This is huge. This is exactly the kind of break that I want and need," he said.

"That's not what I'm talking about!"

"What?" he said.

"It's not what *I* want."

"What? What is wrong with you?" he asked—and I lost it.

"I can't do this anymore," I said, and I started to cry.

"What do you mean you can't do this anymore?"

"I don't know," I said.

I honestly didn't know in that moment if I was talking about staying on the road, all the traveling, all the work—or if I was talking about us.

Thomas Rhett got this terrified look in his eyes, and he pulled into the parking lot of Grace Church and parked the car, and we ended up sitting there for an hour, hashing *everything* out.

"What do you mean you can't do this anymore?" he asked me again.

"I either go with you to do all these things that I don't really like doing, or I don't get to be with you. And that phone call—that's just like one more of the constant reminders to me that my life is not my own. Like, I literally cater to your every need for whatever tour schedule you have, whatever pop-up show happens, whatever interview you need to do, whatever. At what point is it *enough*? Like, at what point is getting ahead not gonna be the only thing we ever talk about? At what point do you become thankful, where it's like, 'Right. Great. This was our goal and we made it. Let's *rest* for a little bit.' There is just no resting and I feel like I don't have a choice, or that any part of my life feels like my own."

Thomas Rhett looked stunned.

I don't know why he hadn't heard me up until that moment. We'd talked about it a lot, and he knew I wasn't exactly pumped to be on the bus all the time, doing the same things every single day. But he never really got it until that come-to-Jesus talk in the parking lot.

> **TR:** As we sat there and I saw that she was in so much pain, which I had obviously *caused* her, I was on the verge of calling my manager and telling her, "I quit." I was like, "If every weekend off the road is gonna be sitting in this parking lot and having this conversation, it ain't worth it. I'll go do something different."
>
> I said it out loud to Lauren, too.

"Is quitting what you want me to do? 'Cause I'll do it. You're more important to me than any of this. You know that," Thomas Rhett said.

"No," I said. "I don't want you to quit. God didn't bring you all this way for you to quit. That's not it."

I didn't want him to quit. I didn't. I didn't know what I wanted. All I knew is that I couldn't keep doing what we were doing.

We hugged each other for a long time, and I wiped my teary, swollen eyes. He said he was sorry. I said I was sorry, too. We both realized in that moment that something had to change, and for the time being, we decided that the best thing we could do was to change our constantly-on-the-road-together routine.

Thomas Rhett flew off without me the next day to whatever interview he had to do up in New York City. But instead of making it a long weekend, he flew right back home for some downtime at our condo. We went to the park and played with Kona. We spent time with our families. We talked about what we were going through, with my parents, and with Paige and Tim. And they all congratulated us for getting through the first year on the road, just like the counselor had asked of us, but they didn't really have any answers for us about what to do next, other than to remember that we love each other and to try and have some patience.

We went to church on Sunday, and we didn't get answers there, either. A bunch of people came up to us before, during, and after, all wanting to talk to Thomas Rhett, and talk about the album, to ask what Jason Aldean was like in person, and to say how fun it must be for me to be out on the road with him. It made us uncomfortable, and it made us realize that it was maybe time for us to move on to a different church.

Thankfully it was late in the year, and as Thomas Rhett's schedule let up we were able to fall back on some of our other traditions.

We went to Opryland, and we decided to do Christmas morning at my parents' house that year, and we surrounded ourselves with family and friends who treated us like they'd always treated us.

"At least some things never change," I thought.

I craved that normalcy, and so we made the decision that I would stay home a lot more often in the new year, so that maybe when I went to see him in concert it wouldn't feel like *Groundhog Day* to me—like I was living the same thing over and over and over again. Remember, and this is true of most artists, Thomas Rhett and his band were playing the same songs (or something close) every night on the tour. That's just the way it works. There's so much that has to be coordinated with lighting and sound that breaking into an impromptu song with no warning rarely happens. And if I was there for sound check and shows, I could end up hearing the same set twelve times in a week. Thomas Rhett loved it. He never got tired of playing, and he was always trying to make his sets better and better for the sake of the fans. But I don't know any fan that wouldn't get a little bored from hearing the same set over and over after a while. Not to mention the venues, sitting in a concrete dressing room or a secondary sports team's locker room, walking through concrete hallways, sometimes underground, eating catering backstage, night after night. After a few hundred shows, being a spectator kind of got old. It just wasn't me.

We knew that the new year would bring all kinds of new experiences that we'd want to do together. Thomas Rhett would have awards shows to go to, and all kinds of events and big moments we wouldn't want to miss. Which meant I couldn't go out and get a full-time job. I needed to keep my schedule open for these things, and I *wanted* to keep my schedule open for them. I still wanted to support him and his career. I was proud of him, and happy for him, and I *wanted* to be his supportive wife. I just couldn't *only* be the supportive wife.

My whole life I'd been passionate about whatever it was I was doing. I loved life, and I thought I was doing it well by doing it with people I loved. Even if I was just playing kickball on summer evenings, my life always felt full and complete because of all the people in it. Being so close to my family and to our Crew of neighborhood friends and their parents always brought me so much joy. But we realized that being out on the road made me feel isolated.

People would try to make me feel better, saying, "You're his wife. You're doing great supporting him." But it just never fit.

And the worst part of it all was because I was unhappy, I wasn't sure I could ever be fully happy for Thomas Rhett. Even after I came off the road, he would come home so pumped about something that happened to him and I'd react like, "Oh, good for you. Glad you're just cranking out your life and being successful and doing all the fun things you want to do." It was unsettling and I felt irritated, maybe out of jealousy, and we would get into fights over it and he'd say, "I wish you could just be happy for me."

I was mad at myself for hurting him.

"It's not that I'm not happy for you," I'd tell him. "It's that I feel like I'm dying. I feel like my soul is empty."

My words surprised even me. I came to the realization that I felt like I didn't have a real purpose in life. Like I had become an accessory to Thomas Rhett's life. And I was pretty sure that wasn't who I was meant to be. And that hurt.

I didn't want to admit that I was hurting that much, for the longest time, because I felt like it was extremely selfish of me. Yet the hurting was deep, and it was real.

It got so bad, I think I actually started pushing Thomas Rhett away. He started sharing his good news with other people in his life first, before he told me. One time, I heard about a big award he'd been nominated for from somebody else before I heard it from him. When I asked him about it, he said, "The reason I didn't tell you first is because I never know if I'm gonna get a good reaction or a bad reaction from you, and I just want somebody to be happy with me."

Being with our friends and family more often picked me up some and made me smile. And Thomas Rhett and I did have fun together whenever he was off the road. We got Kona a buddy, another big dog we named Cash—after Johnny Cash—and we loved on those dogs so much. We even had some fun occasionally when he was working.

One of the saving graces of Thomas Rhett's career is that country music people are just good people. So many of the big artists we met were people of faith, who cared about their families, and who could talk and laugh about all kinds of things. And most of them were humble as could be. They would invite us over for supper in their back yards, and their houses were in neighborhoods, some of them without fences, or on farm properties filled with love, and animals, and open spaces. They didn't live in ostentatious mansions like you'd see from some of the music stars on *MTV Cribs* in the 1990s or something. Most of the country stars we met were just real, and they made the social aspects of being in this new world easy for both of us. In fact, over the course of the next year or so, we started making new circles of friends in country music the way we did back in high school, or college.

Cash licking Sonic vanilla ice cream off Kona's nose in our back yard

I'll never forget getting dressed up and getting my hair and makeup done, feeling like a million bucks in a borrowed fancy designer dress so I could walk the red carpet with Thomas Rhett at the Country Music Awards. I stepped backward at one point and tripped over Keith Urban's boot. I fell right into Nicole Kidman! I was mortified, and so worried how it would look or how they might react, or how Thomas Rhett might react. I didn't want to embarrass him on the red carpet. But Keith and Nicole just laughed, and we introduced ourselves, and they were just as down to earth as anybody.

Having some industry wives as friends definitely helped me (and us) adjust. Some of them understood exactly where we were coming from and what we were dealing with, because they'd been through it. Some of the wives loved going on the bus, to every show, and they were so happy being full-time fans of their husbands on the road. And others were trying to create a balance of family life, and raising kids, and all kinds of things I hoped were in my future.

Industry besties! Top (L to R): Jesse Frasure, Stevie Frasure, Thomas Rhett, Ford Tomlin, Julian Bunetta, Tyler Hubbard. Bottom (L to R): Russell Dickerson, Kailey Dickerson, me, April Tomlin, Virginia Bunetta, Ali Ryan, Hayley Hubbard

Actually, my desire to reciprocate some of those wives' gracious dinner invitations was one of the many reasons I decided it was time for us to look for a house of our own—and a real estate search definitely gave me a new purpose for a little while. We were barely allowed to decorate the condo we were in, mainly because of the HOA rules, and also because it

All glammed up for
the CMA Awards in 2015

was borrowed from Rhett. We needed to leave it pretty much the way we found it. We couldn't paint it or remodel it—with the exception of the baseboards Kona had chewed on. (Still sorry about that, Rhett.) So as much as we loved and appreciated that space, it never felt like "our" house. Especially since there wasn't a yard for Kona and Cash, or for *us*.

We just had this dream of sitting together under the stars in our own back yard. Was that too much to ask?

Thankfully, once Thomas Rhett's recording career took off, he started making some money. After struggling for a little while, barely making it from month to month, the income from his touring started to flow in, and it came in quick. We were so, so glad to know that we had enough money of our own now to make some *choices* of our own.

We found the cutest little house, in a sweet, quiet neighborhood not far from town—since so much of Thomas Rhett's career required him to be in the studio or taking meetings—and we set our sights on remodeling it to make it feel like ours. It didn't have a back porch, or a front porch, and we knew we wanted one or the other or both. It had a garage, and we thought that might be a great spot to turn into a big living area at some point, too. The house was tiny, but we could afford it, and it had potential. That felt nice to me. Safe. Comfortable. As if one of "our" dreams was coming true: creating our own home.

I started looking into some part-time jobs. I even explored a job in a doctor's office where I could use my nursing skills, but nothing. Every time I got close to saying "yes," I'd end up getting pulled back into Thomas Rhett's world and need to fly off somewhere to be by his side. He never wanted to do any kind of big appearance or interview without me, and eventually it became clear that any kind of a steady job in an office some-where just wasn't going to work out for our lifestyle.

So what was I going to do?

A friend of mine—the wife of another musician—had a successful blog, and I thought, "That's something I could do from home, or out on the road. Wherever I want!" But I never really found my groove.

I tried not to stress about it. I tried to let it go. And as 2014 came to a close, I filled up on the beauty of Christmas. We set up a big, beautiful, flocked tree in our tiny new house, and decorated the whole place with as many lights as our electrical outlets would hold. We woke up every morn-ing feeling thankful for every minute we got to spend drinking coffee out of our Christmas mugs, watching Christmas movies, baking the Pillsbury Christmas cookies that are our favorites, listening to nothing but Christ-mas music 24/7, going to our families' homes, and surrounding ourselves in all the lights at Opryland.

And yet, as we turned the corner into 2015, I still felt lost.

Part of the reason for that, I think, was because our life had become so unstructured. Outside of Christmastime, we didn't have any routines, and any routines we tried to establish were always hijacked by Thomas Rhett's work. It was like there were no boundaries. He had to say yes to everything if he wanted to make it, and that meant he could be called out of town on a moment's notice. It was just too much to navigate.

That's why Thomas Rhett fi-nally talked to Virginia and they decided to stop booking him on Sundays, so we could start going to church on a regular basis again. I was so happy he took that step, and it didn't take us long to find a new church, a more modern church, with a

Loving on Thomas Rhett in a hotel room in New York City

young preacher who had pastored Thomas Rhett in college: a guy who was as comfortable sharing the Gospel in a downtown bar as he was in a church building. For some reason, it was one place where nobody cared to talk about Thomas Rhett's career, which was more than fine with us. Even *he* recognized that he'd been obsessing about his career a little too much, and so taking one purposeful day each week to set his job aside and reconnect with family and rest and spend some more time with God was definitely a healthy choice. For both of us.

Going to church again reminded me of something that I had let go of a little bit as I transitioned into adulthood—the knowledge that I had a bigger support system to call upon than my family, friends, and husband.

Since I hadn't found answers on my own, I buried myself in the Word. I prayed. A lot. I read the Bible, pulling new meaning from verses I'd never really paid attention to when I was younger.

The more I read, the more I started to think seriously about what it was that was truly missing in my life. What was it that was causing me such conflict? It was time for me to do some inner work, which means I started to think about my God-given dreams, and my goals, and my callings, going all the way back to when I was a little girl.

I thought about why I wanted to become a nurse in the first place, and how I wanted to make the world a better place, and how I wanted to travel the world and fulfill that opportunity everywhere I went, in any way I could—all of the things that God put in my heart, that I'd known were in my heart for as long as I'd been alive. But even though I'd been traveling quite a bit with Thomas Rhett, I wasn't interacting with the world very much at all. I didn't feel at peace with the way I'd been living my life almost on autopilot.

None of that was Thomas Rhett's fault. I loved him so much and I knew that I mattered to him, that he loved me, too. He let me know it all the time. He was writing more and more songs about me. Beautiful songs. One of them was about how no matter what else he missed in life, or didn't get to do in life, or didn't get to see in life, he would "die a happy man" as long as he had *me* in his life. It was really beautiful to hear him put his feelings into words like that. Honestly, when he pulled out his guitar in the quiet of our home and played it for me for the first time, my heart about melted. He somehow put into words what it felt like when everything was *right* between us. *Everything.* Dancing in the dark, under stars, under September skies, in the pouring rain. Walking hand in hand. And it wasn't just the romance of the words and the melody and having a song sung for me that made me get emotional. I had been worried that I wasn't helping him enough anymore, and it meant a lot that even through the rough year we'd just had, he still loved me. And I adored him.

It kind of blew my mind that he could so perfectly capture how connected we were through his music.

I just wished I could feel less lost in myself.

"I know you'll figure it out, baby," Thomas Rhett told me. "Just tell me what you need."

Who could ask for a better response from her husband? But I didn't know what to tell him. I really didn't *know* what I needed.

So we prayed to God, repeatedly, asking Him to make his path for me clear.

When the answer didn't come as quickly as I wanted, I tried, once again, to answer the question myself.

We were married, I thought, and we had a house now. So: "What's next? Hmm. Maybe we should start a family?"

Thomas Rhett was like, "Really? Because you're bored? Because you don't know what you want to do? You think bringing a baby into this is gonna make things better?"

I appreciated his bluntness.

He was right. We wanted kids, someday. We'd talked about it a million times. But with him gone so much, working so hard, us going through all of this struggle—the timing didn't make any sense.

"Okay, yeah. You're right," I said. "Good call."

Thomas Rhett had been in the studio a ton that spring of 2015, putting the finishing touches on his second album. He'd been working long days and long nights, and playing concert dates on the weekends.

"Look," he said. "Let's take a break. Why don't we go to Hawaii? Sort of relive our honeymoon. Reconnect."

"Really?!" I said. "Can you take time to do that?"

"Yeah, and we can make it a business trip, too. I dunno."

"What? A business trip?"

"Yeah! We need to film a video and wouldn't Hawaii be cool?" he said.

"Uhhh, not really," I said.

"Look, I love you, and I'm trying to make everything work," he said. "I know the 'business trip' side of it isn't a romantic thing to talk about, and I'm sorry I brought it up like that, but I was talking with my business manager and I want us to be careful and respectful of our money. I know you want that, too. And this way, we get the benefit of making it a working vacation."

"I don't want you to *work* on vacation," I said.

I could not understand how he took the idea of reliving our honeymoon and turned it into some kind of a business transaction in three seconds flat.

"It won't be like that. It's for 'Die a Happy Man.' You know I wrote that song for you. We think it could be the second single off the new album, and they want to shoot a video, and I told them: 'There is no way I'm singing that song to some other girl. The only way I'll shoot a romantic video for that song is if it's with my wife.'"

"Wait, you want me to be in the video *with you*?"

"Lauren, there is no way I can sing this song to anyone but you."

"But I told you, babe, I don't want to be in your videos."

"Let's talk to T.K. about it, and he'll walk you through it. It won't even be like we're shooting a video. It'll be like we're on vacation, and we're getting a professional video diary of our time together. Like a wedding video. We had cameras at our wedding, and they didn't bother you, did they?" he asked me.

"No," I said.

"Well, except for my dad's camo cellphone camera," he said, and we both laughed. Thomas Rhett could always make me laugh. Before I knew it, we were reminiscing about our wedding day, and our honeymoon, and the thought of going to Hawaii seemed *so* nice.

"I don't know," I said.

There was a part of me that wanted to go to Hawaii with him so much, I wondered if this whole video idea might actually be God trying to talk to me in some way. It was so far out of my comfort zone, and I couldn't understand how this was going to fix anything I was feeling, but there was just a little flutter in my heart saying, "Yes. You should do this!"

Kamron looking at the two of us, adrenaline overloaded after we landed from our first time skydiving on Oahu, filming footage that would end up in Thomas Rhett's "Vacation" video

We talked to T.K., and he promised me, "There will never be more than a three-person crew. I'll run camera myself, and I'll need a guy holding the umbrella light or reflector, and you guys can go surfing, and swimming, and maybe we'll have you dress up nice for a little bit and dance together or something, but that's it. It'll be easy. I promise."

And so I listened to that little flutter in my heart, and I took a huge leap of faith that somehow this wasn't going to turn out to be the worst idea in the whole world, and I said "yes."

We flew off to Hawaii, this time to Oahu, and not only did we get to live out my surfer-girl fantasies again, but this time we got to stay at the home of one of our close friends, Michael Trisler. It was so beautiful. We fell asleep in each other's arms with nothing but the sound of the waves and twinkling of the stars above, and everything felt right in our world again.

Once we got out on the ocean, we not only got up on boards this time, but we actually caught some pretty nice waves. Then Trisler took us sky-diving, and we went cliff jumping, and we played on the beach. And T.K. was so great about filming it all, I almost forgot the camera was there.

We ended up getting so much good footage that Thomas Rhett was able to use it for his next video, too, for the song "Vacation." To this day those are my two favorite videos he's ever done.

Thomas Rhett was not wrong. By taking a working vacation together, we were able to recapture some of the magic of our honeymoon. We got lost in the romance of being on boards together in the ocean, and laughing, and forgetting about the rest of the world for a few days. Almost like we were falling in love all over again, and it reminded us how much we wanted to be together in the first place. Even though it was a "work trip," even though we were making videos, being together in Hawaii was nothing but bliss.

When we got back to the mainland and T.K. showed us some of the videos, I was just so thankful. How many couples get to take a professional video of their lives together on any day other than their wedding day? He took all of these gorgeous shots. He caught us talking and smil-

Overlooking the stunning North Shore during the "Die a Happy Man" music video shoot

ing in moments when I truly didn't even know he had been there, and it was such a gift. I didn't know if the video would get views, or if the song would get any airplay, or anything else—and I didn't care. I was just so happy to have some honeymoon-style video of the two of us to look back on one day when we're old and gray.

Taking that trip reminded us that it was a good thing to lighten up a little bit. It reminded us just how much we loved each other, and how much *fun* we had together.

That made it perfectly clear what we needed to do in order to make sure that nothing ever caused us to lose sight of us and who we are: We decided to see a marriage counselor on a regular basis after that trip, not because we were in a crisis, but because we wanted to prevent any sort of crisis from happening. We wanted to make sure our marriage was healthy, instead of waiting and trying to fix it after something broke.

This time we reached out to an organization called Porter's Call, which provides free therapy and mental health services to touring musicians. It's an incredible organization, and they set us up with a counselor named Beth, who helped us to gain some perspective on the fact that we were basically still in the infancy of our relationship. Assuming we were going to be together for the rest of our lives, then this phase, less than three years in, was the early toddler stage at best. "And watch out," she said, "because these years might be the terrible twos, but in the years ahead you'll be . . . *teenagers!*"

It sounded funny, but it was really an eye-opener.

Nobody expects an infant to know everything and not to cry when she's upset. A mom and dad wouldn't give up on their toddler just because he's going through the terrible twos. If this marriage was gonna work, we needed to recognize that we were still figuring this stuff out. We needed to lighten up on our expectations of each other, and give each other a little space and grace to understand that we weren't going to get everything right while we were still wearing married-couple Pull-Ups.

That got me right back to thinking about the message my dad always shared: "We *all* make mistakes."

We all mess up. But as long as we're learning, and as long as we're try-ing to do better and better the next day and the next, that's all that mat-ters.

One Sunday in church that summer, we were singing a song that re-minded me of Isaiah 6:8, a verse in the Bible in which Isaiah looks to the Lord and offers himself to do whatever God's calling may be, saying, "Here I am. Send me!"

I stood there thinking about this message of "take me where it is You want me to be, whatever that looks like," and I realized that for far too long, I'd been trying to control where I wanted to go. Even though I had no idea where I was going, I was trying to dictate the direction of my own path. With the blog, the part-time job search, the prematurely trying to make us start a family, all of it—I was doing it without asking for God's help, or God's direction.

The song was "Oceans (Where Feet May Fail)" by Hillsong UNITED, a powerful song that spent forty-five consecutive weeks in the #1 spot on the Billboard Christian chart in 2014, and the lyrics that spoke straight to my soul that morning were: "Spirit, lead me where my trust is without borders. Let me walk upon the waters wherever You would call me. And take me deeper than my feet could ever wander and my faith will be made stronger in the presence of my Savior."

In that moment, as I sang those words, I felt more than ever, "God, I know that you have a life for me. I know there's a purpose." I fully com-mitted to Him—not to myself, or to Thomas Rhett, or to our marriage, or to my parents, but to God—"God, I'm making a promise to you that if you will just tell me what it is you want me to do, I will do it."

All of a sudden I felt my spirit lift, and I had a peace about my life, as if I had turned over this new leaf. In my heart, I knew: *The Lord has a place for me, and I know He's gonna show it to me. It's just a matter of when and where it's gonna be.*

I set aside my fear, and worry, and put it all in God's hands.

My heart and spirit were so overwhelmed by His presence and power that I started to cry, and I looked down at the ground hoping no one else would see me, thinking, "Gosh, the last thing I need is people thinking that our marriage is on the rocks and I'm crying in church."

Honestly, just the fact that I had that terrible thought, in and of itself, was a pretty clear sign that I wasn't supposed to keep dedicating myself solely to supporting Thomas Rhett's career. Suffering the intrusiveness of that worry, the anxiety I had about what other people might be thinking of me, or of us, that was not how I wanted to live.

I left church feeling ready for whatever God wanted me to do.

And then, just a couple of weeks later, God spoke. Clear as day.

Not in some booming voice, or even a quiet voice in my head.

He spoke to me through an old friend.

13

On a Mission

"Landon!" I called out the moment Thomas Rhett and I walked into the park near our house and spotted him.

I hadn't seen my old friend for close to three years, since he'd gone off to live and work in Turkey, a place that felt like the other side of the world to me.

He was only in Nashville for a few days, and I was so glad he called. The moment we hugged hello and sat down and started talking, it felt like we were right back at summer camp in Texas, all those years ago, finding refuge in friendship in an unfamiliar world.

We caught up about everything we'd both been up to, all of his adventures, and my adventures, and Thomas Rhett's career, and he said, "Lauren, you have really been on my heart so much lately."

"Really?" I said. "How? Why?"

"I just—I know I've been telling you this forever, but I really think that you need to meet my aunt. Y'all have got to get together."

There it was. Again. That strange request of his.

"Gosh, Landon, you've been saying this for years now," I said.

"I know, I know, but I really mean it this time. Like, you *need* to meet her. I just know you two will hit it off, and I feel like it's really important. I don't know why. I just feel like you need to meet her."

"Okay, okay," I said. "Let's set it up."

"So her organization, the one I told you about," he said, "they're going on a medical trip next month to Haiti, and I really think you should go."

"What?" I asked, really not sure why Landon would say that.

His aunt's name was Suzanne Mayernick, and the organization she ran was a Nashville-based nonprofit called 147 Million Orphans, which she co-founded back in 2009. I knew a little about that organization. One of the girls I followed on Facebook, the girl I was a little jealous of for all the mission trips she went on in high school and college, had actually traveled with 147 Million Orphans. I'd seen pictures of her at work, helping children and in some cases whole families, in impoverished countries. The name referred to the estimated number of children affected by the worldwide orphan crisis in impoverished nations, and their mission was to provide food, water, medicine, and shelter, in the name of Jesus Christ.

I had almost forgotten, but 147 Million Orphans used to have volunteers on the UT campus sometimes. Back when I was a student, I'd bought a T-shirt from their information table on the sidewalk to show my support. It made me feel like I was a part of it, even if I couldn't go on the trips.

Now here I was, and Landon was telling me he thought I should go to Haiti with his aunt. "Yes," my heart whispered. "Yes! You have to say 'yes' to this."

My voice responded loudly, "What? No. Definitely not."

"Why not?" Landon said. "You said you're looking for something. I think this might be it."

My heart, which in my opinion was the Holy Spirit talking to me, kept saying, "Yes, definitely, yes! You have to," but my mouth said, "No. I don't know anyone or anything about the trip! That is way out of my comfort zone."

"So was going to Texas," Landon reminded me.

That's when my dad's voice popped into my head: "If you're not willing to take a risk, how do you know what's supposed to come? How do you know what could be if you never take the chance?" And in that moment, mixed with fear, and anxiety, and excitement, and maybe a little kick of adrenaline, I responded, "Okay. Yeah. I'll do it."

"You will?" Landon said. He got all excited.

"Yeah," I said, with this weird sense of confidence and assuredness. "Give me your aunt's email. I'll reach out to her tonight."

Thomas Rhett was kinda quiet. He didn't really respond to this whole exchange.

"Can I text her right now and let her know you'll be in touch?" Landon asked.

"Sure," I said.

The moment I got home I went to the website, and my heart sank. The mission trip to Haiti looked exactly like the kind of trip I'd dreamed about going on for years—but it was scheduled for the last week of September. That was the very same week Thomas Rhett's second album, *Tangled Up*, was going to be released. His calendar was already set, and it was huge. He'd be flying to New York City to be on *Good Morning America*, and then flying to Los Angeles to appear on Jimmy Kimmel, and Ellen, with dozens of radio interviews in between.

Thomas Rhett's anxiousness when it came to making those kinds of big appearances had never really gone away, and he told me again and again, "I love having you there with me to help calm my nerves. I couldn't do this without you, babe."

How could I possibly abandon him on the biggest week of his entire career so far? The one he'd been aiming toward for the past three years of nonstop touring and unbelievably hard work? He'd had three straight singles reach the top of the radio-play chart from his first album, and his song "Crash and Burn," the first single from the new album, had already hit #1 when it was released back in April. So the anticipation and expectations for his new album were huge. Which meant he had every right to be nervous. It wasn't only that I felt obligated to be there, but I wanted to be there—for him and with him.

I almost dropped the whole thing. I thought, "I don't want to distract him. Maybe I should just forget it, and see if Suzanne can maybe bring me on the next trip."

But my heart just wouldn't let it go.

Suzanne sent me a detailed email, and after I read all the information I decided to tell Thomas Rhett when the trip was planned and see what he would say about it. I thought for sure he was gonna tell me, "Please, don't go. I've got so much going on that week." Yet that's not what happened at all.

When I told him that the trip was a medical trip, and that a nurse they needed had canceled on Suzanne just before Landon reached out, and that I would be filling that nurse's spot, Thomas Rhett said, "Oh my gosh, that's *amazing*. And they can get you on the trip with this short of notice?"

"Yes," I said. "Suzanne said they can make it happen, just because they don't have enough medical personnel."

"So you'll be working, like, as a nurse?"

"Yeah. They need someone with my background," I said.

"Then you *have* to go. I mean, it's meant to be, isn't it? You've been wanting to do something like this for so long. I remember you talking about it when we were like fifteen years old. God answered your prayers. You've *gotta* go!"

"Really?" I said.

"Are you kidding me? Yes!" he said.

I reminded him how nervous he tends to get before his TV appearances and big interviews, and he took my hand and he looked me in the eye and he said, "I think you have an opportunity here to do something a little bit more important than holding my hand before I go onstage, don't you?"

"Go," he said. "I'll be fine. This is what you've wanted."

He stayed right with me and looked over my shoulder as I excitedly filled out all the forms and then replied to Suzanne saying, "I'm in!"

She told me there was an information meeting coming up in a week that I needed to be at, and she looked forward to meeting me then.

That was it.

I was committed to going to Haiti. With total strangers. By myself. In less than a month!

That's when the *what ifs* snuck in. What if Suzanne and I didn't get along like Landon said we would? What if I didn't get along with anyone in this group? Was this nuts? Was this dangerous? *What was I thinking?*

I confronted my *what ifs* with prayers, as often as I could, and those prayers kept bringing me back to the very same message from my heart: "You're supposed to say 'yes' to this. This is what you're supposed to do."

The day of the meeting came, and I still wasn't sure what to expect. I walked into a little conference room that 147 Million Orphans was borrowing from a friend's office space. The room was mostly full of women, some of whom were maybe twenty years older than me. I was nervous, like first-day-of-school nervous—when you don't want to go in, but you kind-of do, but still kind-of don't. Landon had told me that Suzanne had short blond hair, blue eyes, and long lashes, and I recognized her instantly. She was talking to somebody, so I waited to introduce myself. Finally, I got the chance to talk to her and I said, "Hey, my name's Lauren," and her little body just popped up out of the chair and she just about bounced over and gave me the biggest hug. "I'm so happy to meet you," she said. "Landon's told me so much about you!" and in an instant, she felt like my long-lost older sister.

Over the course of the meeting it became clear that this was a medical trip, first and foremost, and a service trip second. We were going in to assist a philanthropic organization that was based on the ground in Haiti, full-time. That organization was called Respire Haiti. We would be setting up a clinic at their facility there, and examining and caring for adults and children in a region where medical care was extremely limited. We would also be bringing in a bunch of medical supplies to help restock the dwindling supplies they had on hand.

That was the only time I met with the group before seeing them at the airport as we were leaving for Haiti: my first trip to a new country where I would be staying with complete strangers for a whole week.

The night before our departure I packed my bags. There was no need for heels or dresses or makeup or anything that I would usually pack on a trip with Thomas Rhett. Sneakers, lots of T-shirts, towels, toothpaste, and just the most basic supplies were on the list that the organization had given to me. Overpacking with multiple outfits or the creature comforts of home like I was used to wasn't allowed. Electricity would be limited. So would space.

When we got to the airport, my heart started racing, with excitement, with curiosity, with worry, with doubt. A string of "What am I doing? Why am I doing this?" questions played on a loop in my mind.

Before I left for Haiti, I had spoken about my plans with a few people and they said things that just about scared me to death, warning me that women in places like Haiti get raped, sold into slavery, held for ransom, or worse. And I asked Suzanne about those things, and it turned out they were possible but highly unlikely scenarios that were not to be made light of. There are many countries in the world where foreign travelers face higher risks than they do at home. But Thomas Rhett and I prayed on it together. We prayed for safety and for guidance and for protection from harm and to be able to help the people who needed my help. And we came to the same conclusion Suzanne had come to long ago: At the end of the day, if we're all too scared to go to these countries where our help is needed, then who's going to do it? I had to ask myself: Was I going to let fear, or faith, dictate my life?

The fact is, there are risks we face every day, anywhere, even right here in the United States. And a lot of people's prejudices and fears are just that: prejudices and fears. I am wholly convinced that most people on Earth are not interested in doing harm to anybody else. And while it's never smart to be reckless in a dangerous region, I felt safe knowing that Suzanne and her group of volunteers had traveled to Haiti dozens of times without incident. They knew what to expect, firsthand.

I let that knowledge push all of the other people's secondhand, third-hand, and experience-free opinions aside.

I had dreamed of doing mission work—not evangelical work, not trying to convert anybody, but serving people in the name of Jesus—ever since I was a kid, and my heart really did know my deepest desires. I simply would not be living life to the fullest if I let fear dictate my decisions. I had to have faith and trust that God knew what He was doing in my life, even if I didn't. At this point, there was no turning back anyway.

"Alright," I thought, "I'll make the most of it and then see what comes of it."

And I brought it right back to God: "I'm listening. You've brought me this far. I'll go."

There were a lot of hugs and maybe a few tears as I walked away from Thomas Rhett at the airport, but the moment my eyes met Suzanne's, I was okay. Thomas Rhett loved her instantly, and he felt better about everything once he talked to her in those final minutes before we went to the gate.

Suzanne's spirit was like some kind of a contagious magnet. Suzanne may be little, but she's feisty. She has this loving, momlike, nurturing quality. Landon was so right: Suzanne and I were destined to become best friends.

The flight was less than three hours, mostly over beautiful ocean. I could see the mountains out the window of our plane. From a distance, it all looked so stunning. Haiti is the indigenous name for the country, and it means "land of the mountains." The peaks reach over eight thousand feet, and the location gives it the same sort of beautiful climate that vacationers crave from any other island in the Caribbean. Yet for some reason, Haiti lies in the path of an unusually high number of hurricanes. In 2008 alone, it faced destruction from four tropical storms in a row. And then, as most people know, in 2010 it suffered a 7.0 earthquake that killed more than one hundred thousand people and completely leveled villages that were already struggling. The presidential palace in Port-au-Prince was destroyed, so you can imagine what happened to people's homes made of nothing but concrete blocks and thatched roofs.

It had been more than *five years* since the earthquake hit, and yet the people of this tiny, impoverished country, just a few hours off the coast of the United States, were still living in a state of absolute devastation.

I didn't really understand what that meant until we landed.

It was hot, and the smell hit me in the face the moment I stepped off the plane—this strange mixture of burning trash and human waste, topped with a salty breeze off the beautiful Caribbean sea.

We climbed into an old bus that would take us to the commune of

I took this pic to remind me of the devastation I passed on the streets of Haiti

Gressier, west of Port-au-Prince, where Respire Haiti was located. And as we drove a little closer to the beautiful sea, we could see that the waves lapping the shore were filled with garbage, too. I asked and learned that the only way they had to get rid of the mounds and mounds of rotting trash in Haiti was to burn it, and the smell was sickening.

There didn't seem to be any real towns here anymore. Instead, we drove by pieced-together shacks, and everywhere there were kids in tattered clothes trying to collect drinking water off of sidewalks and alongside the curbs. I could see that the water wasn't safe, even from the relative comfort of our run-down bus. There were pigs wading in that water and little kids running around with no parents anywhere. The bigger kids had smaller kids on their backs, and it looked like they were trying to fill containers with that water to take back to their homes. "To drink?" I wondered. "To bathe in?"

There were conversations happening all around me in the bus as we rode along, but I couldn't hear anything that was being said. I was trying to wrap my mind around what I was seeing.

Where I had grown up, if we'd seen little kids running around by themselves, we'd think, "Where are their parents?" If nobody was watching them, we'd think, "What's going on? How do we fix this?"

Here, there were children, even small children, *everywhere,* and very few parents to be seen. Why were these kids all left alone?

When we arrived at Respire Haiti's headquarters, I was kind of shocked to see that even the mission housing was built from nothing more than cement blocks, like so many of the buildings we'd seen on the drive in. The only difference was these houses had doors, and locks, and guards.

I suppose the locks and guards should have alarmed me, but there was no part of me thinking, "Am I going to be safe here?" All I kept thinking about were the children I'd seen on the sides of the roads, and every part of me kept *screaming,* "How can we help them?"

Our hosts showed us to the room I would share with three other nurses who'd flown in from Nashville, all of whom were close to my age, while the rest of the group was shown to a room across the hall in this guest house built for volunteers who were living in Haiti for a semester or even a year or more at a time. I hoped those volunteers wouldn't think less of me, or any of us, for coming in for just one week.

Thankfully, they didn't. They were happy to have help, in whatever form it came in, and glad to have someone new to talk to. They were all so sweet. I had no doubt that we would become friends, and we did. Most of us are still in touch to this day.

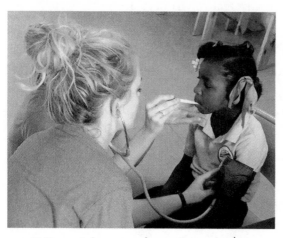

Getting vitals in one of our clinics in Haiti

The housing was very basic, with cracked tile floors, and some running water, but not enough to take a shower. The only baths we were allowed to take were "cup baths," and they were exactly what they sound like. A couple of helpers went out and pumped water from a bore hole out in the front of the building. They put the water in a bucket. They gave us a big cup and we filled it up and that was the water we had to bathe with at night. One cup each night. One time we got a cup and a half of water each and it was amazing how good that extra bit of water felt after going without for even a few days.

I just kept thinking, "This is more than what most people here have been living with for the last five years."

Our job was to set up a clinic at a school in the town of Gressier and to provide medical checkups for anyone who went to school there, or anyone who was part of the community.

I was put to work on my very first day, and it wasn't long before I met a fourteen-year-old boy who was skinny, and sick. He was too terrified to let me take his temperature because he'd never seen a thermometer before. I couldn't speak his language, French Creole, to explain, but through a translator I learned that he walked miles and miles to this school every day, because it was the only place where he could get any food to eat.

I looked into his eyes, full of fear and hunger, and I was stunned at just how much he reminded me of my brother, Grayson. They were about the same age, and the same height, but this boy was so much thinner; he had holes in his clothes, and he was so scared.

If it weren't for the difference of a thousand miles and the fortunate circumstances of where we'd grown up, this boy could *be* my brother, I thought.

"This boy *is* my brother," I realized.

How are we letting our brothers and sisters live like this?

For a moment I started to lose it and had to step outside. The intensity of it all was fierce. I felt a powerful mix of sadness and rage and exasperation and hope and desperation. I tried to take deep breaths, to wipe my tears, and to calm myself so that I could get back to work. Suzanne came out and found me and asked if I was okay.

"I'm sorry. I'm so sorry. I didn't know I would be this way," I said. "I just want to help them all so much. Like, I just got here and I'm already feeling like I can't do enough. I want to do more. I don't understand how people live like this. I mean, why? Why isn't the government helping? Why aren't people helping, way more than we are? Why are they living like this?"

"This is a normal reaction. It's your first time here, Lauren," Suzanne said. "There are things that are so big, so out of our control. But if we can help one child. Just *one*. The ripple effect can make a huge difference in the world."

I knew she was right. In the Bible, in Matthew 25:40, Jesus says: "Truly I tell you, whatever you did for one of the least of these brothers and sisters of mine, you did for me."

I was reminded that I was here for a reason. We were all here in the name of Jesus, acting as his hands and feet in this troubled part of the world. My reason for being here was to do my part. Not everyone's part. *My* part. What *I* could give.

As crushed and sad and upset and shocked as I was by all of the devastation, I pulled myself together and started helping again, just one child at a time. Sometimes it was all I could do to get through the next five minutes with a smile on my face, and with the grace that my mom and dad had empowered me with—the love and the support that I'd known all my life.

"Love one. Love one at a time," I kept telling myself.

I had been filled for so many years with so much love from the friends and family in my life. Now that I had this chance to share my love with these children, I started seeing *all* of the children as if they were my siblings. I can't explain it, but walking through a city made entirely of blocks and sticks and tarps, and looking into the eyes of those struggling children—it changed me.

I was raised with this notion that we should always extend grace to others. That certainly applies to others in places like Haiti. We are all so privileged to live in the United States, and I firmly believe we are blessed to be a blessing. It is our job as humans to take care of each other, and it does not matter if it's in Haiti or right in our hometown. And when we recognize needs in other human beings but then turn a blind eye to it, we are not living the way we were created to live.

And listen, I get it. So often we block things out, especially painful things. Yet if more people could see the lives of these children, if every mom and dad could visit and just see it or share this kind of experience, I thought, there is just no way any parent in our country or any human with a heart could turn a blind eye to it. How could they?

It was all I could do to keep myself from feeling overwhelmed and angry when I thought about how there was only so much we could do. So I threw myself into the work, and I helped however I could.

Outside of setting up the clinic at the school, we made rounds to houses in the area, just in case there was anyone who couldn't—or wouldn't—come to see us in the clinic.

In one house we went to visit, there were two little girls, maybe six or seven years old. They were just there in that house, all day long, by themselves, because their parents had to leave to work. Sometimes the parents wouldn't come back for days, because they had to travel so far to try to make some money. And just as we were getting to the bottom of why these two girls were not at school, we heard a cry and realized there was a baby in the house. The two little girls were taking care of their baby sister when their parents were gone. That's just the way it was, there were no other options for this family. No daycare. No extended-family caregivers. No social services to relieve them.

I admired the fact that these girls' parents were such hard workers, and I had to give them the benefit of the doubt, that they had no choice but to leave their children alone like this. They were clearly doing what they had to do in order to keep their children fed. In that respect, those parents were heroes.

Now, we had to do what we could to be heroes to those kids, too. How could we not?

Seeing those small round faces living in that kind of poverty, it just wrecked me.

Their faces lit up when we brought them food. The few mothers and fathers we saw in the clinic expressed such gratitude for our help in caring for their children. We were making a difference. A small difference, but a difference. For each one of them.

Loving one. One at a time.

I took comfort in that, and I hoped and prayed that every little bit we did caused a ripple that would somehow grow.

As the week went by, the fear of the unknown that bubbled up before the trip faded away, replaced by a love for the heart of the Haitian people.

There was a little coffee shop just down the road in Gressier that we went to for homemade omelets and coffee in the mornings, and the café's owner was

One of my new little Haitian buddies

just so warm and welcoming. She wanted us to enjoy her home, knowing that we were there working to help her people. She poured love into every meal she made, while her little daughter ran around, hopping up on our laps and playing with our hair and bracelets.

Getting to know the families there, it was so clear to me that these were good people who wanted to help their people in any way they could. They lacked resources, but when even the smallest resources were brought in, they put them to good use. They were willing to work, and work hard. And the beauty of their humanity showed everywhere you looked, once you slowed down to take it all in. Everywhere, there were families caring for children who weren't theirs. Neighbors helping neighbors. All they really needed was more money, means, and support for the selfless things they wanted to do, and this entire country could be lifted. Under all of the devastation, Haiti was, and is, a truly beautiful place.

Imagine what would happen if more of us took the time to see it, to take it in, and to do one small thing to make it better.

Suzanne was the embodiment of that. She was such a free spirit, and so much fun to be around, and so fully engaged in her life's work. She rarely let any of it get her down, and she always had a pep talk ready for those of us who struggled more with the emotions of dealing with it all. I'll never forget, on one of our last nights, Suzanne preached a little bit to us, and left us all in tears, feeling the presence of the Spirit of God and so fired up about the mission of the work we'd been doing, and twenty minutes later we were sitting at a little Haitian bar, drinking beer together, and she swore about something and I just laughed so hard. She was just so real, and so alive. "I want to be her when I grow up," I thought.

I wanted to feel that fulfilled, that connected to Jesus, and to be that real with my purpose in life, as well as the loves in my life.

And honestly, it felt like I was at least moving in the right direction.

I thanked God for bringing me to Haiti, and for giving me the courage to take the leap.

The first pic Suzanne and I ever took together,
riding in the back of a truck in Haiti

The Internet service was as spotty as the clean water supply in Haiti. Which meant I couldn't FaceTime with Thomas Rhett to really tell him about any of what I was doing and experiencing, or to talk with him about everything that he was doing back home. Text messages just could not tell the story.

It was hard for me to reconcile: My husband was off in five-star hotels, eating in fancy restaurants, living out his American dream of country stardom and, I'm sure, having the time of his life. I could have been right there beside him, living that life—and in that moment, I wanted to be here more than there.

Not that I didn't want to be with *him*. Not at all. I was so grateful, and I just wished I could share this with him. I *needed* to share this with him. I needed him to be a part of this, in some way, even if we couldn't be here together. I hoped that somehow this mission work would bring us even closer together than we already were.

I made it through the week. I lived without air-conditioning, refrigeration, showers, fresh food, or any of the other comforts we take for granted every single day at home. And as much as I missed my family and Thomas Rhett—and I did, I missed them so much—I wished I could have stayed longer.

I needed to do more.

I had seen the need for these kids to be loved, and to have family and people that cared for them. Some of them needed medical care. Some of them were starving, quite literally, for nourishment, and then some of them were just starving for attention. For a hug. For human contact. For a caring smile.

We take those things for granted, too.

On the flight back home, God spoke to me again. My heart whispered that I had all this love to give, and that I needed to live in that love. Not just my love for my husband and family, but my love for children, and my love for service, and for doing what I can to help.

The Bible talks a lot about doors. Wide-open doors. Doors upon which God wants us to knock. Doors that God opens that cannot be closed.

I realized that I had spent the past couple of years struggling, trying so hard to find my purpose, to find what I could give to the world. I'd been praying, essentially, "God, show me the door and I will walk through it!"

This was my door.

I decided to speak it. Out loud. I told Suzanne, "Listen, I know this was only my first trip, but I know that this is what I'm supposed to be doing.

My heart needs to serve. I want to be a voice for these kids, or just to love 'em at least. To help love on the ones I can reach, just like you said. Whatever that looks like, wherever it is, whenever it is, I wanna go. Thomas Rhett knows I've been trying to find this for a while. We've been praying about it for a long time, so I know he'll understand."

She said, "Well, if you want to do this on a regular basis, it's going to be a lifestyle change, for sure. It's not easy and it's certainly not a glamorous life."

"I know. But it's what I need to be doing. I think this is why I'm here. To maybe help be a voice that can speak to people back home about these children, or just to love them wherever I go."

I wasn't really sure what I meant by saying I wanted to be "a voice." I'd done all I could to stay out of the spotlight. This wasn't Thomas Rhett's cause, so I really didn't know what I could do. "Why would anyone even listen to me?" I wondered. But I knew I had to at least try and help, and try to do what I could to love the children I could reach.

"I want to be there with you. In all of it. I want to help you with the organization or fundraising if I can, back home, on top of the mission trips," I told her. "Wherever you go, whenever you go, I want to be there. If you book a flight, book me a seat right next to you."

Suzanne had the biggest smile on her face, and she agreed to book me with her on the next mission trip to Haiti, which was happening in just a couple of months. "And after that," she said, "we'll be heading to Uganda."

"Uganda? In Africa?" I said. "Are you kidding me? I'm in!"

Suzanne giggled in her little Suzanne way, all giddy and excited to see my heart so full over these trips and these children.

"Are you sure, Lauren? Don't you think you should talk to Thomas Rhett first?"

"Suzanne, I am telling you: I am sure."

14

Blessing

Something crazy happened while I was in Haiti: I got famous.

Well, kinda famous. Like, Internet famous.

I had no intention of getting *any* kind of famous. It just happened. And it wasn't because of the volunteer work I was doing.

Thomas Rhett released his second single just after his album came out, and just like he'd talked about doing way back in the spring, the single he released was "Die a Happy Man." Which meant that he released the video we'd made to go with the song—the beautiful, romantic video T.K. shot with the two of us on Oahu—and for some reason, our video became a bit of a viral sensation. In no time flat, it was viewed more than a hundred million times.

This very personal song that my husband had written went #1 on the country airplay chart and stayed there for six weeks in a row. It became Thomas Rhett's very first #1 single on the Billboard Hot Country chart as well. Before we could even wrap our minds around all of that, it sold over a million copies, went five times platinum, and then hit #1 on the country charts in Canada, too.

As soon as I got back, I met up with Thomas Rhett in Las Vegas, of all places. Which meant I went from serving in an impoverished country to landing in a city full of gaudy displays of excess and what felt like wasted wealth. My heart couldn't handle it. I felt so conflicted. At one point I locked myself in the hotel bathroom and just cried and cried. How could I reconcile this life I was living with everything I had just seen? I'm not sure that struggle will ever go away.

Thomas Rhett was so glad to see me when I got there, and I was so excited to see him, too, we just couldn't wait to tell each other everything we'd both been through over the course of our week apart. He told me all about *Good Morning America,* and Kimmel, and Ellen, and how crazy it was to watch the views keep going up on the video, and how he'd posted something on Instagram after he'd been on TV, and more than ten thousand people liked it in a matter of *minutes*—and I was so, so happy for him. And then his jaw dropped when I fully described what I'd done and seen in Haiti. He got a little scared for me when I told him about the crumbling buildings, and the burning trash, and the security guards; and his heart broke when I told him about the fourteen-year-old boy who reminded me of Grayson, and the two little girls who were caring for their baby sister, and he was just so proud of me for everything I'd done, and so excited that I wanted to go back and do more. He knew his travel schedule wouldn't allow him to come with me, especially after the success of "Die a Happy Man" and all the new requests he was getting to make appearances and play concerts, but he offered to help in any way he could.

It was strange: Being apart for that week while we were both doing things we loved and felt so passionate about, it's like we came back together and we were somehow closer than we'd ever been before. The two of us just got all tangled up in how happy we were to be back together and alone in the comfort of our little house, even if it was only for a couple of days before he had to head right back out on the road.

Before we knew it, it was Christmastime again—and it turned out it was a little bit of a chore to go to Opryland with our family. Every ten feet people were stopping Thomas Rhett and asking us to take pictures with them. Not just him. *Us.*

"No, no, no. We want Lauren in the photo, too! Please?"

I was used to fans asking me to hold the camera and take the picture. I was used to professional photographers at red-carpet events shouting at me to move out of the way so they could get their magazine-worthy shots of my country-star husband.

That all changed after "Die a Happy Man."

Suddenly, Thomas Rhett fans were talking about me on social media. My Instagram, which had mostly been used to share pictures with family and friends, blew up with thousands of new followers every day.

Total strangers started responding to the posts I made. And when I posted about my work with 147 Million Orphans, lots of strangers responded to that, too.

It was *wild*. Because of my posts, traffic increased on the 147 Million Orphans website, and their Facebook and Instagram pages started to blow up. Not only did awareness increase, but donations and merchandise sales increased as well.

It felt like God just opened up a channel for me to help in ways I couldn't ever have imagined.

It was weird, though. I was flattered sometimes and, to be quite honest, annoyed sometimes. All the magazines I'd grown up looking at suddenly ran pictures of the two of us, and wanted to set up interviews with the two of us, and people started tagging us in Instagram posts with the hashtags #MarriageGoals and #RelationshipGoals. People were like, "Oh, we wanna be *that*. That's what every couple should aspire to be in *life*." And it was really cool at first, like, "Wow, people think our love story is sweet. They think that we're such a cute couple." But then it didn't let up. It was almost like some kind of an obsession. I wasn't sure how comfortable I was with people looking to us as role models. It was surreal. And I understood that none of them knew the full story, the real story of our marriage.

The fact that we had stayed true to who we were, stayed true to our values, that we'd lived in love and shown our love to the world, ended up being a bigger part of Thomas Rhett's success than anyone could have ever predicted.

Weirdly, even though the whole world now knew us as a married couple, some girls out in public seemed to become even more aggressive in their flirting with my husband. These older women would even walk right up to him and grab his arm and pull him away from me and go, "Oh my gosh, I just *love* you." I won't even tell you some of the things some young girls said on Twitter about what they'd like to do to him. And at a Halloween concert that year, two girls who were barely wearing any costumes at all jumped up onstage and started touching him and trying to dance all over him—while I was standing right there on the side stage watching.

"Security got rid of 'em as quick as they could. And you know I'm not interested in other girls," Thomas Rhett told me. "You know that. Please don't let it bother you."

But it *did* bother me. A lot.

There were parts of this business that still *really* bothered me.

When those kinds of crazy things happened, I found myself praying something I could not believe I was praying: "God, please just take us out of this business. We don't *need* this!"

And yet, God never did that.

Both of us in complete shock when Thomas Rhett won Single Record of the Year at the ACM Awards

In fact, on April 3, 2016—the night of the Academy of Country Music Awards—"Die a Happy Man" won ACM Single Record of the Year.

There are certain awards that hold more meaning than others in the record industry. We've all seen Best New Artists fade and never have another hit in their lives. There are other awards that are more a tip of the hat to the producers and executives who created a sound or signed an artist to a deal. But the Record of the Year categories are huge. They're the kinds of awards that mark the arrival of a major artist—one whose career is likely destined to last a long, long time. At least, that's how Thomas Rhett and his manager, Virginia, and a few other people on his team described it.

It was, for a musician, and especially for a songwriter, a major dream come true.

That's the reason Thomas Rhett was so pumped up and felt like partying all night long.

And that's the reason I stopped in the middle of our celebration, took a look around at everything that was happening, and asked the same question that had nagged at me since shortly after we got married: "What about *my* dreams?"

I was genuinely thrilled that Thomas Rhett had received this kind of acknowledgment from the industry that meant so much to him. He deserved it, and I was so proud of him, and so proud to be *with* him.

I was also thrilled that I'd found a calling in working with Suzanne, and that my little brush with fame had brought a lot of really positive attention to 147 Million Orphans. Beyond that, though, I just couldn't understand what God was up to. Why was He doing this? What was His plan? What was He trying to tell us? How was any of this going to lead to Thomas Rhett and me starting a family, or enjoying the sort of simple life I'd longed for since I was a little girl? The life we'd both enjoyed so much before we were married? I mean, Thomas Rhett was starting to write songs about that simple way of living, but what he wrote was nostalgic, as if that life was all gone and he wished we could get it back.

I couldn't help but wish that this was somehow leading us someplace good.

Actually, I prayed about it: "Thank you for Thomas Rhett and for helping all his dreams come true. But please, God, help us and guide us as we walk through these brand-new doors you keep opening."

★ ★ ★

Thomas Rhett went on a whirlwind of press appearances and concerts after that night at the ACM Awards. And within a few days, I was packing a suitcase for my first-ever trip to Uganda.

Suzanne had prepared me for the trip. First of all, she warned me that it would be a really long flight: thirty-two hours of straight travel time just to *get* there.

Second, she clarified that this would truly be a service trip. The four of us who were going wouldn't be focusing on medical care quite as much as doing an assessment of needs: physical needs, medical needs, monetary needs, supply needs, and more, in the children's home that 147 Million Orphans supports on the ground.

Third, she prepared me for the conditions. In the United States, when people picture an orphanage they tend to imagine something out of *Little Orphan Annie*. The children's home we would be working at in Uganda wouldn't be that. Instead, she said, it was a group of mostly cement buildings in the city of Masindi, surrounded by a big cement wall that goes all the way around the children's home. There was no air-conditioning. There was only sporadic electricity. There were maybe two lights in the whole place, and there would be somewhere close to two hundred kids there when we got there. That's in part because the facility is also a boarding school. Some of the kids there, of varying ages, had families, but their families couldn't afford to take care of them. So they sent them to this boarding school so they could get food, and an education, and occasionally some clothes. But some of the children there were truly orphans, abandoned children or children whose parents had died, who now had no family to take care of them at all. We would be meeting some of those children who had just recently come in.

In truth, nothing could have prepared me for the experience of walking into that children's home.

After thirty-two hours of travel and a short night's sleep at the hotel, the next morning we pulled up to our destination. Suzanne hopped out of the van and got right to work, giving me a brief tour as she said hello to the staff. A whole bunch of kids recognized her right away. I walked around in a bit of a jet-lagged haze, noticing the fine red dirt that covered just about everything. Every floor. Every surface. I could feel myself breathing it in with every step we took.

There was a girls' area and a boys' area, and both were crammed full of metal bunk beds all lined up on the poured-concrete floor. They were draped in mosquito nets, but those nets all had holes in them. One of our missions on this trip was to count the mattresses that needed replacing, because when you ripped them open—as Suzanne showed me firsthand— the bedbugs scattered everywhere.

Yet I looked around at the faces of the kids who were living there, and they were all smiles. They looked like the happiest kids in the world. One little boy had a hole in his shorts, right on the seat of them, and he didn't have any underwear on. I asked someone about it and they said those were the only shorts he owned. He wore them every day. This was a middle-school-aged child, and I just kept thinking, "At that age, if my hair wasn't parted the right way I got embarrassed." But he seemed as happy as could be.

Everything depends on perspective, doesn't it?

Suzanne showed me to the bathrooms, and as soon as we walked in, the smell triggered my gag reflex. I held my breath and covered my mouth with my hand. It was hard for me to comprehend the fact that this was the best housing available to the orphaned children who had no families to speak of, and maybe the best housing available to any of the children who attended the boarding school, too.

There are no words I had ever read, no scenes in any movie I had ever seen that prepared me for experiencing these conditions with my own five senses. For whatever reason, we have this ability as humans to block things out. I had seen documentaries and commercials on TV for non-profit efforts in this part of the world, which had made me think, "Oh gosh, that is so sad." Yet I never felt the alarm, the sense of urgency, and the profound responsibility to do something about it until I walked on the red dirt and concrete floors in Uganda myself.

I was twenty-six years old when I set foot into that space for the first time. I'd been on this Earth for a little more than a quarter of a century, and was only just now fully grasping how much work there was to do for so many children.

I tried not to get overwhelmed by it all, the way I had in Haiti, but it was truly overwhelming. There hadn't been an earthquake here. No one was trying to rebuild after a hurricane. Because of the broken economies and governments riddled with corruption, combined with the limitations on transportation, poor health care, food shortages, and poor water supplies, this was how life *was* here.

All the time.

"Just one," I reminded myself. "One at a time. Love and care for just one. It'll make a difference."

"Let's go into the office and I'll introduce you to everyone," Suzanne said.

As we walked toward the office in the back, I noticed a baby laying on her stomach on the cement floor. There was red dirt all over her. She was dressed in a little onesie, laying there all by herself. No mattress. No blankets. She didn't look old enough to even roll herself over.

"Is that where she plays?" I wondered.

It was filthy.

It made me so sad, but I just walked right past her. Some part of me didn't want to pick her up. I'm not sure why. My normal instinct had always been to pick up any baby I saw. Especially one laying on the floor. Maybe it was all just a little too much for me to take in all at once.

That afternoon, after assessing how many diapers we needed to buy, and how many mosquito nets needed replacing, and meeting the staff full of warm and welcoming men and women who seemed so thankful to have us there, I ended up playing with some of the older kids, both inside the buildings and out in the yard. And I kept seeing that little girl, wondering what her story was, and wondering who was taking care of her.

It turned out she wasn't the only infant that had recently come into the children's home, and some of the staff weren't used to dealing with children who were so young. We would end up spending hours over the next couple of days educating some of the caretakers on what they needed to be doing for these babies: how they ought to be feeding them, how often

The children's home in Uganda

they needed to sleep. We showed them ways to keep them from rolling off tables and getting hurt when they changed their diapers, and all the kinds of things new mothers are taught in basic parenting classes back home. We showed them how to make formula properly, and explained its nutritional value. We even taught them basic hygiene for babies, and I held some of the other children as Suzanne showed them what to do.

For some reason, though, I never held that little girl I'd seen on the floor.

Suzanne, the other two volunteers in our group, and I slept in a comparably comfortable setting of the Masindi Hotel, less than two miles from the children's home, and I wished we could have taken all of the children to sleep there with us. Truly. It broke my heart, and I wanted to do everything I could to help improve their surroundings as soon as possible.

"We'll get there," Suzanne told me. "One step at a time."

When we were wrapping up our work with the staff on the second day, I went outside thinking I might go play with the bigger kids again, but Suzanne stopped me and said, "Hey, will you hold her for a sec?" She was holding the little baby I'd seen on the floor. "I need to go show them something," she said. "Here," and she handed me that baby girl and walked away.

"Uh, okay," I said—and the moment she handed me that five-month-old baby, I felt something.

It was instantaneous, and overwhelming. She was just such a sweet, sweet baby—and she was so scared. She stared at me all wide-eyed, but never once cried. And I smiled and touched her face with my hand, and she smiled back, and my heart just about melted.

I really can't explain why I had avoided holding her before that moment, but I wonder if part of me knew that once I did, I wouldn't be able to let her go.

Suzanne came back a few minutes later to take her back, and I was like, "No, no. I'll take care of her. I'll hold her. Y'all go do what you need to do."

I wish I could explain it, but I felt such an overwhelming *responsibility* for her. I just wanted to protect her and cuddle her and never put her down.

I took a selfie while holding that little girl, and I posted it on Instagram when I had a free moment. I wanted my parents and Thomas Rhett and everyone I knew to see her, to see how beautiful she was.

"What is her story?" I asked her caretakers. "Where is her family?"

"She has no family," they said. "We've tried and tried to find anyone related to her, and we have found no one."

"No one?"

"No. There was a full investigation, and nobody has come forward."

They called her "Blessing."

"Blessing." What a beautiful word to describe her, I thought.

She had a cough when she came in and in fact, the first test they ran showed that she was positive for HIV. Later tests came back negative, and it was explained to me that a false positive in an infant can sometimes be an indication that the mother had the disease. HIV is still a major issue in Uganda, and there are still lots of taboos and prejudices around those who have it.

All I saw when I looked at her was a sweet little girl who deserved to be loved. As she slept in my arms toward the end of that day, as the sunset lit up the red dirt all around us, I held that baby, and held her, and held her, and I just couldn't stop thinking about her future: "Okay. So, she has no relatives. Which means *this* is her future. Period. Unless somebody takes her in, this is all she's got."

Some of the kids in the boarding school had family members who they might see at holidays or on special occasions. But the kids who were truly orphaned, only occasionally would they find a home. Every once in a while an American or European would go through the adoption process and take a child in. It didn't happen often, Suzanne told me. I just could not fathom what would happen to this baby girl if she were to stay in the children's home for her whole childhood. Somewhere deep in my heart I felt like it was up to me to help her find a real home. And I committed to doing something about it that very night.

I was able to get on FaceTime with Thomas Rhett late that night, and I expected to hear all about the big show he'd played that afternoon, but instead, all he wanted to talk about was the picture I'd posted on Instagram.

"Babe," he said. "I've never seen a more beautiful baby, and it looks like you're glowing. Tell me about that baby."

I thought, "Perfect. That's exactly what I wanted to talk to you about."

So I told him all about her. How they'd searched for any possible relatives. How she had no one in the world except for the caretakers here, and how this children's home was *it* for her unless she found someone to adopt her.

"We know so many people where we're from," I said, "so many people who are ready to have kids, who've gotten married and have said they might want to adopt some day. And this baby, she is just *precious*. I know we can find her a home. I just know it. One of our friends, or a friend of a friend, we just have to find her a home."

And without even skipping a beat, I mean, with no hesitation, Thomas Rhett said, "We'll do it. *We'll* bring her home."

"What?" I said.

"Maybe she's meant to be our daughter," he said.

I never expected him to say something like that.

The picture and moment
that started it all: my first
moment with "Blessing"

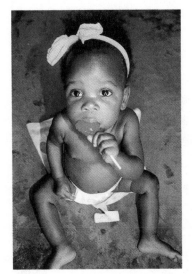

The sweetest little baby ever,
Willa Gray, eating a "sweetie," as
it's called in Uganda

Cuddling my sweet baby
one more time before heading
to the airport to fly back home

All my life I had thought I would like to adopt someday. My mom being adopted made me a by-product of a healthy, loving, adoptive family. Granted, my mom's white and her parents are white, and they were all born and raised in the same country, so it's not exactly the same thing as adopting a baby from Africa, but I'd always thought, "Maybe one day I'll adopt, too, and help to create a happy, loving home for a child in need of a family."

Thomas Rhett and I had talked about adopting before. It had been something we considered as a direction our family could take, and although he had never shot it down he was never like, "Oh my gosh, yes, let's adopt!" So I just kind of thought, "You know, if it's meant to happen, it'll just happen one day."

Never, ever, in a million years did I think that day would come so soon. And I definitely didn't expect that Thomas Rhett would be the one to take the initiative on it and say, "Yes, we will adopt her. We'll bring her home! We can do this! We have so much love to give!" Which left me thinking: "Who *are* you? Like, what are you even *talking* about?"

I don't even think I had a response for him at the time. I was just so shocked.

"Whoa, whoa, whoa. Okay," I said. "Well, I don't know about that, but we can definitely talk about it."

"I think we should do it, Lauren," he said. "I don't know why, I just feel like we're supposed to do this."

"Well, at the very least," I said, "we agree that we need to find her a home."

Before I left from that trip, I paid the fees that were needed to start the paperwork for the international adoption process. We also committed to financially support this child until she got to a safe home.

I prayed for the other kids in the children's home as well. Was the work we were doing enough? Were we being helpful? I kept seeing all of their beautiful faces in my mind. But I kept coming back to the idea of "Love one. Just one at a time."

* * *

When I told Suzanne about my conversation with Thomas Rhett, she was all for the idea.

"You can do this!" she said, encouraging me and Thomas Rhett to think about adopting this baby girl ourselves.

Suzanne had adopted a child from Uganda herself about six years earlier, her precious daughter, JosieLove.

"Laur, I won't lie to you. It's going to be tough," she said, "but I'm here for you. Go home. Talk about it. If this is what y'all feel like God is really telling you to do, I will stick by your side through all of it. I've walked this journey before, so I know what it's like."

I said goodbye to that sweet baby and made the thirty-two-hour trek back home at the end of April, and neither Thomas Rhett nor I really spoke to anybody else about what we were thinking. We wanted to make up our minds first about whether or not we should try to adopt her ourselves, which meant we began talking to each other about it all the time.

Faced with the reality of life at home, we had doubts. Big doubts. *So many* doubts.

We just weren't sure we were ready to start raising a five-month-old child. We had been thinking about starting a family for a while, and for the last six months we had *not* been taking steps to prevent it, just to see what would happen. But if I'd gotten pregnant, we'd have had nine months to prepare ourselves for a baby to come into our lives. This was different. So we questioned whether we were really ready. Yet the more we talked about it, the more we prayed about it, we both felt God speaking to us about this little girl in Uganda, and telling us that He would take care of all the details.

Even then, adopting her felt like such a huge decision—way beyond anything either of us had any experience with at all. It was tough. We felt like our hearts were in the right place, but we really needed to work this thing out, and maybe we needed a clear sign that this was what we were supposed to be doing.

So we did what we usually did when we had trouble with a decision in our marriage: We called our counselor, Beth.

"Okay, so, we've had this situation come up. We're not really sure what we should do about it," we told her. Then we shared a list of our concerns.

"One: Is this the right thing for this baby? I'm just going to be blunt about this, but we're worried about whether we're prepared or educated enough about what it means for white parents to raise a black baby. What will it mean for *her*?"

We knew the color of her skin meant she'd face challenges that we might not know how to help her navigate. I was anxious about all of the things I simply didn't know as a white mother, and whether I would be capable of handling everything this baby needed.

"Two: How is this gonna work with Thomas Rhett's career? And how will the adoption process work with his career? I mean, are we thinking about this clearly? Will he have the time to be able to go through an international adoption while on tour? Plus, all the attention from his second album isn't letting up. It's only getting stronger. What is all that attention going to do to this baby and her life?

"Three: Are we even ready to get into this? We don't know if we're ready for this. We don't know if we can even do this. What kind of parents are we going to be? Are we sure we're ready to adopt first? Because, how do we even know we're going to be good parents? What if we suck at this thing, and then we're bringing a child into our home who doesn't get to choose, knowing someone else could have taken her in? At least our biological kids, we're just what they get, you know? If you're taking another child into your home, though, it's a different story. What if we're just not good enough parents?"

We were panicking.

Beth listened attentively and caringly, like she always did, and then she just about laughed out loud at the both of us.

"Oh my gosh," she said. "I'm not worried about y'all not being good parents. It's just a matter of, 'Is this your child or is it not?'"

She could tell we were both just so scared. So Beth said, "You know, y'all just need to be very intentional about praying for this answer."

So we started to pray seriously about it at that point, and we prayed for a very clear sign.

In mid-May, Thomas Rhett was off doing a gig somewhere and I was coming home from Paige and Tim's house, where I'd been at the pool that day. I was driving back home late at night and I was so tired and so ready to go home. I was on the phone with Thomas Rhett when I remembered it was our friend Russell Dickerson's birthday.

Russell, who's a country artist, too, and his wife, Kailey, had become two of our really good friends. To find a couple in the music industry who shared our faith felt like a blessing, and we clung to them hard. They had asked me to come by the bonfire they were having at their place. It was about 11:00, and I was at a red light where I could either turn one way to go to their house, or the other way to go home. Right at that moment I got a text from Kailey saying, "We're still up! Come on over." And I just got this feeling.

"You know what? I think I'm gonna go," I said.

"Where?" Thomas Rhett asked.

"To Russell's house."

"Why?"

"I don't know. I'm just gonna go."

"What? That doesn't sound like you."

"Well, no, but I'm just going to."

"Alright, well, drive careful. I love you. I'll talk to you tomorrow."

"Alright, love you too. Bye."

So I hung up the phone and drove to Russell's house, where the party was still going strong. Kailey and I started talking, and every time I talk to Kailey, it always gets to be real talk, real fast. So I went upstairs with her to grab something out of her bedroom and I really wanted to tell her about everything that was on my mind, but I hesitated.

Kailey has dreams. Prophetic dreams. Since I'd known her, some of the dreams she had that came true were just insane. The details were just spot-on. So I asked her, "Have you been having any dreams lately? Maybe, say, dreams of me having a baby?" And she was like, "What?!"

"I was just wondering if you'd gotten anything lately. And if you do, would you let me know?"

She started laughing and asked me, "What is going on?" So I told her the whole story about what we were trying to decide, and then I asked if her and Russell could just be praying about it because we needed an answer.

"Absolutely," she said. "We will!"

We walked back downstairs and went outside to the bonfire. On the other side of the fire there was a girl. She had a cigarette in one hand, a whiskey glass in the other, and she kept looking at me from across the fire. I'd just watched her shotgun a beer, so I was sitting there thinking, "I think this girl may be drunk."

I continued to talk to Kailey, but it was hard not to notice that this girl kept staring at me. It looked almost like she was angry at me or something. Then before I could even say anything, she looked directly at me and said, "I gotta tell you something."

"Okay," I said, a little intimidated and caught way off guard. I was thinking I wanted to say to this girl, "Listen, I don't know what you think I did, but I am not that girl. I am not dramatic. I don't want you to think that I've been looking at *you* weird, I just saw you've been staring at me and thought it was a little weird, that's all." Yeah, I completely chickened out. Me being Miss Nonconfrontational, I just waited to hear what she wanted to say.

That's when Kailey got this serious look on her face and looked at this girl and said, "You got a word?"

"What?" I said. "You got a *word*? What does that mean?"

"This is my friend—" Kailey started to say, but the girl interrupted.

"God wants you to know that you can't fit Him into a box," she said.

"Okay," I thought. "This girl is definitely drunk."

She continued: "He's telling you, 'I'm so much bigger than that. You have this idea of what you think I can do and what things should look like. You have no idea and you have to get Me outside of this box that you have created for Me in your head.'

"God needs you to know that He sees you right now, standing on this cliff, and you're thinking about whether or not you should jump off. And you're close, you're really close to jumping, but you just don't know if you should do it or not."

At this point I'm thinking, "This girl's lost her ever-loving mind!"

Then she said, "Well, God is telling you that you have to jump."

"Okaaaay," I said, with complete skepticism, bordering on sarcasm.

"God is telling you to jump off this cliff and to not be afraid," she continued. "God has put you in the position to do this, because He needs the world to see what you're doing."

At that point I looked at Kailey, like, did she somehow tell her something about what I was thinking about in the last ten minutes? Because I hadn't even seen them talking, and I had told Kailey all of that in confidence!

But Kailey closed her eyes and just said, "Yes, girl. Yes!" to everything this girl was saying.

She looked me right in the eyes. "You're trying to make this decision, right?" she said.

"Yeah."

"It's a life-altering decision, right? I mean, life-altering—implying somebody's life."

"Mm-hmm. Okay, I'm listening," I said.

"He's paving a path for you. You think you're living in someone else's shadow. Whatever's happening in your husband's career, you think that it's happening for him. You and your husband think that his career is there to make a way for *him,* but what you don't realize is that God put your husband in his career path to make a way for *you*—because the world needs to see you do this."

"What?"

So now I start to get really freaked out.

"If you do not take this step, your husband's faith is never going to change. Your heart is there. His is not. He is doubting."

"What is your husband's name?"

And I said, "Thomas."

"Do you know whose name is like his in the Bible?" she asked.

"Yeah," I said. "Doubting Thomas."

She nodded. "Exactly. God is telling you the next step may hurt, or postpone, or cramp your life, but it is what your husband needs for his faith to grow. You have experienced and known the Lord's love. He doesn't yet know the Lord's true love. He's telling you, 'Do not be afraid. Have faith.' It's going to look wrong to some people. You're going to think it might keep you from going to the next level. You're going to think that it's going to stop you, but it's actually going to change lives."

She went on, and got more specific. "There are all these worries that the two of you have—mostly him," and she started listing off all of the things we had spoken to our counselor about. All of them. Things we hadn't spoken to anyone else about at all. I'm telling y'all, she listed them off in perfect order. Verbatim. And then she said, "God needs you to know: He's already taken care of all of it."

At that moment, I'm pretty sure all of the blood just went out of my face.

"What does your husband do?" she asked.

I told her.

"Okay, I don't know who that is. Is that a big deal?" she asked me.

She was originally from Australia. She didn't listen to country music. She did not know who we were.

It was mind-blowing. *Mind-blowing.*

She said that was all she had, and she walked away, and Kailey explained that she knew the whole time that this girl was a visionary who had the gift of prophecy. I didn't know anything about that kind of stuff. I grew up Church of Christ, where you don't even talk about those things. There were people in our church who thought visionaries were touched by Satan himself. I'd encountered a little bit of voodoo, faith-healing type of stuff when I was in Haiti, and it scared me a little bit, I'm not gonna lie.

Well, let me tell you, when somebody comes out and spits that kind of detail and truth right out in your face, there is no way you can't talk about it.

As I drove home that night, my mind was spinning. When I got home, I tried to write down everything she said because, I thought, "I'm never gonna remember all of this."

The more I started to think about it, the more it started to kind of make sense. It would make sense that people would think my husband's career was for him, of course. But then, at that time, "Die a Happy Man" had done its thing and people were looking to me, like, "Why are you starting to have such a big following when you don't even *do* anything?"

The part that really got me, though, was when she said: "Whatever it is you are worried about, God has already taken care of it."

I couldn't stop thinking about it.

Our days and nights had been spent worrying and praying a lot lately, and it was draining both of us and making life feel really heavy—and it felt to me like this girl had been sent to us for a reason.

The next morning I called Thomas Rhett and I told him everything, and he said, "You've got to be kidding me."

"I just know it, Thomas Rhett. God sent her to share this," I said. "God wants us to do this. This was the sign we had asked Him for! What if we chose to deepen our faith and to believe in love and the love God has for us and the love we have for each other and the love that God would want us to share with this little girl?"

Could we do this?

Somehow, talking it out that morning with Thomas Rhett, it was like the clouds parted and a light of clarity shined down from heaven onto the both of us.

"It's funny," he said, "because I woke up thinking about that picture of you, that very first picture, and how comfortable and content you looked, and she looked, and the first thought I had was, 'Yeah. That's our little girl.'"

"Thomas Rhett," I said. "You believe she's our baby?"

"I mean, yeah," he said. "I think she is."

"Oh my gosh," I said. "She's our baby. *She is our baby girl!*"

15

Our Baby

The long flights back to Uganda that summer felt twice as long as they had the first time around, just because I wanted to get back there so bad. To hold our baby girl in my arms and to let her know that she would now have a family to call her own.

Thomas Rhett and I told our families all about our decision, and they were so happy for us. Of course our parents, and even some friends, expressed concern about whether we'd thought this through, and how much it was going to cost, and whether we were ready to raise a child who'd come from such a different community, and we told each and every one of them, "Whatever it is y'all are worried about, God has already taken care of it."

I would say those words out loud quite a bit before we were through.

I would doubt them at times.

Thomas Rhett would doubt them even more than I did.

Neither of us had any idea what we were getting into.

Standing in the red dirt, holding this baby girl in my arms was the most miraculous feeling in the world. I felt in my heart and in every cell in my body that she was our child now.

We had already decided on a name for her: Willa Gray. Willa came from Thomas Rhett's Papaw, Willard, who had been such a rock for our family. He was a source of strength and support for so many of Thomas

Rhett's relatives and we wanted this little girl to have that sort of strength and support with her, always. Gray was short for Grayson, my little brother. I had a circle of girlfriends back home who would be my prayer warriors, who got together and made bracelets with Willa Gray's name on them, so that each of us would be reminded to pray for Willa Gray every day.

Knowing that our daughter was living in that children's home only made the urgency of our 147 Million Orphans mission all the more real, and all the more pressing. As much as my heart went out to every child in that orphanage and every child in that school, and as much as I trusted the hands of those amazingly dedicated caretakers who lived there full-time, the idea that I was going to be leaving Willa Gray behind on those floors, on those mattresses, under those mosquito nets every time I had to go back to the States, made every bit of what we were trying to do there seem so much more important.

That summer, Macy flew to Uganda with me and Suzanne, which meant my sister was the first person in the family to meet Willa Gray. That trip was a service trip, where we got busy repainting things and ran a Bible school for kids in the children's home. We were able to replace all the mattresses on that visit, and seal them in rubber covers to keep the bugs out for good. My sister and I were down on our hands and knees and walking around with mops in our hands, participating in a deep clean of the entire place in the hopes of trying to keep the kids a little healthier. Basically whatever needed to be done, we did it.

Over the course of that summer, I doubled my efforts to spread the word about our mission on social media, and I threw myself into the work of caring for every child there with more passion than I'd given to anything I'd ever done in my whole life.

During a summer trip to Uganda, Macy came with us: (L to R) Macy, Suzanne's daughter Grace, me, Willa Gray, Suzanne, and our friend Beth

Suzanne and everybody else warned us that the adoption process wasn't going to be easy. We would face all kinds of red tape, she said, and delays, and potentially some corruption as people tried to get money from us, illegally, as the process went along. We were warned about individuals who would promise they could move the adoption through faster if we paid them, and we were told that we should avoid that temptation. The last thing I wanted to do was to make any missteps, so we worked with an adoption agency stateside and they helped us hire an attorney in Uganda to walk us through the process.

Thomas Rhett planned to make the long flights with me that October so the two of us could sit down with the attorney together and go over every detail. But there was an even more important reason why he cleared his schedule in order to take that trip: It would be the very first time he got to meet our baby girl in person.

TR: I think we were there for ten days the first trip.

Lauren: Yeah. We were there for our anniversary.

TR: That's right. So, when we walked in the gates to the children's home, I was like, "Do I say, 'Hi, I'm Daddy?'" How do I talk to her? How is this gonna go? I was so nervous.

Lauren: Maybe more nervous than I'd ever seen him.

TR: I was terrified to meet this person, because I already loved her through Lauren, and I really wanted her to love the crap out of me, but I had no idea how this was gonna go. Who knows what she was going to do? So me and Lauren were literally in the children's home for like an hour before we could even see Willa Gray. And the whole time I'm just freaking out inside going, "Where is she? Why haven't I seen her yet?"

Lauren: I think she was napping, and then they were giving her a bath.

TR: So finally, we walk into this little room, and Willa Gray was laying on a towel, on her stomach, with her head turned to the side and her legs bundled up on the concrete, sleeping. And we sort of tiptoed in there, and kinda scratched her back real gently, and Lauren picked her up. She opened her

The first day they met; the first kiss they had

pretty eyes and I started waving at her, trying to see if she'd grab my pinkie, and she was looking at my baseball hat, so I took it off and put it on her head and she just kept looking at me with no emotion at all. Like, none. Not a laugh. Not a smile.

Lauren: She didn't know what to think of him! I don't know if it was the beard, or the hat, or his white face. He was so nervous, and he didn't want to make her cry.

TR: We went back every day after that, and I just started to play with her, and hold her, and the first time she fell asleep in my arms, I just melted, man. I fell so in love with that little girl.

Seeing Thomas Rhett so nervous to meet her was really, really sweet. My heart was just feeling so many different emotions. Africa had always felt like a part of my calling, and when I was able to go, and I met my daughter there, and she made me a mother, it became a big piece of my heart. It was really hard not having him there to experience that with me, and with her. It was almost like it didn't feel complete until Thomas Rhett was there: until we could all three be together.

It went right back to my wedding vows to him: "I don't want to do any part of life without you."

He completed the circle.

Seeing Thomas Rhett just love on her, like he had known her forever, was one of the most beautiful things I had ever seen in my entire life. I really think it made me fall in love with him all over again. Especially because it wasn't something that was guaranteed to automatically happen. We were worried! "Was she going to love us?" He was really worried she didn't like him that first day, and I had to tell him, "Honey, she hasn't been around that many white men in her life. You look weird to her!"

By the time we left, she was so comfortable with him, and him with her, that it nearly killed us to leave. He struggled with it even harder than I did, because he knew I would be able to travel back and be with her a lot more than he would.

And this was going to be a long process.

Right in the middle of us making our decision to adopt Willa Gray, the laws in Uganda changed. What used to be a fairly short, still difficult process was altered in an effort to keep more children in Uganda safe. We were required to foster Willa Gray for twelve full months before the Ugandan government would allow her to be considered "our daughter" and grant the adoption. And that meant twelve full months from when Thomas Rhett came over and we first met with an assigned probation officer, with our lawyer. We realized the process would take even longer than we thought. All the months we'd spent supporting her financially and getting the paperwork started and dreaming about starting our family for real didn't count toward the fostering process at all.

We met with our probation officer and lawyer on the last day before flying back to Nashville, and they left us with doubts about whether the adoption would go through successfully, whether we would ever be able to bring Willa Gray home as our daughter.

The process they laid out for us involved so many meetings, approvals, and hearings in front of a judge, it sounded nearly impossible. It quickly became clear that I was going to have to come back in just a few weeks, and that I'd need to stay in Uganda for an extended period of time if we were to have any hope of getting the paperwork approved before the end of the year.

"Even then," we were told, "a judge could simply say 'no.'"

"Why?" Thomas Rhett said. "Why would a judge do that?"

"Because he can," I said. "It's the judge's duty to keep the children in Uganda safe, and sometimes judges decide that the safest thing for the child is to stay right where they are."

After bonding with Willa Gray for more than a week, Thomas Rhett went to the airport feeling heartbroken. Loving her and being with her felt so complete, to both of us, but the reality of the situation made it feel like we had the world against us in our efforts to bring her home.

I remember thinking, "How are we ever going to get through this tunnel when we can't see any light at the end, at all?"

Thomas Rhett clearly felt the same way.

He kept staring out the window as we took off.

Finally he said, "Babe, I don't know if we should even get attached to her. Maybe that's a mistake. Like, what if this doesn't happen? It's going to crush you. It's going to crush me now, too."

That's when I remembered I wasn't alone in this. We weren't alone in this. We needed to not lose faith.

"Just remember," I said, "God told us, whatever we're worried about, it's already been taken care of."

"Oh, come on, Lauren. Do you really believe that? After everything the lawyer just told us? After all the warnings we got from Suzanne and everybody else, do you really believe that?"

Thomas Rhett with Willa Gray on a swing set in the children's home

I had doubts, I won't lie. I felt *so* much fear when we left that lawyer's office. I was terrified that this might fall apart. And I knew Thomas Rhett was right: If this adoption didn't go through, it would crush me. It would crush *us*. Our families were invested in this now. Our friends. Everybody we knew was praying for Willa Gray. It would crush them, too.

Yet even while all of that fear and doubt rattled around in my head, I *knew*. Way down deep in my heart, I knew the answer to Thomas Rhett's question.

I turned his face toward mine and I looked into his eyes, and I said, "Yes."

I knew in my heart there was nothing that could stop our efforts to bring our girl home with us, no matter how long it took or how hard it might get.

He looked at me kinda funny, almost like he was confused by my response. Then he dropped his eyes down.

"Well," he said, "your faith is definitely stronger than mine."

I called on my prayer warriors the moment we got back to Nashville. I sent out a group text message and explained how tough this process was gonna be, and I asked them all to pray for Willa Gray, and for God to bring her home with us before the year was out. I'm not sure why I added that last part. It made no sense, knowing we were supposed to foster her for twelve months before they would allow us to take her home. I just had a feeling that it was important to pray for that, and so that's what I did, and that's what I asked for.

At this point my prayer warriors included pretty much everyone I knew: the Crew, cousins, grandparents, my mom's best friends, college friends, high school friends, industry friends, everyone! I had a handful of group texts going daily, and I was sending out prayer requests to up to seventy people each time. Then my mom forwarded my prayer requests to her prayer group, and Paige forwarded my requests to hers, and members of those groups forwarded them on to some of their extended prayer groups, too. Which meant that before long, there was truly no telling how many people were praying for Willa Gray. Daily.

Even with all that support, people back home and at our stateside adoption agency kept telling me, "Lauren, it will never happen that quickly."

That's why I was thrilled when I touched base with the people we were working with in Uganda a couple of weeks later, and our lawyer seemed to be all over it. The paperwork started moving. Some of the first approvals came in. And

Teaching Willa Gray how to walk

when I prayed to God, with a Willa Gray bracelet wrapped around my wrist, I heard a whisper from my heart that was as clear as any whisper from God that I'd ever heard: "You will be going home with your baby before Christmas."

So I told everyone I knew, "I swear to you, He told me! I'm going to have this baby before Christmas."

Suzanne, Thomas Rhett, even my mom kept trying to warn me not to get my hopes up.

"Miracles do happen," they would say, "but I think you need to prepare for the road ahead in case it doesn't happen."

"I know," I said. "I hear you. But I'm telling you, I'm coming home with a baby for Christmas."

Everybody had doubt but me.

Thomas Rhett flew over with me in late November. We missed Thanksgiving with our families for the first time in either of our lives. But here's the thing: Getting to spend such an important holiday to us in our daughter's home country was special. Sure, there were certain foods that we had to avoid in Uganda, just so we wouldn't get a stomach bug, and I missed my family's home cooking like crazy. But what hurt my heart was that for the holidays, part of our family was in Uganda while the other part of our family was thousands of miles away. I desperately longed for our family to all be together.

"One day soon," I told myself.

Then December came, and I definitely caught some kind of stomach bug, because I started feeling really sick. All the time.

I was sick and miserable, and the adoption process stalled out completely. We stayed in Uganda as long as we possibly could, bonding with Willa Gray as she fell in love with a downloaded copy of *Finding Nemo* on my iPad, and looked at videos of Kona and Cash and laughed and laughed at the sight of our two goofy dogs playing with each other.

For the first time in nine years, we had to miss our annual ugly Christmas sweater party. Macy and her new incredible husband, Tyler, who got married that October, were amazing. They took the reins and threw the party for us. But it was so hard to break that tradition. There are friends who look forward to that party all year, who come from really far away. There are some people I only ever get one chance to see all year, and it's at that party. I missed them.

I missed home.

Thomas Rhett and I wanted Willa Gray to be a part of our home *and* our family. She was still sick, still coughing, like she had been the whole time I'd known her, and I wanted to bring her back to Nashville where I knew she could get the kind of medical care that simply was not available in Uganda.

We impressed upon the lawyer just how badly we wanted to wrap up this adoption before Christmas, and he promised to try. Through Suzanne, we were able to ask some other prominent officials who were supporters of the orphanage to please help us as well. Mostly, we prayed. I asked my prayer warriors to pray, too, texting all of them and knowing they were sending up so much love—but the process did not go through.

"That's it," our lawyer said as he hung up the phone with someone he'd been trying to reach at the courthouse for days. "The judge is away for the holidays. There is not a chance we can move any of this forward until mid-January, at the earliest. There is nothing more we can do."

I looked at Thomas Rhett, and I burst into tears.

"Come on, baby," he said. "Let's go home."

We were devastated.

As the two of us got ready to fly back home before Christmas, I just could not understand why God had whispered in my ear and told me I would be going home with my baby if it wasn't going to happen. *How could God tell me something so clearly and it not come true?* I wondered.

Then, suddenly, unexpectedly, it all became perfectly clear.

It turned out that I didn't have a stomach bug at all.

The reason I'd been so sick?

I was pregnant.

We found out in the middle of a safari trip to Tanzania, where we met up with our good friends Hayley and Tyler Hubbard (of Florida Georgia Line), who just happened to plan their trip to Africa right before we were scheduled to fly back home. It took almost two days to get a pregnancy test delivered to us out in the bush—and just a few minutes to realize what God had been up to all this time.

God hadn't misled us. In fact, he had given us the greatest Christmas gift ever. Thomas Rhett and I were overjoyed. We were going to be parents times two! God's blessing was twice as good as we'd ever imagined.

Which also meant we now had twice as many plans to make.

*Our very first family photo, on the bed in our hotel room
in Masindi, Uganda*

Like somebody a whole lot wiser than us once said, "We make plans.
God laughs."

I wanted to tell our families so bad, but we decided to make it a big
surprise. We wrapped a whole bunch of baby announcements and put
them under the Christmas tree, so our whole family could open them all
at once.

I don't think any of us will ever forget the scene, as we sat around the
Christmas tree on Christmas Eve (because I couldn't wait any longer),
and everyone realized they had the same box from us, and we made everyone wait and open them at the exact same moment. I can still smell
the scent of the tree and hot chocolate, and hear the sound of all of those
boxes opening at once, and feel the anticipation as Thomas Rhett put his
arm around me and held me as our parents and siblings all gasped and
said, "Oh my goodness!" and jumped up full of excitement and happy
tears at the news that nobody saw coming.

We sent the news out to our prayer warriors right after, and they reminded me that God had kept his word. In a slew of happy text messages,

they said: "See? You *did* come home with a baby before the end of the year! Willa Gray's gonna have a baby sister or brother!"

As we turned the corner into January 2017, I was getting ready to enter my second trimester. That meant we had a pretty exceptional reason to want to bring Willa Gray home with us as quick as possible. At some point, my doctor was going to tell me I couldn't fly back and forth to Uganda anymore. At some point the airlines were going to refuse to let me board in my condition. And soon after that, I would be giving birth to a brand-new baby who would need my attention at home as a newborn. All of that combined meant that if we couldn't get Willa Gray home with us soon, I could end up going months without seeing her—and during those months apart, the adoption process could end up getting delayed further, or even denied.

I could not let that happen.

Thomas Rhett insisted on hiring a bodyguard for me when I went back to Uganda. We hired a wonderful guy with a lot of military experience who basically stayed by my side at all times while I was in Uganda that winter.

For the most part, whenever I was there I felt safe. Most of the people in Uganda were so peaceful, and when it came to those who weren't, I didn't really worry about someone targeting me in particular. There was just a worry that you could end up in the wrong place at the wrong time. We weren't all that far from the Congo, and there were rebels transporting weapons through the area. There were also people living in desperate conditions, and sometimes desperate people take desperate measures. It's definitely a different world than we live in back home, in too many ways to count, and had it not been for the love and connection we felt for Willa Gray, I don't think anyone would have blamed us if we'd used any of these things as an excuse to drop the adoption process, saying, "This is just too hard, this is just too much."

But there was just no way we were going to do that.

TR: Traveling in Uganda isn't like traveling in the United States. It was dangerous. There was one night when the bodyguard brought us into a room and said, "I just want to teach you all something." He sat us down and taught us step by step how to assemble and disassemble the type of gun he carried. "Because," he said, "if I go down, you need to learn how to use this thing." There was one time when we were on the way to the airport in Kampala and he got a call from an American official in the area, telling him to take a different route because someone had been assassinated on the route we were taking.

My mom insisted on flying over with me from that point forward. And my dad was ready to fly over, too, at some point, if this dragged out for very much longer.

Unfortunately for all of us, it did.

Every time we thought we were getting a meeting we needed, or a form signed by the correct official, something would go wrong. Somebody would change our appointment at the last minute and tell us to come back three days later. Or they'd tell us we had the wrong form and needed to go back for another one, even though they'd told us to get the exact form we had a week earlier. We'd spend days on end putting a file together, then turn it in, and come back to hear that they'd lost it. The whole file!

TR: We had to learn a set of patience skills that we had not been taught in America. During this whole process, it seemed like everything took hours. If someone said, "Be there at 2:30," it was just a suggestion.

On our first trip to Uganda, Jude took Suzanne and me
into town on a bota bota—one of the many dirt bikes
that swarm the city streets

* * *

Things certainly don't move as fast in Uganda as they do in the States, but
we began to see the beauty in that slower pace. We found more time to
appreciate small moments and gestures of kindness than we sometimes
did back home. Like, we could spend an entire afternoon playing on the
floor with Willa Gray and not even realize that hours had gone by. And
we fell in love with the people there. Just like I found in Haiti, the Ugandan people had such beautiful hearts. They cared for each other, and each
other's children, often in nearly unimaginable circumstances. They also
took great pride in their country and wanted to show it off. We had people take us out on safari, to see their wildlife and the beauty of nature.
And they were always sharing food with us. One day I commented on the
gigantic jackfruit growing on trees in town, and Jude, one of the young
men who helped to run our organization on the ground there and who
became like a Ugandan brother to me, climbed right up into a tree and cut
one down so I could try it.

It was strange, but whenever I went back home to Nashville, I actually started to feel homesick for Uganda. With every trip, the people there became more and more like family. And that feeling was only made stronger because they were caring for our daughter when I couldn't be there. They took such good care of Willa Gray, and when you see someone love your child, you can't help but love them back.

We also just had so many angels who showed up and went out of their way to help us. People like our bodyguard, who helped us in ways we never could have imagined when we first hired him. It's just that so much went wrong. Suzanne would have to remind us sometimes, "Don't be fearful. It will all work out. God will take care of everything." And He would. I knew that—even if Thomas Rhett didn't quite believe it the same way I did. He had good reason. Things were just not going as planned. There was a lot of judgment, too, which I wasn't prepared for. People would aggressively stare at us sometimes, as if they were angry to see us holding Willa Gray. One day at the hotel, a large, intimidating-looking Ugandan man came over to me while I was walking around with Willa Gray in my arms. He started shaking his head. I looked up at him and said, "Hello?" and he said, aggressively, "She is not your baby!"

"She's not?" I said, and he came closer as he kept shaking his head. It was the first time I felt my Mama Bear instinct rise up inside me, and in a moment of anger I responded to him with more than a hint of American sarcasm and attitude. "What?" I said. "She doesn't look like she came out of my *body*?"

I couldn't believe those words came out of my mouth.

He looked at me kinda confused. I was alone, it was dark outside, and my bodyguard had stepped away for a moment, but I wanted to be very clear to him that I was not going to back down. Thankfully, my bodyguard happened to come back a few seconds later, and the guy walked away before anything escalated. But it was eye-opening, for sure.

Up and down the system there were people who simply didn't care if Willa Gray came home with us or not, and then there were some people who didn't *want* her to come home with us *at all*. I didn't realize before we started this process that there are people of all different nationalities who don't believe that *any* foreign adoptions should happen.

Sometimes it felt like Satan himself was trying to keep us from giving the love of our family to Willa Gray. To be honest, I know he was. So we just kept praying to God to send His angels to help us through.

It turned out that our bodyguard was a very spiritually connected man. And Joseph, our Ugandan driver, was a father to adoptive children. Which meant he knew people in and out of the system who might be helpful to us in all kinds of ways. And one day, he managed to get us a meeting with a Ugandan supreme court judge, so we could tell him about our case, just so he could make sure we were doing everything correctly, and perhaps offer us some advice. This judge didn't have jurisdiction over our case, but our bodyguard and Joseph both said it wouldn't hurt to have some extra eyes and ears looking out for us.

When we walked out of the supreme court judge's room after our meeting, our bodyguard said, "Did you not see that?" And we were all like, "What are you talking about?"

"The light," he said.

"What light?"

"There was a light above him the whole time he was talking," he said. "It was so bright, it was just right behind him and on top of him. I did not want to freak you all out, but I was just watching that light the whole time, like he was an angel."

I had chills. Moments like that reminded me to have faith, to recognize that the Holy Spirit was moving and remember that He was working supernaturally on our daughter's behalf.

We just kept praying, and again and again we found the strength we needed to keep going. I mean, it felt like Satan was trying to stop it all from happening, by causing all kinds of delays and lost paperwork, but through all of it, I saw where Jesus kept stepping in to say, "You have no power over this family, and as long as they keep proclaiming that I'm the one doing this for them, you have no power in this situation."

I had to remind myself, "This is not about me. This is not about her. This is not even about Satan or anybody involved in the adoption process. This is all about God and what He can do, and what He *says* He can do is what He's *gonna* do."

If I didn't believe, I truly don't know how I would have made it.

When people would see how much of a toll this was taking on us, with all the flying back and forth and the lack of movement on the part of the government, they would ask me, "How do you know she's really meant to be your child? Maybe these delays and the change in the law and all of it are signs that you should give up?" I would tell them, "I know because He told me. No, really. He *literally* told me."

Loving on Willa Gray in our hotel room, under a mosquito net

I think some people thought I was crazy, and I hate to say this, but I think Thomas Rhett was one of 'em. There were times when the difficulties we faced during this process wore him down. He had no choice but to fly back home and leave me there when the process dragged on, and it nearly killed him. I think there were times when he wanted to give up. But he saw how God gave me the resolve to keep going, and something about that resolve really started to change him.

In the middle of all of this, under the ticking clock of my pregnancy with our second child, Thomas Rhett and I had no choice but to cling to our faith whenever something went wrong. "You've gotta tell us the next step," we would pray together, "because we are *lost*."

We spent more time apart trying to complete this adoption than we'd spent apart in any of the first four years of our marriage; maybe even in the whole time we'd known each other. And that was tough. FaceTime can only bring you so close. Calling my husband at odd hours, catching him on his way to the Super Bowl or living it up at some after-party or backstage after a sold-out show while I was throwing up in a Ugandan toilet and feeling uncomfortable with my body, stuck going back and forth to a run-down municipal building in Uganda while trying to take care of Willa Gray between meetings, I couldn't help but feel sad, lonely, and a little resentful again.

"I'm sorry, babe," he always said. "You know I'd be there if I could."

I truly believed that he meant what he said. It just hurt my heart that he *couldn't*.

The reality was, his tour dates were on the books a year or more in advance, before the adoption even started. He was contractually obligated to do shows and make appearances, and he could have gotten sued if he'd gone and canceled.

But those same old worries about his career and "when is enough *enough*" came back and haunted me like crazy in my increased hormonal state of being pregnant on the other side of the planet.

TR: I was out on my first headlining tour, ever, and at one point we added two nights in Nashville and every single one of our friends were there—and Lauren was in Uganda, pregnant, and throwing up in a bathroom.

Lauren: I had people calling me in the middle of the night going, "We can't get backstage." And I'm like, "Ummmm, hello? I'm in Uganda and I'm trying to sleep. I am not there!"

TR: And she's right, I went to the Super Bowl while she was in Uganda. For like a month I said, "Babe, I can't do this. I don't want to go. If you're not there, I don't want to go." And she convinced me to go. So I went. And we all had a great time. But during this time there were nights where I'd get off the phone because I knew that if I kept talking to her, it was just going to get worse. We had awful fights.

Lauren: I mean, nothing was going to make it better. It was his job. He had to be home. That's all. I could've been there with him, but I had to and *wanted* to stay for Willa Gray. It was just a hard situation.

TR: There were probably three straight weeks of me being in America with her being in Uganda and being pregnant when she would call and it would be the next morning Uganda time, but 1:00 a.m. my time, and she could hear people in the background and obviously we're having a great time, and I just felt awful about it. There were countless shows where I thought, "There's nothing in the world I would rather *not* do than go play this show." Like, my wife is in Uganda, we just had a blowout fight on a cellphone, and I've got to go pretend like I'm the happiest human being on the planet for ninety straight minutes. A big part of me wondered how we were ever gonna make it if this thing dragged on much longer.

At the beginning of February, we finally got our hearing date with the judge.

We walked in, and our attorney presented our case, and the judge looked almost like he was angry about it, like he didn't want to hear anything more about what we had to say. My attorney made a case for granting the adoption on an accelerated timeline because I wouldn't be able to fly in a matter of weeks, and I wouldn't be able to return to Uganda with a newborn. He did a great job, and we truly walked in there feeling confident that the judge would give his approval on the spot. He already had our files: We had everything signed, every letter we needed, every form we needed. It was all there, and not a single person had any objection to the adoption, which was a rarity in some of these cases.

But when our attorney asked for his decision, the judge said, "No. I don't see how I can grant this adoption quickly." Then he looked right at me: "It is not my job to take care of your unborn baby," he said. "It is my job to take care of the baby that is sitting in your lap, and I don't see how her adoption happening sooner than expected is good for her. So my answer will be 'no.'"

He dismissed us, and I burst into tears. I mean, I *bawled*.

I thought for sure that no was a hard "no," and all hope was gone, but then our attorney told us the judge postponed the next hearing, which meant we had to extend our stay in Uganda.

That's when I turned to my prayer warriors again.

I texted home and begged them to pray for the judge to change his mind; to say "yes" to Willa Gray. "Yes" to us. "Yes" to our baby.

The number of texts that went back and forth were far too many to count. For the next three days there were literally hundreds of people praying for Willa Gray, praying for us, praying for that judge to say "yes"!

And on the third day, the attorney called. "The judge is making his decision," he said.

As we drove to the courthouse one more time, I wasn't as nervous as I was feeling defeated. I felt the judge had already told us his answer, even if it wasn't "official" yet. And then? Because of a miscommunication, we arrived late. Mom and I waited in the car as the hearing unfolded, with Willa Gray asleep on my shoulder.

Joseph knew the court clerk, so as soon as we saw people leaving the courthouse, meaning court was likely over for the day, he went inside to see what he could find out. A few minutes later, he came back to the car with some paperwork in his hands.

"Well, do you want to know the judge's decision?" he said.

"Yes!" I responded, with a lot more attitude than he deserved. I was just angry, and hormonal, and felt hopeless after all the waiting we'd done.

He handed me the paperwork and said, "Well . . . according to Uganda, she is your baby."

I looked at him in shock, with this blank look on my face, not quite understanding what he was saying. And Joseph looked right at me and said, "She's now your baby. She's your daughter."

I had not cried like that in my entire life. I couldn't even speak. Thank goodness Willa Gray was asleep, because I probably would have scared her half to death. My mom, like me, is not really an outwardly emotional person, but she started crying, too. All she could do was just put her hand on my back as I bent over, just weeping with relief and thankfulness.

I clung on to Willa Gray and held her so tight to me.

"You're our baby, Willa Gray," I whispered. "You're our baby!"

Holding on to my baby girl in the car when we found out the adoption had been granted

In the quiet of the car as Joseph pulled away from the curb, I started speaking out loud: "I just . . . I cannot believe that God actually made that happen."

I had clearly let too many doubts creep in about God's whispers to me. I had done my best to keep the faith, though, and I'm pretty sure that my faith in God grew stronger than it had ever been, right in that moment. I was just so, so thankful that my doubts and fears didn't turn out to be real!

What was real was God's promise.

When I finally felt ready, I handed Willa Gray to my mom, pulled out my phone, and texted our entire prayer circle: "WE DID IT. (Well, God did it.) According to Uganda, Willa Gray is now our baby!"

Oh my gosh. I will never again in my life feel that much weight lifted off my shoulders. Ever. *Ever.* God came through.

I called Thomas Rhett and he was so, so thankful, and so happy.

I'm pretty sure that phone call changed him forever.

Thomas Rhett's doubts that this was ever going to happen were bigger than mine. They always had been. He didn't just doubt the system, or doubt the officials in charge, or doubt our own ability to have the patience to make it through this. He doubted God's word.

So that phone call? It changed his faith in God.

"You never stopped believing," he said to me. "And what you believed . . . it was *real*. God's words to you were *real*, Lauren. 'It was already taken care of.' I'm just so blown away right now."

I could hear him start to cry on the other end of the phone. All those thousands of miles away, and somehow I felt closer to him than ever.

"I'm so happy," he said.

I smiled.

"Me too."

16

The Long Way Home

It wasn't over. We weren't finished yet. There was still a whole lot more to go through before we could get Willa Gray home. We had to get her a new birth certificate, with her name on it. We needed to present proof that she was healthy enough to travel. We needed to get an I-600 approved by someone at the U.S. embassy, which is a petition to declare that this former orphan was now our "immediate relative." We needed to get her a passport so she could fly, and a visa so she could enter the United States with us.

Not one bit of it would be easy, and every part of it would take time. Frustrating, agonizing amounts of time.

The clock was ticking, so we paid a fee to expedite the final paperwork—the same way you can pay a fee to expedite a passport back home—and we put Willa Gray back into the trusting arms of her Ugandan caregivers. Those men and women were angels, and we knew she was in good hands.

It was time for me to go back to America and check on my health, along

Clinging tight—knowing our adoption journey was far from over

with the health of my baby. So Mom and I flew home to Nashville. I did my best to try to see this as a good thing: It meant I could be with Thomas Rhett for his birthday that March, and that I would be able to celebrate with family and friends on our annual spring break trip. We were able to set aside all the stress for a few days, to reconnect as husband and wife, and then to spend some time in our home thinking about the blessings of the two babies we had on the way. We had already started setting up a beautiful room for Willa Gray; now we had to hurry up and put together a nursery for our second baby, too.

That April, a few days before we were set to go back to Uganda, my growing baby bump and I walked the red carpet with Thomas Rhett for the 2017 ACMs, where he won one of the most prestigious awards in all of country music: Male Vocalist of the Year.

At the ACMs in 2017, after announcing our adoption— and our pregnancy

Thomas Rhett was becoming more and more accustomed to the ways that his fame opened doors for him. Producers and people in the business who never would have taken his call when he was first starting out were now happy to talk with him. But in Uganda? We were just two Americans trying to adopt a baby in a country that didn't make it easy. Not at all.

When we returned to Uganda that spring, we stayed in one of the nicer hotels within driving distance of the U.S. embassy. It was a spot that other Americans and Europeans tended to frequent—including other couples who were mired in the new twelve-month foster period and the endless paperwork of trying to adopt children from other orphanages in the area. We wound up talking to some of them, listening to their heart-wrenching stories, including stories of some extended waiting on the part of the U.S. embassy. They all had been tied up in red tape for months. One couple had just gone before the judge and they were told their adoption would never be approved. After a year of trying, they were out of options. They were getting ready to go home without their baby. For good. It was awful.

I started to get nervous again—and that's when something really special happened.

Thomas Rhett turned to me and said, "You can't listen to everyone else's story. That is not *our* story." After seeing how God had come through for us in the Ugandan courts, and realizing how many miracles had happened to bring us to where we were in that moment, Thomas Rhett found more strength to support me when my spirits got down. He became more of a rock to me than ever before. I was further along in my pregnancy. I was tired all the time, sometimes mentally and spiritually, too. Only now, when I started to feel weaker, Thomas Rhett became stronger.

When I got angry that we were waiting yet another day, and then another, and another—not on the Ugandan side, but now on the American side of this adoption equation—Thomas Rhett would stop me from fuming, and say, "We should be praying about this."

The three of us (with a baby on the way) at the new hotel next to the capital city in Uganda— so ready to be home as a family

He did for me now what I had done for him early on.

Clearly, God knew what He was doing by putting the two of us together; my weaknesses are where he's stronger, and vice versa. That's how a marriage, a true partnership, should work.

My anger and frustration were certainly warranted. We'd spent enough time together that our family unit was established with Willa Gray. I was Mommy, Thomas Rhett was Daddy, and Uganda had officially declared that she was our baby girl. She was staying with us at the hotel. Full-time. She was getting loved on by her grandmother, my mom, like she'd never been loved on before. We just wanted to go home. I was like, "Come on, America! Let us come home!"

Thomas Rhett and I vowed that we were going to stay right there together with each other until Willa Gray came home with us. We couldn't imagine the process would take all that long now that the adoption decree was approved and we'd paid to have her passport expedited. Yet for some reason, we still didn't have all the paperwork we needed, and we couldn't seem to get an appointment confirmed at the U.S. embassy. It just dragged on and on, until finally Thomas Rhett had to fly home. He had a summer tour to get ready for.

When May 3 came around, I had to leave, too—doctor's orders—and the adoption still wasn't complete. The paperwork we needed from the government was *still* not finished. I had no choice but to leave, and thankfully, my dad was able to fly over so he and my mom could stand in our place, finish up the paperwork and any last-minute interviews, and finally bring our baby home.

It was like a dagger through the heart having to board that plane after this thirteen-month ordeal and to leave without Willa Gray. Even though I knew she was in good hands.

After a tearful goodbye at the airport and an agonizing trip back to Nashville, all I could do was wait. And wait. And wait. I swear every hour felt like a day, and every day felt like a week. I kept my phone on my nightstand with the ringer turned up so I wouldn't risk missing any important messages when I slept. I put the prayer warriors to praying again until my parents went to the U.S. embassy for Willa Gray's visa appointment.

Finally, on May 9, at 4:00 in the morning (11:00 a.m. Uganda time), the chime of a newly arrived email woke me out of a deep sleep.

It was the U.S. embassy, emailing to tell me that our daughter's visa was *approved*!

That was the final step. We were *done*.

My parents boarded the next plane out of Uganda with Willa Gray in Mom's arms, and texted me a picture as they were backing away from the gate: "Taking off now. Shutting phones off," they said. "She's almost home!"

On May 11, 2017, Thomas Rhett and I drove to the airport to meet my parents' flight.

It was, from start to finish, the craziest year that we'd ever experienced.

God was bringing our baby home now, and part of me could not believe it was actually real. We had arranged a private spot where we could meet them at the airport as soon as they got off the plane, and I was ba-sically jumping out of my skin with excite-

Willa Gray boarding her first flight ever

ment as the minutes went by. There are no words to describe how relieved, and safe, and complete I felt when my mom texted to tell us they'd landed.

When we finally laid eyes on them, Willa Gray was asleep on Mom's shoulder, and we couldn't get to her fast enough. Mom woke her up, and Thomas Rhett and I basically fought over her. I hugged her, and he picked her up and showed her around to everything. She kept pointing at the planes and trying to say the word: "pane, pane, pane!" Clearly Dad had influenced her already. She was so excited.

She was home.

I stood back for a minute and watched Thomas Rhett holding Willa Gray and looking out the window at the airport with her. As I broke into the biggest smile I'd ever felt cross my face, tears started pouring down my cheeks. I don't know if it was partly the late pregnancy mixed with the extreme lack of sleep and the realization that we had our baby home at last, but I just couldn't stop crying. I thanked my mom and dad, and God, and I sent out a thankful text right then to all of our prayer warriors. I couldn't thank them enough for this moment if I thanked them for a million years. My heart had never been this full.

Thomas Rhett looked at me and smiled this glowing, fatherly smile, and he carried her over and we all hugged and thanked Jesus, and then we just looked at each other, like, "Can you believe this is real?"

"You want to go home?" Thomas Rhett asked Willa Gray, but I was the one who responded: "Yes!" I could not get her in the car fast enough. I could not get back to our *house* fast enough. I was dying for her to meet the rest of our family, who had only gotten to know her over FaceTime. (Thank you, technology!) I was dying for her to meet the dogs, and for the dogs to meet her. I was dying for her to see her bedroom and her big bed with a comfortable mattress, and to taste ice cream for the first time. I was dying for her to see the rosebushes in her back yard, and to meet the rest of her family and to give her a long bubble bath, and her first taste of ice-cold juice. I was just dying all over the place with wanting to be home with her and wanting to share the home we'd created for her. A home built with so much love, I hoped, like the one I knew growing up.

Willa Gray wouldn't ever have the exact childhood I had. None of my

Willa Gray is home!

Thanking God
He brought our baby home

Our first family photo, taken right outside our front door

Willa Gray on the
tour bus with her aunts,
Kasey and Macy

kids would, because they're not me. But more than anything, I wanted to give her a childhood that she could look back on with sweet memories. One day, many years from now, I wanted her to be able to say, "I was loved well, and cared for, and had so much fun that I would do it all over again in a heartbeat!"

I couldn't wait to sit on our beanbag chairs and watch anything other than *Finding Nemo,* which she'd made me watch again and again. I'm pretty sure I could quote every line of that movie by now.

The whole drive home I just kept thinking, "I cannot believe she is finally *here*!" It was truly a dream come true.

We drove up the driveway and our dogs started barking and she got really excited, but when we opened the door, they jumped up and scared the absolute snot out of her. "Ahh! Ahhhh!" she screamed. They were just so big. She had watched videos of the dogs and had fallen in love with them on my phone. She knew them by name. When she saw 'em in person, though, and experienced how big they were in real life, she clung to me like a cat about to be dropped in a lake.

Our families were waiting for us to call them the minute we got home, and they came bounding over to the house to meet us almost as fast as the dogs had run out to greet us. Macy and her husband, Tyler, and Grayson, and Paige and Tim, and Kasey, and little Tyler, and Rhett along with his fiancée, Sonya (I almost forgot to mention that Rhett got engaged to an amazing woman!), and some of our friends came over as fast as they could, too, and we all took pictures and hung out, and Willa Gray did not stop moving from the moment we walked in the door. She just wanted to see everything, and touch everything, and hug on everybody—especially Macy, who she had taken to the moment they first met, way back when Macy came with me on one of my earliest trips to Uganda. Having Willa Gray home made it feel like our little house had come to life in a whole new way.

This wasn't just Thomas Rhett's and my house now. This was our *family's* house.

* * *

Willa Gray slept right through the night, the very first night. And the next morning, waking up with the three of us was just the most magical morning ever. Our little girl was so excited about every little thing. She loved her bed. She loved our couch. She loved the blast of cold air when we opened the refrigerator door. She drank up her juice like it was water in a desert. And we played and laughed, and walked her around our neighborhood in her stroller, and watched Disney movies. (*The Jungle Book* and *Moana* quickly topped *Nemo* on Willa Gray's hit list.)

But it wasn't long after that when Thomas Rhett had to go on the road again.

He was doing so well, he didn't have to ride the bus anymore, except on extended runs that were far from home. He now had the option to fly in and out for concerts in just a day or two, and he was so excited to get back home to me and Willa Gray that he scheduled every trip to be as short as possible.

I was so sad to see him walk out that door, though, and I was nervous about caring for Willa Gray all by myself for the very first time. She was a lot to handle. She never stopped moving. Ever. Plus, I was feeling a little off and gaining all kinds of weight in my third trimester, and I wasn't sleeping well at all.

It took about three days before Willa Gray got up the nerve to actually pet Kona and Cash, or to sit on the floor next to 'em without trying to climb up my leg to safety. And she got so comfortable after a week or so that she started driving the dogs nuts. She just wouldn't stop jumping on them. She jumped on Cash's back one time when he was laying on the floor, and he jumped up so quick that Willa Gray tried to grab on to whatever she could, and she ended up grabbing both of his ears and riding him across the room like a horse.

Honestly, I saw my mom in a whole new light after just that first week, picturing her raising me all by herself while my dad was off flying a lot. It was exhausting! And I wasn't even dealing with a newborn keeping me up all night. I mean, I was dealing with a soon-to-be-born keeping me up all night, but I knew it wasn't the same. In fact, my mind was just about split-

Just like we posted on Instagram: "Georgia boy, Tennessee girl, Uganda cutie pie = our new all-American family"

ting open at the thought of having a new baby on top of keeping up with Willa Gray.

Nearing the end of my third trimester, with Thomas Rhett gone so much and me a new mama, I have no idea how I would have handled it without my beautiful, ever-present family, and especially my mom. I was so grateful for her thoughtfulness and attentiveness and support. And for Paige and for Macy and Kasey and Sonya, and all of my besties who showed up and formed a circle of love and care around me and our daughter.

It was strange, but it seemed like the whole world cared about Willa Gray. We celebrated the Fourth of July with our family, with fireworks and hot dogs, just like old times—except for the new addition of our wide-eyed girl, who got to enjoy every single bit of that celebration for the very first time—and when Thomas Rhett posted a picture of the three of us dressed in red, white, and blue and holding sparklers on his Instagram, *People* magazine picked it up and put up a whole article on their website about it. They picked up quotes from other magazines, where Thomas Rhett talked about what it felt like to be a father, and how he wasn't sure if Willa Gray fully understood that she was going to have a sister soon, but he thought she was gonna be a really great big sister. He got tens of thousands of comments about it. I posted the same photo: "Georgia boy, Tennessee girl, Uganda cutie pie = our new all-American family," I wrote. "Thankful for the men & women of our country who give us this freedom and make our sweet family possible." And thousands and thousands of people responded to my post with loving comments.

I wasn't sure what I really felt about all that attention. I was proud of our family. I felt like we were helping to start a public conversation about adoption and love and all the different ways families can be created—and I hoped that was a good thing. I liked that we were representing a different vision of an all-American family. And it seemed like our fans liked it, too.

Just after the Fourth of July holiday, though, Thomas Rhett took off for more shows and I happened to come across that *People* article online, and reading it felt really weird. It was like I was looking at and reading about somebody else. Like we weren't real. Like we were just some made-up family.

Thomas Rhett had come and gone in what felt like an instant to me. Like he'd flown in for the fun family vacation and then split.

I suddenly felt really alone again. And although I knew it wasn't the case, it was hard when his job involved interviews to talk about Willa Gray, when I felt like the two of us had *barely* had enough time to process everything we'd just gone through ourselves.

On August 11, exactly three months after Willa Gray arrived, I was induced into labor.

I stayed in labor for thirty-six hours, and twenty-eight of those thirty-six were natural labor. Talk about exhausted.

Thomas Rhett was at my side, holding my hand, at 10:28 in the evening, in the comfort of an all-American hospital, when our second baby, Ada James Akins, finally came into this world.

In the hospital, after the
thirty-six hours of labor
and delivery it took to
meet this sweetie . . .

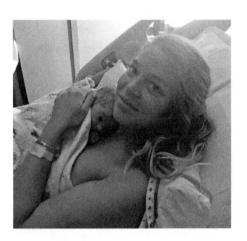

Ada James Akins
♥

Willa Gray loving
on her new baby
sister

It was the most amazing, painful, excruciating, exciting, incredible day-and-a-half journey I'd ever been on. I swear, only Jesus got me through it. (And my mom.) That's a long time to be in labor by almost anyone's standards. But oh my goodness, it was worth it. It was worth every contraction, every push, every bit of pain and agony. And compared to the yearlong labor of trying to bring Willa Gray home, I could confidently say it was a breeze. I mean, thirty-six hours was just about the length of a one-way trip to Uganda.

Ada James was seven pounds, three ounces of the most beautiful little bundle of joy I'd ever laid eyes on. Thomas Rhett and I were both instantly over the moon.

So was Willa Gray. She fell in love with her little sister before we even brought her home from the hospital. She was so gentle with her, and so caring, always bringing her stuffed animals to play with and making sure she was okay. She would touch Ada James's cheek so gently, just the way I always touched hers, and give her kisses on the forehead, and my heart would melt every time.

Being parents for the very first time to an infant and a twenty-one-month-old all at once is a pretty crazy thing to do. My heart goes out to any parents trying to raise back-to-back babies. And because of the way this all happened, Thomas Rhett and I didn't have the first twenty-one months to get used to raising a first child before number two came along. We were *fresh* at this parenting gig. And it was a *lot* to adjust to.

When the four of us were together, cuddled up and hanging out at home, it was perfect. We were happier than we'd ever been. But a couple of weeks after Ada James was born, those cuddle-up-at-home times became fewer and farther between.

Thomas Rhett's third album, the fittingly titled *Life Changes,* was going to be released on September 8—less than a month after Ada James came into this world. That didn't leave time for him to be lounging around with the three of us at home. He had all kinds of work to do.

I realize a lot of men go right back to work after their wives give birth, so this wasn't anything all that unusual. I just missed him. I loved it when he was home. Willa Gray squealed with delight every time he walked through the door. And we needed him. As much help as I had from the people around me—our moms, sisters, friends, family— there were times when I just wished my husband could be there a little more.

The four of us in the parking lot after church

I felt awful for thinking these things. Like, who am I to complain? We were so blessed to be living the life we were given, and I was so grateful that we weren't facing some of the stresses and pressure so many young families face. We had a home. Our children were healthy. We lived comfortably and in a safe area. I knew that my circumstances could not be compared to those of the families I'd lived and worked with in Uganda, or in Haiti, or even families all across the United States. So I tried to tell myself to get my big-girl panties on and to be grateful for my blessings.

Still, let's face it: Parenting under any circumstances can be stressful.

It might not have looked like it in the pages of *People* magazine, but some days—actually, on a lot of days—I was miserable. I had never felt so completely uncomfortable in my own skin. After giving birth to Ada James, my body changed. A lot. I had gained a lot of weight and I was so busy taking care of two baby girls that it felt nearly impossible to take care of myself or to put the work in to lose the weight. I was stuck in a body I didn't recognize while Thomas Rhett was getting up early, going to the gym, and getting ripped. He had to look and feel good onstage, and he was looking and feeling better than he had in his whole life. That was a big part of his job. How could I argue with it? Still, I looked in the mirror and didn't recognize myself.

Thankfully Thomas Rhett never, ever made me feel like I wasn't exactly what he always wanted me to be. He'd catch me saying something about how awful my body looked, and he would say, "Stop it. You're more beautiful now than you've ever been." And he meant it. He still looked at me with those longing, puppy-dog eyes of his, as if I were the prettiest girl in the whole world.

He was the best husband that way, always telling me how proud he was of me, but the fact that he had the freedom to go work out and live his life while I held down the fort for him at home left me feeling kind of lonely and, frankly, kind of broken.

It was really hard for me to have Thomas Rhett traveling so much. Maybe I just wanted my husband to be home more, like my dad was when I was growing up. My dad had always been around to share things with my mom. He came home every night and gave his family all of his attention. He wanted nothing more than to love on his wife and family, as if they were his greatest happiness, the most important part of his life.

That was how I had grown up, but that wasn't our reality.

Thomas Rhett loved us. He *showed* us that. He was attentive and affectionate as could be whenever he was home. And yet the bigger his career got, the more famous he became, the more I felt that his career was number one.

Even on the days that were supposed to be his off days, Thomas Rhett would start out playing with the kids but then he'd end up taking phone calls or texting with industry people, because his mind was always on the next show, the next "thing."

It's so hard to explain, but I started feeling like I just missed him. I felt estranged from my husband. Even when he was in the same room with us.

It wasn't that Thomas Rhett did anything to hurt me on purpose. There was no malice behind any of it. It was just that he didn't understand. He wasn't gonna stay home with the girls. He had a career to keep alive. He was the man of the house. He was providing for us. So there was no way for him to understand what I was going through—and I didn't really know how to explain it to him.

I missed him so much that I made up my mind to get back to traveling with him before the kids and I were really ready. The weekend his album came out, we got the girls and flew up to New York City as a family (plus my mom), so at least we'd get to see him in between TV appearances.

That Sunday, Thomas Rhett did a signing at Target and then went to Atlantic City to serve as a judge in the Miss America contest. I stayed at the hotel with my month-old baby girl and her sister, who hadn't yet turned two. I was up feeding Ada James and trying to get Willa Gray to fall asleep in the strange hotel room when I turned on the TV and there was Thomas Rhett, live at the Miss America pageant.

At first, I just felt sorry for myself, thinking, "There he goes, all dressed in a tux at this fancy event and I'm sitting here with forty pounds still to lose. I'm in a hotel room in New York City, because I had no choice but to fly thousands of miles with an infant and a toddler or else I was just not going to see my husband. So now I'm nursing a newborn and watching him on TV. He's dressed to the nines escorting a model down the aisle and they're taking pictures of all the judges with these gorgeous women in beautiful dresses and I'm sitting here with throw-up on my shirt." I looked at my husband's beaming face on the TV and said, "Well, this really sucks," as if he could hear me.

As the words came out of my mouth, I realized I was upset about a lot more than my postbaby body and being worlds away from my husband. That night, in a hotel room with my baby girls—two girls I loved more than anything and had fought so hard for—while their daddy appeared on national television, I realized that a life I had always dreamed of living was gone. I had grown up in such a happy, easy, low-key, *normal* home. Our family was everything and our neighbors were part of the family. Every night we'd play in the street and then get called in to supper where we'd sit around the table and eat together, talk about our days, just be around one another. I had always thought Thomas Rhett and I would create a family like that. One where our kids would run between our house and their neighbors' houses, where we'd just love each other.

That night, seeing my husband on television, I think it finally sunk in that the type of family life I had always thought we'd build together just wasn't going to happen. As I watched Thomas Rhett play his part to help make another girl's dream come true as she was crowned Miss America, I felt my own dream slip away.

I found myself grieving.

"Why?" I wondered. "Why didn't anybody tell me it was gonna be like this?"

Everybody's out there looking at life through the pictures in *People* freaking magazine, and thinking we're this family fairy tale. But nobody tells you about *this* part of the story.

Nobody ever *sees* this part of the story.

Some fairy tale, huh?

17

The Long Way Back

Part of what I was feeling might have been brought on by a predictable postpregnancy rush of hormones. I'll admit that. But if anybody dared to blame my feelings on "hormones" at that point, they'd just better back it on up!

Looking back on that time now, I don't think I was overreacting. I think I was feeling exactly the way I should have felt. Hormones or not, those feelings were real. Maybe God gives us this perspective to help us see things more clearly and to give us the strength to speak our minds.

It was only a week after the Miss America pageant when Thomas Rhett came home all excited to whisk me and one of our closest couple friends off to a Bruno Mars concert in Memphis. I like Bruno Mars. My husband *loves* Bruno Mars. I *for sure* needed a date night. It should have been fun.

What I needed even more than a night out, though, was just a night in. A moment where Thomas Rhett wasn't the superstar country music guy with another #1 album, but the man I married: a down-to-earth man who loved to hang out under the stars talking with me for hours. Those days now seemed so long ago, like another time when things had been simple. When just being together had felt like enough.

I needed Thomas Rhett to just sit down with the kids for a while. To witness the magic of Ada James's smile and Willa Gray's laughter. Or maybe, just maybe, to help me clean up the kitchen.

He wasn't even home for an hour that day before he came out of the bedroom in his gym shorts and said, "I've gotta get a workout before we go. I didn't get one in this morning before the flight. I'll be back in an hour and a half, so be ready to go. Love you."

He gave me a kiss on the cheek and went jogging out the door. I watched him drive away in his truck, headed for the gym, and thought, "Well, you *go* to the gym. I'll just be here with my extra forty pounds. And your *kids*. And this *mess!*"

Okay, so I was a bit salty. But the sink was full of dishes. Ada James was crying. My mom wasn't there yet to babysit. Willa Gray was jumping on the dogs, and I was still in my dirty PJs, with spit-up on my shoulder and something sticky in my hair, and definitely some pee on me somewhere.

Going to the gym was important to Thomas Rhett. I understood that. Looking good on camera and feeling good onstage were parts of his job. This was about more than the gym. It was starting to feel like having these two babies, making a family—our family—was just something Thomas Rhett did on the side. I felt like he was constantly prioritizing his career and everything that went along with it over our family. Going to the gym, yes, and traveling and public appearances and taking calls at all hours. I hated myself for feeling this way. I was so lucky to have such a wonderful and talented husband. He was providing more for us materially than I could have ever dreamed. But he wasn't providing for us emotionally. His attention, his focus, always seemed to be elsewhere. We weren't "doing life together," like our vows had promised, and it felt like his job was an excuse for everything.

I would watch Thomas Rhett sleeping peacefully while I got up with Ada James, who woke up multiple times during the night and always, *always* woke up at the crack of dawn, and I couldn't help but feel annoyed. Once, when I was getting out of bed to feed our daughter, I accidentally woke Thomas Rhett up from what seemed to be a very blissful sleep, and instead of offering to help he just rolled over and went right back to sleep. To say I felt resentful toward him would be the understatement of the year.

He had been out at an industry event the night before. His new album

*Willa Gray watching her daddy, sidestage in her pajamas,
on the* Life Changes *tour*

was a huge success. Thomas Rhett was the toast of the town. He deserved to celebrate. He deserved all the accolades. But where was our family's place in all of this? He was being celebrated for songs he had written about our life together, yet I felt like we were now almost an afterthought. I missed our time together. I missed sharing our kids with him.

I told him at one point, "Our lives could not be more opposite."

And he *laughed.* He thought I was being *funny.*

Earlier that week, a package had arrived at the house and he opened it and pulled out a pair of Gucci shoes. Thomas Rhett always liked to dress nice. I didn't hold that against him. I liked that about him. But these shoes were crazy expensive. He had to go to a party or maybe it was a dinner where he was going to be photographed, and he had to wear things that were sent to him—celebrities get those kinds of perks. Or he might have spent a fortune on them himself. I'm not sure. It was all part of his job. *Whatever.* (No, I'm not bitter . . .) But I looked at him pulling those shoes from the box and said, "Dude, are you kidding me?"

"What?" he said.

"Babe, you get a box like every other day and you're constantly getting the nicest things. I don't order *half* this much crap."

"It's not crap," he said. "You know—"

"Yes, I know. But it's like you're ordering Ruth's Chris steaks to the house every night, and I'm stuck with McDonald's cheeseburgers."

"That's not true, babe. Order what you want!"

"That's not the point. That's just what it feels like. And yeah. It kind of is true."

The next day, another package showed up, and he opened it and pulled out a ridiculously expensive designer jacket.

I was just so annoyed.

"I need to wear this to that event I have next week," he said.

"Oh, do you *need* to wear it?" I replied.

"Look!" he said with a smile. "You got a box, too."

"Open that box, and let me see what it is," I said.

He opened it up, and it was Lysol.

Lysol.

"See," I said.

At that point he just cut his losses and walked out of the room.

All of that was weighing on my mind by the time he got back from the gym—after I'd fed the kids, cleaned the sink full of dishes, tidied up the living room, taken a shower, blow-dried my hair, and passed the kids to Mom. I was ready to go just like he'd asked. Right on time.

"Two minutes," he said, rushing to the bedroom. "I've just got to change, and make a quick phone call."

Through the bedroom door, I could hear him talking. Going on and on about some business thing. Willa Gray kept asking for me, pulling away from my mom, getting all teared up and making me feel guilty for even thinking about leaving the kids that night at all. Mom and I finally corralled the two of them into the back room, where they settled down in front of a Disney movie, and I thanked her as I walked back out to the front door.

Fifteen minutes later, Thomas Rhett finally got off the phone and came out, looking sharp and telling me, "We have *got* to go. We're late."

Why was he telling *me* we were late? I'd been standing next to the door waiting for *him*!

He looked at me and he could tell I was fuming.

"What is it?" he said.

"Honestly?" I said. "I think I hate you."

Hate was a word that was never spoken in my family. In the Gregory house, we were never allowed to say we "hate" anybody, ever. It didn't matter who it was: friends at school, people who were mean to you; you did not "hate" anybody.

So when those words came out of my mouth, it felt like everything shattered.

How did we go from such bliss two years ago to this point where I just said the unthinkable?

To me, we had hit rock bottom.

I looked at him, and I saw just how badly I'd crushed him.

He didn't even see it coming.

In a flash of regret, I started hating on myself, thinking, "How could I say that? Of *course* I don't hate him. I *love* him. I just don't *like* him very much right now. Lord, how did we *get* here? How do we get *back*? Are we ever gonna be the same now?"

Thomas Rhett finally came out of his state of shock and spoke to me, timidly, like he was afraid of what else I might say. "Do you mean . . . we're not surviving this? Are you saying you want to leave me?"

"No," I said. "No. Geez, don't be that dramatic. That's not what I mean. Like, divorce is not even anywhere in my brain. I mean I want to fix this. We *need* to fix this, but it's like you don't even hear me. A part of me just wants to quit, but I don't *want* to quit. I'm just trying to tell you how I feel, and it's *not good*."

"Okay," he said. "Well . . . we're gonna cancel going to this concert tonight and we're gonna stay here—"

"No," I said. "We're going. I'm not going to cancel on our friends like that."

When I commit to something, I follow through. That's who I am.

That's who Thomas Rhett is, too. You don't just go and change your plans because of your personal problems and then ruin everyone else's night because of it.

We didn't finish the conversation. Thomas Rhett had hired a van with a driver for the night and they were already there waiting for us, so we hopped in and went around the corner to pick up our friends from the neighborhood, Ford and April. They instantly recognized that there was some tension between us. Thankfully they knew us well. We'd gotten super close. So we were able to talk through a little bit of what we were feeling and they were more than supportive. They'd been through their own ups and downs, and they reminded us that if we were both committed to fixing whatever was wrong, we could find a way to fix it.

I won't lie: The tension between us wound up hanging in the air all night. And yet, I knew that Thomas Rhett heard me. *Finally.* And I knew for sure that we were both committed to fixing it. But having two close friends there to help soften the blow and to keep us from getting into an argument again without even trying was exactly what the two of us needed in that moment. I don't think the two of us could have planned it better if we'd tried.

Being out of the house actually felt good. We made the best of the night. Bruno was amazing. Inspiring, actually. And the next morning, Thomas Rhett called Beth, our marriage counselor. "We need, as soon as possible, to do a very quick mini couples intensive," he said.

We set it up for just a few days later. Thomas Rhett cleared his schedule. Our moms took the kids and the dogs, and we spent two whole days working through everything that was going on.

Thomas Rhett isn't always good at waiting, but he is really good at working, and he's definitely a fixer. That's part of the reason he's so successful. He works hard to learn, and to get things right, and to get things *done.* So the second he saw just how serious this problem was, he committed to fixing it.

Beth brought in a second counselor, and we started talking things out, individually and together, and trying to trace it back to when the problems really began.

I ended up tracing it back to Super Bowl weekend, back in February, after he'd flown back from Uganda to meet some of his "obligations." This was right when I was dealing with all the legal issues, and finally getting the meeting with the judge who held Willa Gray's entire fate in his hands. Thomas Rhett and I FaceTimed one night, and he was all pumped getting ready to head out and spend the weekend at the Super Bowl with some of his guy friends.

I was really pregnant, and really sick at the time, and he was not there to help. I felt like I was carrying the family we were trying to build all by myself. He was not there taking care of our daughter, who we were trying to bring home. He was going to parties, doing the Super Bowl thing, and he seemed really excited that he got to bring all of his guy friends because I wasn't in town. Like even though I wasn't there, I was easily replaceable. And it was in this moment where I realized that normally, that would be *me*. I would be with him, because I did *everything* with him. We were a *we*. Since we were little kids, we had always been a *we*. We did *life* together.

It felt to me like he was saying, "Well, sorry you can't be here, but I'm still gonna go on and do exactly what I want to do."

Under the guidance of the counselors, we both got super comfortable. They made it feel safe for us to talk openly. So I just started word-vomiting.

I talked about the house, and the sink full of dirty dishes, and how I felt like I was alone doing all the feeding and caretaking for the kids, and taking care of everything in the house. Then I heard these words come out of my mouth: "I feel like you are not *in it* with me. Like I'm doing life by myself." As soon as I said it, I knew that I had finally been able to tell him what was really bothering me. It wasn't the dirty dishes or getting up early to feed our daughter, it was that I was doing all of that alone. It was that my husband and I were living separate lives. We had created a family and I was lonely. How could that be? And what were we going to do about it?

"Well, let's get more help," Thomas Rhett suggested.

"No!" I said.

"Why not? I'll check with our business manager, but I think we can afford a nanny," he said.

"No, Thomas Rhett. No. That is not what I'm trying to say. I don't want to just hire more people for us to manage. I want *us* to take care of our kids. I want it to be what you and I had when we were kids, what we've done in our life for so long. Can we just do 'us' now? Can't you just wake up with me in the morning?"

"Well, I've gotta sleep because if I don't sleep I don't sound good," he said.

"So go to bed earlier," I said.

"Sometimes that's not an option," he said.

"Really? You don't have the option? Staying up for one more drink, going to hang out late in the vibe room, that's not an option where you're choosing yourself over us? Come on. You live in this world where you've got a manager for everything and everyone takes care of everything for you. What about our family? Including me? Us?"

"Are you saying I'm not taking care of you?"

"You're *providing* for us. You're providing for your family. I get that. I value that. And I don't take that lightly. I know how hard you work at your job. I'm grateful for that. And I understand this is your passion. You were born to do this. God gave you these gifts. But that doesn't mean that you necessarily have to do everything that you're doing that keeps you from your family. You're making choices that are not bringing us together. There is a line where the priorities have to match the values. You do *not* have to stay up to party so you can then sleep later the next morning. You do not have to work out every single day instead of spending time with me and the girls. There are a lot of things you don't *have* to do. You're *choosing* those things over your family."

Thomas Rhett's face just about went white.

I didn't want to hurt him, but I needed him to understand. I needed him to fight for us.

"I've said this to you before, but sometimes . . . it's like we just live in Thomas Rhett's world. Like we *all* just live in Thomas Rhett's world. And I need you to come around to *our* world for a little bit. I miss you. The kids miss you. I need to feel like this is a partnership rather than me just following you around like I'm the personal manager of our family."

"Babe, that is not at all what it is," he said, and he started to try to defend himself.

"I'm sorry," I said. "I can't . . ."

I could feel the tears coming on.

"Do you want me to quit?" he said.

I knew with 100 percent certainty that he meant it. This man would've given up his entire career to make this right. So why was this so hard?

"No, I do not want you to quit. I mean, you know I've prayed to God to take us out of this business, on numerous occasions, and that's not what God wants. He's made that very clear. You are doing what you love. And doing what you love is what brought us to where we are now. All of it, including the kids. I know He has you in this business for a purpose."

"Then *what?*"

"I just need you to come home to us. Be with us," I said. "I've got to feel like we're in this together."

TR: I guess I used to be from the mindset of "The man gets up, he goes to work, he comes home, tucks the kids in, and that's that." Obviously my job is a hundred times different, though, and that mindset is pretty old-fashioned. That is just not the kind of man I want to be.

Lauren's words cut me so deep. I mean, I could tell she was just *done.* She didn't have anything left to give. She felt like she'd already given it all. Which meant this wasn't going to be about the two of us working on our marriage together. This was on *me.* I had to step up, or I was gonna lose her. It was *my* job to try and fix this.

Thomas Rhett looked into my eyes and said, "What do I do?"

"Here's the thing," I said. "We just need *more* from you. Not money. Not stuff. More *you.* Your time, and I guess, effort. At home. In general. I don't know . . ."

"Okay," he said. "I get it. I understand."

I hoped to God that he really did.

The next week, Thomas Rhett sat down with Virginia to talk about reducing his schedule—starting with clearing three straight weeks at the end of December so we could get back to all of our holiday traditions with our kids, with no interruptions whatsoever.

"I'm really glad you're doing this," Virginia said.

He'd been scared to ask her, nervous about what it might mean to place boundaries on the unpredictable nature of his business.

"No," she said. "This is good. If you're not taking care of yourself, your family, and your priorities, none of this will work."

Sometimes, the things we're scared of are exactly the things we need.

He couldn't give up his morning workouts, but he decided the kids and I were worth sacrificing a little sleep. So he set his alarm for an hour before the kids woke up, and tiptoed out to the gym—that way he could make it back in time to have the morning with us.

We all had breakfast together when he got back that first day, and it was so nice to see his face at our kitchen table. He was just so good with our kids. I'd almost forgotten. I loved watching him play little games with Willa Gray to help her eat her breakfast, and the way he leaned over to kiss Ada James on the forehead when he stood up and asked me, "Do you want some more coffee?"

"Yes, please," I said. "Thank you."

I mean honestly, is there anything more attractive than a man who's a really good dad?

I was already starting to like him again.

It seemed like things were going really well, until a couple of days later when he raced right out the door after breakfast to go to a full-day songwriting session with some of his buddies. The sink was full of dishes. He hadn't asked what our plans were for the day. It felt like we didn't exist once his obligations to us at breakfast were finished. *And here we are again,* I thought. Worst of all, when Thomas Rhett kissed all of us goodbye—barely grazing my cheek—he hadn't even looked me in the eye. He was too busy reading a message on his phone.

Nothing's changed, I thought. *He still doesn't get it.*

I left the mess, packed up the kids, and drove up to see my mom. I figured Thomas Rhett and I could fight about it when he came home—after I'd come back and cleaned it all up by myself.

Like always.

The kids loved going to my parents' house, and my mom embraced her grandmother role as easily as she embraced her mommy role with us when we were kids.

"I'm just so blown away at how well you handled everything when we were growing up," I told her. "I don't know how you did it," I said.

"What do you mean?" she asked.

"Like, you were always the 'fun mom,' even after Granddaddy died. Even *more so* after he died. And you had *three* kids. I'm barely getting started with two and I already feel like I'm falling apart. I mean, how did you do it? You were always in a good mood, and smiling, and playing, and somehow keeping this house so pretty. How did you find the energy and the capacity to do all that?"

"Honestly, Lauren," she said, "I think I was depressed."

"What?"

"After your granddaddy died, I was just so broken. I think all of that fun and smiling and craziness was just me coping with the pain I was feeling. Like, I did everything I could to lose myself in having fun with all y'all, and cleaning the house and keeping busy all the time was so I wouldn't have to face my own feelings."

"Mom," I said. "I had no idea. I thought you were just, like, living life to the fullest or something."

"I was. But not because I necessarily wanted to. It's just what I did to survive."

"Wow."

All those times I thought my parents had all the answers, they didn't. And all those times I thought I knew the whole story, I didn't. I supposed I was probably too young and naïve to understand it until I had kids of my own, but sharing that moment, having my mom open up to me like that—it felt like full-on mom-to-mom validation. I was just so thankful for everything she'd given to us kids. And so thankful that God allowed her to cope with her grief in such a positive way.

Just then, Willa Gray ran up to me, completely out of the blue, and yelled, "Mommy, Mommy!"

"What?" I said.

She crawled up into my lap and hugged my neck, and then leaned over and kissed Ada James on the cheek.

I looked at my mom and she just smiled so big.

"It's so worth it, isn't it?" she said.

I shared a knowing smile right back as I hugged my girls to my heart and relaxed in the beauty of that moment.

Holding our girls at dinner

"Oh my gosh," I said. "*So* worth it."

18

Doing Dishes

I'm so glad that Thomas Rhett and I believe in counseling, because everything we had ever learned in counseling would come into play at this moment—especially what we learned during an intensive four-day couples counseling retreat called Onsite.

A retreat neither one of us will ever forget.

"Are you sure we want to do this?" I asked.

"Are *you?*" he said.

"I guess so," I said. "I don't know."

"We could turn around right now."

"No," I said. "We should do it. We *need* this."

Thomas Rhett parked the car in front of this surprisingly big, stately manor in the hills, surrounded by woods and cabins.

They handed us a schedule when we walked in, and it looked like we were in for a month's worth of therapy all crammed into four days. The calendar was *packed,* from sunrise till lunch, then all afternoon, and after dinner right up until bedtime.

I was worried that whatever this "intensive therapy" was, it might make us uncomfortable, and then neither one of us would want to follow through. But I was surprised to see just how all-in Thomas Rhett was for this process.

TR: There were a couple moments right off the bat where I felt like, "Okay, I'm not doing this." Like at one point, we were talking about how frustrated I was with someone I work with, and they put a pillow in a chair and wanted me to pretend the pillow was him. I thought, "This is ridiculous." But I knew this was for the sake of Lauren's and my relationship, so I tried talking to the pillow. "Dude, you made me so mad over X, Y, and Z." And then the counselors pressed me. "Why did that make you mad? Don't tell me. Tell *him*." And before I knew it, I'd spent like an hour and a half talking to a pillow. It kinda worked. Through that "conversation," I somehow got down to the root of why I felt a certain way in the first place. And then I could deal with it. It helped me to think about how I handle situations when I'm face-to-face versus when I'm talking about them to somebody else. And I think that helped me start to think about how I was maybe avoiding some face-to-face confrontation with Lauren.

Lauren: I was right there in the room when he did it, which meant I got to experience it right with him. And he stayed in the room for my pillow talk, too. It was weird, but it was okay—because it was us, doing it together.

One day they took us out into the woods, where there was a big piece of plywood placed over a log, like a seesaw almost. And they made Thomas Rhett stand on one end of it, and me on the other. We had to work together to make it to each other's side without either end of the plywood ever hitting the ground.

We had to balance it first. One person had to get on, and then the other person, and we had to figure out our balance point. And that was tough enough as it was. Then we had to try to step together and around each other and keep that wood balanced up off the ground and it seemed impossible. I don't know how many times we tried it. And we got frustrated with ourselves, and with each other, and it took us like an hour and a half but we finally figured it out. Then, just when we were all proud of ourselves, they said, "Great! Now do it again without talking."

"What?"

"Trust us. It will tell you a lot," they said.

We somehow worked just with hand signals and body language and did it again.

Then they made us do it with only one of us in charge, and then the other person in charge, so each of us had a turn just being quiet and listening and basically taking orders.

TR: It seemed like a game at first, but when we talked about it afterward, what it really showed us was, "How do you argue? How do you talk to each other in different times of trial and stress?" It was wild.

It was revealing. The exercise was super frustrating for both of us, but both of us had this determination. We both felt, "Well, if you would just let me do it *my* way, it would work fine!" Then when we got a chance to do it our way, it still didn't work like we thought it would. So we had to work together. It taught us a lot about communication. *Real* communication.

I realized, "Okay, I see why you wanted to do it your way, and it's different than the way I wanted to do it, but it still worked." I may have done it completely different and it still would have worked, but that means neither one of us was really *wrong*. It's just that both of us had different ways of doing it. That was eye-opening.

It led to us learning how to fight better—because couples fight, and we learned that sometimes it's the fight itself that makes things worse, not the things that the two of you are fighting about in the first place.

In the end, we realized that we couldn't even *do* that balance exercise without each other. It's impossible to do with just one person. We had to really be in it together to make it work.

We did another exercise where we had to climb a rock wall and get all the way to the top, blindfolded. The only thing we had to go on were the instructions each of us shouted to the other.

Reconnected—and sidestage kissing—
before a show

It's crazy how many different issues the exercises tapped into, and how it started to show us how to communicate in a healthier way. We were learning new ways to respect each other, and to listen to each other.

What I learned through all of our counseling is that what I needed to do was to let go a little bit, and to realize that just because I was right did not mean that Thomas Rhett was wrong.

Maybe I needed to give him more of a chance to explain himself. Maybe he just doesn't explain things well, or maybe I wasn't explaining things to him in a way that he could understand. We both needed to develop more empathy, which sounds like something that should come easily and automatically with your partner in life, but clearly it was missing. Like, maybe we were taking for granted that we were giving our best selves to each other, when actually, we weren't. It became so clear that the most important thing was learning *how to listen to each other*. I think we both were so stubborn, and got so caught up in proving that we were right, that sometimes neither of us was listening to the other.

TR: Lauren's never been one to back down from a fight. So before we went to counseling, I got to a point where I knew, "If I keep trying to press my point, it's just gonna cause a bigger fight. And it's not even gonna be worth it." Which meant I was backing down so much that I wasn't even trying to come up with solutions that worked for me anymore.

What I learned is that the more you understand somebody, and where they're coming from, and even how their parents were and how that influenced the way they interact, it just makes you process the way you want to argue better. Like, at one point we did this thing called a Trauma Egg, where your counselor's in the room, and your backs are toward each other, and you have a gigantic piece of paper on the wall and you draw a large egg with markers. And then inside the egg you draw these little boxes and then try your best, even if you're not good at drawing, to draw every pivotal memory you had from birth until now, including the earliest memories, or memories that impacted you in good or bad ways. The pivotal moments in your life. It could be the first time you got in trouble, your first kiss, an accident you had, just that kind of stuff. And at the end of it, even though Lauren and I had known each other for so long, we realized there were a few things in each of our histories that we didn't know about each other. For example, I didn't really know why Lauren wouldn't talk to me before we'd go to bed if we had an argument at night. Well, it's because her way of dealing with something is different than mine. I like to talk it out, to get to a resolution. I grew up with that mindset of "Never lay your head down angry." The way her parents argued was different, though, and that influenced her. I didn't realize it when we were growing up, but Steve and Lisa fought like everybody else does.

Lauren: They fought like cats and dogs sometimes, but there was always love there. It always came back to how much they loved each other. They knew they weren't walking away from each other just because they were fighting. They would always work things out.

TR: And Lisa was one who just needed some quiet time to herself to process things rather than to just keep getting into everything all night. Lauren learned from that, whether consciously or unconsciously. So when things got bad with us, when Lauren and I got into it, I would literally stay awake till one, two in the morning, totally frustrated—and frustrating her—going, "Yo, what is happening? Like, are we getting *divorced*? Are we *good*?" I couldn't let it rest. I'd want everything to be fixed before we stopped talking about it. And for Lauren, what she needed was to cool off and have time to think. She was more of the mindset of "You really made me upset and I just need to go process it, go to bed, and more than likely I'll forget about it while I sleep."

Lauren: I would *not* forget about it, but I would calm down and rationalize in my mind what's important to talk about or whether it was a dumb fight and I just needed to let it go. Like, what's worth talking about and what's not? How do I really feel about it? Because in the heat of a moment maybe it's not something that's really that important to me. Maybe it's just the way that he said it that really ticked me off. And maybe *that's* what I needed space from.

TR: I was able to apply things we learned really quickly. I mean, no matter how much counseling you do, you're always gonna fall back a little bit into previous ways. But now I feel like a few years into marriage, I'm pretty good at keeping things in perspective, like, "Okay, she's mad. I'm just gonna let her go stand in the shower and give her an hour or so and not bring up anything, and then I'll figure out the nicest way to bring it back up later." It has helped, tremendously.

I feel like I'm a pretty chill guy most of the time, but I do get pretty anxious and have a hard time being "off," if that makes any sense. In my career, there are just so many hours and days of just going and going and going, to this interview, that interview, meet-and-greets, shows. And most of the time, to a fault, I feel like my purpose, my job, is to keep going. So when I'm at home, if I have a week off and I don't have to be in the studio or I don't have to write or I don't have to do this or that, it makes Lauren nuts how stir-crazy I get. I just need to do something musical, or do *something*. I'll bring up starting a business or be on the phone with a manager, just trying to be how I'm used to being. It's something that I've had to apply differently now that we have kids.

Through counseling, I learned to talk to *her* instead of channeling all my energy into work; to say, "Lauren, I don't know what to do today." And she learned to answer me rather than get mad at me. She'll say, "Well, what if you just don't think about work and just sit with our kids?" That's all it takes usually, and I manage to refocus and turn my stir-crazy energy into focusing on them, and us.

I'm still working on it, but I really had to learn how to be "off." How to really be present, and how to relax when I'm home. And to let Lauren know how much I appreciate all she does.

It wasn't long before Thomas Rhett was back in the studio, starting work on his next album. I took the kids to run some errands on one of his first days, and when I drove back to our house just before suppertime, I was surprised to see Thomas Rhett's truck in the driveway. His days in the studio usually went well into the night.

I walked in, and he was sitting on the couch.

"Hi," I said. "I didn't think you'd be home till late."

"I know," he said. "I told them we'd pick it up tomorrow. I thought we could maybe take the kids out to dinner or something."

I noticed the pillows next to him, back where they belonged instead of all over the floor. I thought that was really weird.

I walked into the kitchen, and it looked like he'd cleaned the countertops.

Then I looked over at the sink—and it was *empty*.

"Did you do all this?" I asked.

"Yeah," he said. "I'm sorry I couldn't get to it before I left this morning. I'll try to give myself more time tomorrow."

"Wow." I smiled.

We took the kids out to eat. We watched a movie till they fell asleep. We tucked them in, together. When we went to bed, I kissed him. I mean *really* kissed him.

"*What* is *up* with *you*?" he asked me.

I'll leave out the behind-closed-door details here. But let's just say, that night, I think Thomas Rhett was a happy man.

"Just because I did the dishes?" he asked me.

"Pretty much," I replied.

It wasn't just about doing dishes.

It was about wanting to share my life with an equal partner—the man I loved—and not allowing some old-fashioned stereotypical view of how marriage is supposed to work get in the way of making our marriage actually work. For both of us.

If I was ever going to find peace with the fact that we weren't going to live the kind of simple life I always dreamed we would, I for sure needed to know that I had a partner in this new life we were building. *Our* life. With *our* family. And from that day forward, there was no doubt in my mind that Thomas Rhett was seriously committed to finding our shared happiness again.

He started making us number one—and I did the same for him.

They say in order for a marriage to make it, you have to be good communicators. For us, that was not the answer. Thomas Rhett and I "communicated" all the time. You can "communicate" and still hate what the other person is saying to you. You can also choose to ignore what the other person is saying, and that's where things go wrong. Really wrong.

Marriage takes work. Actual *work*. It takes commitment, too. It takes faith and values. And it also takes help. Whatever it is that causes the magic to wear off at some point, you have to remind yourself, "Okay, well, *there is a reason why I love this person*." And if you ever really loved them, then I think there's always a way to bring it back together.

We had a long way to go. The parts of our marriage that weren't working didn't develop overnight, and they definitely wouldn't get fixed overnight. In a lot of ways, we were just getting started.

But Thomas Rhett doing dishes was a pretty good start.

It really came down to setting priorities, and we're working together now to keep our priorities straight.

The things I was angry about weren't because I "hated" Thomas Rhett. I was fighting because I loved him, and the reality was I *needed* him. The kids needed him. We wanted *more* of him—not less.

I didn't "hate" the music business. I didn't hate my husband's job. I hated the way it seemed to be pulling us apart.

Thomas Rhett is such a present dad and husband now. In fact, I'd argue and say he's *truly* the best. My heart absolutely melts at the man he is for our family today, even more than it melted when he kissed me that night on my parents' front porch. He says "no" to more work things, and "yes" to us, and that's actually helped him to write even more successful songs, and to sell out more concerts in big venues as the headliner. His fourth album, *Center Point Road,* which came out in the spring of 2019 and has so many songs about us and how we grew up, went #1 on the Billboard 200

album chart in its very first week. That's not a country chart. That's the chart that measures sales and airplay and downloads of *all* albums, in every genre. Which means *Center Point Road* was the #1 album in the country! (Proud wife right here.)

In other words, what he gave up wasn't much, and what he got in return was a whole lot.

And the best part of all is now that we're more centered in our marriage, we both enjoy the kids and each other so much more. Instead of growing apart, we're growing together through life's changes.

The influence of having kids has had a direct impact on Thomas Rhett's writing. I make no apologies for standing up and reminding him that he has a responsibility to his two children, which means that he better be keeping his lyrics family-friendly. I remind him that Willa Gray and Ada James are listening to and singing those lyrics, and he'd better think twice about what he puts on his records. There's a lot of pressure in the music business to keep things "edgy" and "cool," but honestly, the fact that he's choosing a more family-centered approach to songwriting these days doesn't seem to be hurting his career. Just the opposite. And the large number of parents who bring their kids and teens to his concerts makes that pretty clear.

I'm not bitter anymore about the work he has to do, or the times when he has to travel without us, because the two of us are on the same page now.

I can't even count the number of times last summer, in the middle of the week, when we would end up going on a walk around the neighborhood, or just sitting outside, firing up the grill, while the lightning bugs started glowing and Willa Gray went running around, chasing the dogs all over the place, and Ada James started taking her first steps. It seemed like every few nights, Macy and her husband, Tyler, were stopping by, and then Rhett and Sonya came walking in, and Ford and April from the neighborhood showed up with their kids, who started running around with ours. And then my parents came over, and Paige and Tim, and Kasey and little Tyler swung by, and when we sat down to eat, my dad said the prayer and made every one of us tell God what we were thankful for before we ate our food.

I looked around at all those faces, and I knew what I was thankful for the most. These people were, and always would be, the center of our world.

Having kids is funny. They always surprise you. Whenever Dad performed his pre-dinner ritual, Willa Gray tended to say she was thankful for *The Little Mermaid,* or Kona, or Cash, or her Barbie dolls, or ice cream.

Then, one night last summer my dad said, "And Willa Gray, what are you thankful for?"

And Willa Gray looked around the table and thought about it really hard, and said, "I'm thankful for my baby sister Ada James. I love her sooooooo much."

Talk about hearts in a puddle on the floor. To hear my little girl put her love for her sister into words like that, and to stop and think for even one moment about the incredible odds that had to be overcome in order for these two girls to *become* sisters, it just blew my mind. Like, I

Sister hugs,
while on tour in Australia

can hardly believe that we get to live *this life.* The one our family is living *right now.*

How incredibly lucky are we, every single one of us, to get to live this life that we've got?

"That was so good, baby girl," Thomas Rhett said to Willa Gray, picking her up and sitting her down on his lap.

I caught Thomas Rhett's eye across the table in that moment and I could tell he was thinking the exact same thing I was. We smiled at each other with this loving, shared smile of a husband and wife who'd been through a thing or two—knowing that if either of us had given up at any point along the way, we wouldn't be here. We wouldn't be living *in love*, in this perfectly imperfect life of ours.

We knew it.

We recognized it.

And we were *grateful*.

Afterword

Starry Nights

Thomas Rhett and I are building a life together.

That is such a gift.

While I continue to work in the field a few times a year, Suzanne Mayernick also asked me to join the board of Love One International. That's the new name for the organization formerly known as 147 Million Orphans, and we are now totally focused on our mission to help children and families in Uganda: to rescue, rehabilitate, and (when necessary) resettle children into new homes, in the name of Jesus. The idea is to dig deep in that one spot in the world, to do everything we can right there in the hopes that we'll be able to have a greater impact on the lives of more children than we did when our resources were spread among Uganda, Haiti, and Honduras. As I hope is clear by now, the whole idea of loving "just one" and how big of a difference that can make in the world means everything to me and my family, so the work I'm doing just fills my heart.

The public doesn't see me working every day, but Thomas Rhett jokes that I am way busier than he is these days. He also complains that I talk to Suzanne on the phone more than I talk to him. There are always decisions to be made, and a lot of times there's a new baby found or an emergency situation and we've got to act. *Now.*

There's some irony in the fact that I have an extremely hectic work life. It's brought a level of unpredictability into our home life that's not unlike

Our little family, out at our farm

the very thing I used to get mad about in Thomas Rhett's career. Oh how the tables have turned. But we're adjusting as we go.

As I'm working on this book, Love One is in the middle of a campaign to raise capital. We're trying to raise millions of dollars to develop our reclaim center, where children come after being hospitalized for malnourishment or other conditions. The goal is to give them a place where they can rehabilitate and/or get educated on ways to avoid repeating whatever situation they're in. And the fundraising is so we will be able to care for many more children than we currently do. There are more than two hundred little villages around the city we serve, and we're only really active in four or five of them. So we've got a long way to go.

In these last few years, with everything that's gone on, our family has needed a place of refuge more than ever. A private space. A place where the outside worlds of work and fame and attention seem very far away.

I'm happy to say we found one, and it's turned into a refuge. For all of us.

We don't live our daily life in a neighborhood where our kids are free to run outside and lay down in the middle of the street, but Thomas Rhett and I want our kids to grow up with as many of the same opportunities for fun and adventure that we had growing up. And we thank God we were able to buy a beautiful farm where that can happen. We keep dirt bikes there, and four-wheelers, and we go fishing and hunting, and there's an amazing place for building bonfires, too. It's the most beautiful, dreamy little slice of heaven.

Sometimes, I can't help but stop and think how much Hunter would have loved doing all of this with us. Gosh, we miss him. All the time. But if anyone ever inspired any of us to live life to the fullest, and to appreciate every day, it's him.

Dealing with fame definitely affects our ability to do some of the things we used to do, and we'd like to do. For example, we had to skip out on three years of going to Opryland, and I was really sad not to be able to share that with Willa Gray and Ada James. The rest of our Crew went, but it just got too complicated for us. There are too many people who recognize us when we go out to any kind of a crowded public place like that, and the kind of attention that comes from a crowd makes the kids really uncomfortable. It makes *me* uncomfortable. I missed it so much it hurt. We took the time to watch some old videos over at my mom and dad's house with the kids, and to show them pictures of our past visits, and the nostalgia of looking back made it seem even more special.

Finally, for Christmas 2019, we were able to arrange to take the whole Crew to Opryland on a private, guided tour. Our girls got to spin around under the big tree of lights, and I'm just so happy that they got to taste a little bit of one of my happiest childhood memories.

Thomas Rhett has been writing more and more nostalgic songs about our family and our life growing up together, too, and those songs have been really well received. We're so thankful for that. I think his fans have

a lot of nostalgia for their own childhoods. Anyone who's tuned in to Thomas Rhett's lyrics is clearly tuned in to the importance of love and family and relationships, and that gives us so much hope.

Thomas Rhett was able to cut back to something like sixty-five shows last year, which is still a lot, but nothing like what he used to play. And he's made the shows more of a family affair, too: In 2019 he headed out on his own summer headlining tour, with his dad, Rhett Akins, along as one of his opening acts. Talk about full circle. He's playing arenas he only dreamed about playing when he was a kid, and he's doing it with his dad, and a group of other friends from the business (including Russell) who've all worked hard to make it in the industry they love.

And me and the kids? We go with him as often as we can—with help. Our amazing assistant not only helps us run our lives but has stepped up as a babysitter on lots of occasions. And at some point along the way, I had to swallow my pride and realize that I could not do this all on my own; nor could Thomas Rhett and I keep putting so much of the babysitting burden on our extended family. So we hired a nanny. At first the thought of it made me feel like a failure as a mom. But now? I look at it as a godsend. Our nanny is an angel to me and our kids, and the relief of not having to always scramble for help has lowered the stress levels at home, and on the road. And that makes *everyone* happier.

Our family and friends are the key to everything, so we put a lot of effort into making our time together sacred. We still go to church on Sundays when we're in town, and we always try to start our day with God, letting Him know we are *so* thankful for this beautiful life and praying He keeps showing us clearly the open doors He wants us to walk through.

We still say a prayer around the dinner table in our family, too.

And when it comes time to make tough decisions at home, Thomas Rhett and I always turn to the three of us: me, him, and God. If all three don't agree on something, we don't do it.

I wish every couple could go through counseling like we did, or a process like we did, at Onsite or elsewhere. Maybe do it before they get married—and definitely after having children. Going through counseling gave us the skills and knowledge we needed so we don't have to be afraid

Daddy singing to his girls at his show—
as if we're the only ones in the room

to confront our own demons. Instead, we can pin them down (like snakes) and wrangle them however we want.

One thing we definitely agree on? Making time for us.

Family comes first. Our marriage comes first. Our love comes first.

Backstage with my honey in St. Paul, Minnesota— with baby girl number three on the way!

Willa Gray and Ada James are still a little too young to sit still long enough to really do much stargazing with us. But their "Stevie" (my dad) is already teaching them about constellations, and telling them all about NASA and space travel. And they've already got a taste for airplanes. On top of all of our travels for Thomas Rhett's tours, they've gone up flying with my dad. And now that my little brother Grayson got his pilot's license, too, I have a feeling they'll be calling their uncle to fly them around soon enough. And they'll be sharing it all with their little sister. And maybe more siblings after that.

In the summer of 2019 we found out I was pregnant with another little girl, and we could not be more thrilled. (Truth be told, I wasn't so thrilled about the morning sickness, which was more like an all-day sickness. It was *bad* this time around.) We expect she'll be in our arms by the time this book is on shelves. And we haven't ruled out adopting again, either. We're both in a place where we love our little family so much, we keep thinking, "How much more love would we be able to give if our family was just a little bit bigger?"

But that's a conversation for another time.

I think we've managed to navigate plenty of life changes for the time being. We know there'll be plenty more to come. As God opens the doors, we'll walk through.

For now, though, I think we're just gonna tuck the kids into bed and go sit out on the Adirondack chairs in our back yard, where we can take in the night air and stare up at the stars together.

My heart is constantly melting around these two and how much they love each other

Our perfectly imperfect family in a perfectly imperfect family photo: giving kisses at Thompson-Boling Arena on UT's campus before one of Thomas Rhett's shows

At the end of the day, whatever this day brings, we're happy knowing that we have each other, we have our family, and we have our friends. We're surrounded by love, the things that matter most, and as long as we're working hard to keep those close, we're good.

Why?

Because we're living in love.

"Whoever lives in love lives in God, and God in them."

Acknowledgments

Writing this book was not something I ever knew was possible for me. And just like my life would not be what it is without the people I'm beyond blessed to have around me, this book wouldn't exist if it weren't for the incredibly talented and dedicated team I have around this project.

First of all Mark, my co-author, you made this story come to life in such a beautiful way. Your carefulness, attention to detail, and passion you have for my story means more to me than I can put into words. You and your better half, Terry, are so precious to me! Thank you both for your hard work and patience with me through this whole process.

To my editor, Whitney Frick, I knew I loved you the moment I met you! Thank you for helping to keep this book and its messages so true to who I am. To the entire Ballantine team, all of you have been absolutely incredible to work with: Kara Welsh, Kim Hovey, Debbie Aroff, Colleen Nuccio, Jennifer Garza, Karen Fink, Allyson Lord, Cindy Berman, Gina Centrello, and the Random House Audio crew—thank you for making this so fun for me!

To Cait Hoyt, my agent, thank you for seeing the unwritten story and believing in it so fiercely—way before I did. Emily Wright, I can't believe I get to work with someone like you, who I'd choose to be friends with in real life. Thank you for making "work" fun. To Kate Childs and everyone else at CAA, you all are so supportive in all I do. I'm so lucky I get to work with an agency as amazing as y'all.

To my sweet Virginia, the big sister I never had, you have been through so much of my life with me and held my hand through all the good and all the chaos. Thank you for loving me and teaching me with such kindness through this wild ride. I couldn't do any of this without you. I love you!

To Nichole and our entire G Major family, you are too good to me, TR, and the girls. Your hard work does not go unnoticed, and I hope you know how grateful we are for y'all on a daily basis.

Duane—you, Fred, and Danielle take the best care of us. I cannot thank y'all and the whole FBMM team enough for your constant support and guidance.

Thank you Tyne Parrish and the Greenroom for helping me to share our family with the world while protecting us and keeping what's important to us a priority.

To our three angels who make our daily life go 'round, this book wouldn't be here if I didn't have you helping me. Mo, thank you for keeping me organized and looking like I have my life somewhat together. Elbia, thank you for keeping our house feeling like our cozy home that we love. Mack, thank you for being the best and most loving extra set of hands to care for my babies. Our life would not be possible without you three. You each love and care for us so well—I hope you know how much we all love you!

Suzanne—I have to thank you for introducing me to Uganda: the country that stole my heart and introduced me to my baby girl. I also have to thank you for modeling what it looks like to stay close to Jesus, be a devoted wife and mama, and stay true to the woman God created me to be in the middle of a chaotic world. Love you sweet Suz.

To my precious friends—you know who you are. Thank you for always supporting me and loving me just as "Laur" no matter where life takes me. And for praying Willa Gray home, with me and for me, when I wasn't strong enough. I will forever be grateful to y'all for helping to bring my baby home. Your hearts are threaded through my entire life story and I am beyond blessed with the best friends ever created.

Thank you, a million times thank you, to our perfectly imperfect family. Rhett and Sonya, thank you for being there for us and our kids and for loving each of us so well. Your advice and constant supply of laughter is something I truly treasure. Tim and Paige—y'all have been like parents to me since high school and now I consider you both best friends of mine who I look up to so much. I can't believe I get to call all four of y'all my "in-laws"! Thank all of you for being a constant support and rock for me, TR, and the girls. I love each of you so much. To my bonus siblings Kasey, little Ty, and big Tyler—I cannot thank y'all enough for being the best siblings to me and the best aunt and uncles to my girls. I get to call you family but choose to call you my best friends. I love y'all more than life!

Macy and Grayson—thank y'all for never, ever leaving my side as long as you both have lived. I had the best childhood and a lot of that is because of you two. Y'all never fail to make me laugh, you love my girls as if they were your own, you don't hesitate to tell me when I'm wrong, but most important you love me so incredibly well. My life would be absolutely dull without you both. I cannot put into words how much I love you, Mace and Buddy.

Dad and Mom—my goodness. Seeing as the entire first part of this book is about y'all, I think it's pretty obvious how hugely you both have impacted my life, my decisions, and ultimately who I am. Thank you for being the most honest, down-to-earth, fun, loving parents to me. You have always pointed me to God and taught me what's most important to value in this life. Thank you for leading our family so well these past thirty years and for helping my little family get started by bringing my first baby home all the way from Africa. I love you both so much.

To my magical, stubborn, kind, joyful, wild little princesses Willa Gray and Ada James: thank you for teaching me to live life in every sweet and chaotic moment and to not take it too seriously. Willa Gray, thank you for making me a mommy and for undeniably lighting up every room brighter than any other human can. Your heart will move mountains, baby girl, and I can't wait to sit back and watch your light change the world. Ada James, thank you for being my calming little angel in my tummy when I needed it most. You have no idea how your gentle spirit brought me so much peace through Willa Gray's adoption. Your strong-willed, hilarious, loving heart is going to rock this planet and I'm so grateful I get to be your mommy through it all. Lennon, although you're so new to our family, you've already changed us all in the best way. Thank you for making me slow down in life when it was most important. I cannot believe God gave me you three precious angels to raise on earth. My heart could explode just thinking about how much I love each of you girls.

Thomas Rhett, words will not do my heart any justice when I try to say how grateful I am to God for giving me you. You are beyond my most special dreams. I don't deserve how well you love me, how patient and gentle you are with me, and how carefully and boldly you lead our family to Jesus. Thank you for being my best friend, my number one encourager, and supporter, making me laugh, challenging me to be better, loving me better than anyone can, being the most devoted husband and truly the most incredible daddy to our three little girls. God was showing off when He created your spirit, honey. Thank you for picking me to spend your life with and in the midst of you living out your dream, making a way and a special place for mine. I wouldn't be who I am today without you pushing me to be who God created me to be. I would be lost without you, Thomas Rhett. I love you more and more every single day. You and me, babe.

Last, and definitely most important, thank you Lord for this life, and for the people you have put around me to teach me and love me. I do not deserve all you have done for me. Thank you Jesus for showing us how to love, and for loving me so unconditionally. Thank you for your daily patience with me and for never leaving my side. I love you, and everything I have and do, I owe it to you.

About the Authors

Lauren Akins is a devoted mother, wife, and philanthropist who lives in Nashville, Tennessee, with her husband, country superstar Thomas Rhett, and their three little girls, Willa Gray, Ada James, and Lennon. Lauren has worked as a missionary nurse for years and is enthusiastically continuing to support children in Uganda through her efforts with Love One International.

Laurenakins.com
Facebook.com/AkinsLaur/
Instagram.com/laur_akins

Mark Dagostino is a multiple *New York Times* bestselling co-author who is dedicated to writing books that inspire and uplift.

Markdagostino.com

Isn't she just the brightest beam
of sunshine you've ever seen?

LOVE ONE INTERNATIONAL
PROVIDING ACCESS TO LIFESAVING MEDICAL CARE
FOR CHILDREN IN UGANDA

Many critically ill children in Uganda don't have easy access to medical care, so Love One ensures they receive the emergency health care they need. But emergency medical treatment is only the first step. Without ongoing care, children who are returned to their communities often become sick again.

To put them on a path to complete healing, we bring children to the Love One Center, where they receive rehabilitative services—including physical therapy, nutrition education, and spiritual support—and where their parents learn how to keep them healthy once they return home. Our goal is to keep families together.

We can transform entire communities—one child at a time. But we need your help!

For more information or to make a donation to Love One International, visit:

LoveOneInternational.org